# Postcolonial Surveillance

# CHALLENGING MIGRATION STUDIES

This provocative new series challenges the established field of migration studies to think beyond its policy-oriented frameworks and to engage with the complex and myriad forms in which the global migration regime is changing in the twenty-first century. It proposes to draw together studies that engage with the current transformation of the politics of migration, and the meaning of "migrant," from the below of grassroots, local, transnational, and multisited coalitions, projects, and activisms. Attuned to the contemporary resurgence of migrant-led and migration-related movements, and antiracist activism, the series builds on work carried out at the critical margins of migration studies to evaluate the "border industrial complex" and its fallouts, build a decolonial perspective on global migration flows, and critically reassess the link between (im)migration, citizenship, and belonging in the cross-border future.

## Series Editors:

Alana Lentin, Associate Professor in Cultural and Social Analysis at Western Sydney University

Gavan Titley, Senior Lecturer in Media Studies at the National University of Ireland, Maynooth

# Postcolonial Surveillance

## Europe's Border Technologies between Colony and Crisis

Anouk Madörin

ROWMAN & LITTLEFIELD
*Lanham • Boulder • New York • London*

Published by Rowman & Littlefield
An imprint of The Rowman & Littlefield Publishing Group, Inc.
4501 Forbes Boulevard, Suite 200, Lanham, Maryland 20706
www.rowman.com

86-90 Paul Street, London EC2A 4NE

British Library Cataloguing in Publication Information Available

**Library of Congress Cataloging-in-Publication Data**

Names: Madörin, Anouk, author.
Title: Postcolonial surveillance : Europe's border technologies between colony and crisis
  / Anouk Madörin.
Description: Lanham, Maryland : Rowman & Littlefield Publishers, 2022. | Series:
  Challenging migration studies | Includes bibliographical references and index.
Identifiers: LCCN 2022027649 (print) | LCCN 2022027650 (ebook) | ISBN
  9781538165034 (cloth) | ISBN 9781538196250 (pbk.) | ISBN 9781538165041 (ebook)
Subjects: LCSH: Border security--Europe. | Electronic surveillance--Europe. | Europe--
  Emigration and immigration--Government policy.
Classification: LCC JV7590 .M3254 2022  (print) | LCC JV7590  (ebook) |
  DDC 325.44--dc23/eng/20220825
LC record available at https://lccn.loc.gov/2022027649
LC ebook record available at https://lccn.loc.gov/2022027650

# Contents

# Acknowledgments

This book would not have been possible without the research training group *Minor Cosmopolitanisms*. I warmly thank Dirk Wiemann and Regina Römhild, whose advice and support at every stage have extensively guided this project, and the fellows for being wonderful friends and colleagues. My special thanks goes to the editors of the *Challenging Migration Studies Series*, Gavan Titley and Alana Lentin, for having so thoroughly engaged with the manuscript and for providing invaluable feedback in the last stages of the project. I also want to thank Joseph Pugliese for sharing critical insights on parts of this book and Gordon McGregor, Howie Rechavia, and Yann LeGall for offering their expertise on German Southwest Africa. A very special thanks goes to those who have so generously answered my last-minute call to proofread chapters of an earlier version of this book: Laurel Carmichael, Tobias Holzer, Ashley Bohrer, Jens Temmen, and Timothy Chandler. I am further indebted to many people who have offered support and encouragement during the project, either as friends, compelling interlocutors, critics, and commentators, or with other acts of generosity. In no particular order, my gratitude goes out to Mariya Dimitrova Nikolova, P. G. Rubin Maciotti, Yener Bayramoğlu, Michelle Pfeifer, Billy Holzberg, Eddy van der Leer, Meret Wagner, Mia Sánchez, Agatha Jakubiec, Jasco Viefhues, Helen Ramseier, Radiwan Phanthurakulnan, Jack, Tina Buchen, Maxi Wallenhorst, Rahel Schrohe, Joseph Appleton, and Alison Shuman. Lastly, I dedicate this book to my friend and intellectual companion, Viviane Zitzer, a fierce feminist and critical thinker, who is resting in power between the rocks, fossils, and sediments of ice, or the strata of time.

# Preface

This book emerges out of a political moment in which we are witnessing the consolidation of racialized border regimes across the globe, a situation exemplified by the circulation of Covid-19, which intensified border protections despite warnings from the World Health Organization that generalized border controls do little to control the virus and might even accelerate its spread.[1] This reaction highlights how the intensification of border regimes defines our political present in which national protectionism and racist systems of segregation have emerged as the preeminent strategy for dealing with wider economic, political, and environmental destitution. Western and Global North states' nefarious disease management has cost millions of lives across the globe and deteriorated the situation of migrants, refugees, and people traveling outside regular channels. During the pandemic, European Union (EU) member states have pushed for stricter border controls, harshened conditions in detention camps, and further normalized the already existing practice of nonassistance at sea, which substantially widened the rescue gap in the Central Mediterranean.[2] The border restrictions to curb the spread of Covid-19 obstruct the free movement of people across borders, with the year 2020 marking the lowest rates in irregular migration to Europe since 2013.[3] Alongside the drop in registered cases of irregular border crossings, travel restrictions led to a shift from air to land and sea journeys, making the routes of those traveling outside legal corridors more dangerous and lethal. Frontex, the European border and coast guard agency, has illegally pushed back forty thousand refugees attempting to cross national borders during the pandemic, actions that led to two thousand migrant deaths.[4] The border agency has been clear in positioning itself apt at controlling migration and the spread of Covid-19, which has substantially strengthened its mandate.[5] While its budget has been rising steadily since the agency became operational in 2005, under the EU's New Pact on Asylum and Migration, a policy proposed by the European Commission in September 2020, it has become the largest EU agency in terms of staff and budget, which allowed it to double its uniformed border guards, marking the first time in history the EU maintains an armed police force.[6]

Pandemics have offered useful templates for governmental aspirations concerning the circulation of goods and people and to establish new forms of surveillance and control.[7] During exceptional epidemiological situations, the power of city authorities grew and produced the conditions for the emergence of the health police or "policey"[8] as the foundation of the fabrication of social order. Viral states of exception enabled the production and legitimation of identification technologies, such as the emergence of the pest letter and the passport in the fifteenth century in the form of the *bolletini di sanità* (health bulletins) that either authorized or prevented movement. Pandemics further provided the crisis framework to distribute power and control measures unevenly and often evoked the specter of contagious and improper circulation in the figure of the nonsedentary migrant worker, such as when in fifteenth-century Venice, migration from today's Balkan region was inhibited by pointing to the dangers of the pest.[9] Also in 1713, when a new Plague wave was announced, the sanitary cordon drawn around Vienna could only be passed with a health passport (*Gesundheitspaß*), a strict border control measure primarily directed against the Turkish population who was thought to be deliberately bringing the Plague into Europe.[10] It was also in the context of disease control when cities discovered statistics, which presented an early attempt to generate big data in the form of mathematizing population health. Pioneering these early efforts in population statistics was William Petty, who, as a physician under Oliver Cromwell, was commissioned with fighting the Plague and found in Ireland a colonial laboratory to experiment with statistics in disease management.[11] Petty was interested in the economic damage of diseases, comparing the Plague in London and Ireland. In his political arithmetic, society was not a given but a produced one, so besides promoting a racio-eugenic program in which the mixing of the British and the Irish population would heal the poor and the sick, he projected his fantasies of data-informed population control to England's colonies in North America where a transmutation scheme would primarily target Native Americans.[12] Fortunately, Petty's Atlantic extension of political arithmetic remained little more than a thought experiment, but his reflections on colonial population and disease management present an eerie resemblance to today's pandemic context in which disease control is tied to capitalist value production and in which the disenfranchised of the former colonies present the primary targets for testing new modes of surveillance and control.

A first glance into the pandemic's technological environment seems to confirm a key contribution of postcolonial research, namely the fact that it was the historical colonies that served as laboratories for European (late) modernity, with technologies forged within these contexts gradually moving from their peripheral application to the metropolitan center. When Michel Foucault noted that the pushback "colonial practice can have on the juridico-political structures of the West" to allow that the West, eventually, "could practice something resembling colonization, or an internal colonialism, on itself,"[13] he was echoing Black intellectuals who understood European fascism along with its annihilating technologies and protocols as a kind of European imperialism turned inwards, a dynamic Aimé Césaire termed the "boomerang effect of colonization."[14] The subsequent call from postcolonial scholarship to "treat metropole and colony in a single field"[15] uncovered the reciprocal relationship in a range of areas such as military tactics, medical and virological experiments, and statistical data collection, with these practices first having to conclude their experimental phase in the colony before being applied to the European population. Before the advent of the digital age, data collection frenzy in the colonies included knowledge about geographic regions, political structures, and the meticulous ethnographic categorization and description of peoples and their lifestyles—scientific disciplines and bureaucratic apparatuses to be eventually put into the service of colonial population control. The mortgage bond as a debt-based system for creating surplus capital, for example, is now standard practice in finance but was first used as a financial and legal instrument to create the conditions for unequal trade with Indigenous and enslaved populations that empowered primitive accumulation in the Americas.[16] Also, the United States' domestic policing apparatus was fundamentally shaped by the colonial counterinsurgency campaigns the country waged as part of their 1898 occupation of the Philippines in the aftermath of the Spanish-American war.[17] Smallpox vaccination programs in colonized regions of Africa presented one of the earliest and most extensive health campaigns and were applied to European populations only after their experimental phase was concluded in the colonies.[18] The dynamic is most poignantly rehearsed in today's context when in the early months of the pandemic, two French doctors suggested to trial a Covid-19 vaccine technology "in Africa . . . where there are no masks, no treatments, no resuscitation,"[19] marking the continent as a regressive space shorn of medical infrastructure and a ground zero awaiting Western interference. A range of European states have increased digital tracking under the pretext of disease control, such as the sifting through geolocation data and social media to track infected persons and those breaking the nationwide lockdowns. Migration data used for population modeling was co-opted to model flows of the novel coronavirus,[20] and the disease surveillance system to track and trace contacts in Germany was invented and trialed in Nigeria.[21] These controversial, data-driven initiatives to track population movements were often first applied to predict migration and manage border control,[22] confirming that not only the historical colonies but also contemporary borderlands and those inhabiting their (post)colonial zones of exclusion frequently function as laboratories for new technologies with the migrant as test subject.[23]

It is not coincidental that quarantines—invented in fifteenth-century Venice at the height of the second global Plague pandemic—are reminiscent of today's offshore detention measures practiced by border regimes across the globe.[24] Today's border archipelagos in the Mediterranean Sea effectively create spatial and temporal exclusion to become enclosed zones surgically sealed off from mainland Europe. The proximity between today's offshore detention and historical quarantines is rehearsed in the many instances where refugee detention camps have been de facto declared as quarantines, such as in the case of Moria camp on the Greek island of Lesbos, where authorities enforced a mass quarantine and let the virus ravage within the detainment facility. People held in immigration detention generally live with a lack of adequate health care, personal protective equipment, and access to legal advice, along with the increased use of solitary confinement legitimized as a Covid-19 prevention mechanism.[25] In Australia, the former Christmas Island Detention Centre was put to use as a quarantine where Australian evacuees from Wuhan, China, spent their incubation period. Although the conditions inside the detainment facility were substantially better than those faced by thousands of asylum seekers in Australian offshore detention centers in recent years, the reutilization of the facility speaks to the fact that the carceral architecture of immigrant prisons serves as a suitable pandemic infrastructure and is in convergence with the "quarantine nationalism"[26] put forth by many Western states, which, although proven ineffective, has promoted a racialized understanding of health and disease in which the virus, as claimed by Jacques Derrida,[27] is always the foreigner, the other, the one from elsewhere. If the previous use of technology is any indication, refugees and people on the move will be disproportionately targeted as even before the current pandemic, a worldwide roll-out of migration techno-solutionism has continued apace and provided technological solutions, most often from private industry actors, to tackle social, political, and humanitarian challenges. Far from unilaterally moving from the former colonies to a crisis setting to be equally applied within the social strata of the privileged, border and surveillance technologies, as I will show in this book, are in constant migration, and they gain legitimacy precisely through these circulations.

This book will advance a postcolonial reading of border and surveillance technologies by locating technologies between Europe's former colonies and the current border crisis. From the days of colonial conquest to the economic exploitation under the Mandate System and recent years' interventions in the "Orient," I provide a *longue durée* perspective to uncover the unacknowledged legacies that have sedimented into the bureaucratic and technological backbone of the European border regime. The border and surveillance technologies of the contemporary European border regime are genealogically linked to the era of conquest. As such, EU border technologies, including its media infrastructure and bureaucratic systems, do not present qualitative distinctions from pre-digital apparatuses but new declinations of already established colonial technologies such as panoptic surveillance, biopolitical registers, body tags and labels, and deterrent infrastructure. Europe's pre-digital colonial history continues to shape the political present and has morphed into EU border technologies, media infrastructure, classification apparatuses, and weaponry. By locating border and surveillance infrastructure between Europe's former colonies and the current migrant crisis, the book lays bare the colonial fabric of late-modern surveillance technologies—the colonial antecedents of today's border apparatuses.

The European border regime forms part of a racial–colonial complex that stretches from the contemporary refugee crisis to the colonial era. The "between" signifies a spatio-temporal framework that acknowledges the chronological and spatial emergence of both the colony and the crisis, respectively. It presents a methodological take on past and current events based on the assumption that the political administration of colony and crisis is instrumental in mediating Europe's postcolonial border crisis. The media and border architecture of the European border regime applies these concepts as a matrix to cope with, narrate, and visualize the event that commonly became known as the European migration crisis. The spatial ordering of colony and crisis permits to (visually) dislocate the migration event into Europe's former colonies via externalizing the border apparatus while at the same time situating the crisis in the putative elsewheres, outside of Europe. Chronological ordering articulates the event as a contemporary exceptionality (i.e., crisis) by severing it from colonial history. What emerges from this framework is the durability of both colonial and crisis formations. It allows fragmenting the colonial over time and space while acknowledging the presence of multiple crises that spill over from the former colonies into the current crisis context.

The postcolonial condition of the European border presents this book's imperative starting point from which to approach a theme often disarticulated from the colonial period: the EU border and surveillance technologies that are an integral part of what scholars, activists, and migrants have dubbed the "European border regime." While there have been scholarly accounts of the constitutive role of technologies in the colonies, demonstrating, for example, that each stage of imperialism involved certain key technologies such as the gunboat, quinine, steamship lines, submarine telegraph cables, and colonial railroads,[28] the perspective still missing in discussions about the European border regime places race, empire, and the (post)colonial condition at the center of surveillance critique while seeking out their enduring effects in structuring today's political landscape. Public media debates and scholarship on (Critical) Surveillance Studies have long overemphasized not merely the novelty of contemporary technological developments but the novelty of surveillance itself. The often-evoked term of the *surveillance society* is misleading, as there are not only a variety of surveillance societies across the globe but the term temporally encloses the emergence and the many bearings of surveillance in a particular Western time and place, thus foreclosing the multiple genealogies that led to surveillance landscapes in the first place.[29] One example of this shortcoming is the technological trope of 1990s surveillance culture par excellence, the camera gaze of closed circuit television (CCTV) that still today frequently stands in as a general icon for surveillance but made visible a specific paradigm that emerged in Western cities and particularly the UK at the time: a neoliberal urbanism characterized by the privatization of public space through commercial management and private security[30] that sought to enclose and make public space legible and ready for profit.

Media scholar John Fiske argued in the late 1990s that although Foucault and Orwell conceptualized surveillance as integral to modernity, surveillance has been racialized in a manner they did not foresee: today's seeing eye is white.[31] In recent years we see a resurgence of scholarly contributions that hone in on the racial and racist repercussions of surveillance, including its manifold prefigurations that stretch back to the colonial period and the time of the Middle Passage. In *Dark Matters,* Simone Browne reminds her (white) readers that Black and other people of color have lived for centuries with surveillance practices aimed at maintaining a racial hierarchy and guaranteeing the property relations at the heart of chattel slavery. Her genealogy of racial surveillance disrupts the claim of newness often attributed to surveillance technologies as it situates surveillance in "strategies that first accompanied European colonial expansion and transatlantic slavery that sought to structure social relations and institutions in ways that privilege whiteness."[32] Also, Deepa Kumar and Arun Kundnani have insisted that discussions on national and international security and surveillance that have emerged in the wake of 9/11 are "woefully inadequate" precisely through this analytical shortcoming because it is "racist ideas that form the basis for the ways national security surveillance is organized and deployed, racist fears that are whipped up to legitimize surveillance to the public, and the disproportionately targeted racialized groups that have been most effective in making sense of it and organizing opposition."[33] This holds particularly true for the European context, which has been aptly described as a postcolonial space with past and present racisms and racializations; however, scholarship in this context lacks a detailed account of racialized surveillance regimes and their racist implications.[34] "Histories of surveillance," Robert Heynen and Emily van der Meulen claim, "are inextricable from broader histories of colonialism and imperialism, and the global movement of goods, people, diseases, ideas, and technologies." Such histories, they continue, "reflect the profoundly unequal ways in which surveillance has been applied to different people and populations."[35] For them, the term *modernity* is too imprecise when analyzing the history of surveillance as surveillance critique needs to consider the specific dynamics of capitalism, industrialism, and urbanization that have given a particular shape to the global histories of the past centuries. While colonies foreground a key dimension of surveillance, namely its role in "social sorting"[36] as part of longer histories of population management, the colonial and slavocratic history of surveillance is also marked by erasure: more often than not, colonizers did not record but erase the records of those they sought to govern. At the same time, they were disturbed by what they perceived to be "the seeming unknowableness of Africa,"[37] for they lamented a lack of biopolitical data such as the systematic registering of births, marriages, and deaths. To compensate for the lack of information, biometric systems developed as a blunt mechanism for tracking labor in many colonial contexts.[38]

Taking the intricate relationship between the slave ship and the migrant boat as the starting point, "The View from Above" traces panoptic border and surveillance technologies from the Atlantic and Mediterranean world into current EU border politics. By racializing the panopticon as an apparatus of surveillance and discipline not born in European penal institutions, but the slave ship and the tropical sites of European colonies, I complicate present European border panopticism by involving their colonial and slavocratic legacies. The genealogy discussed in the chapter consists of two case studies: the application of drones in the Mediterranean Sea and Eurosur. I discuss the postvisual engagement of these distinct surveillance technologies—a mode of surveillance and control that extends beyond vision—and present the current border crisis as a complex defined by (post)colonial governance, maritime power, and racial capitalist surplus production—features that were defining for the Middle Passage.

The chapter, "Data on Bodies," traces the technologies that put information—data—onto migrants' bodies as moments of colonial ordering that link the racial surveillance infrastructure of the colonial era to today's border regime. In the colony and at the border, data are attached and inscribed onto bodies both physically and bureaucratically with wristbands, tags, pens, and by ordering individuals into groups labeled according to ethnic and racial categories. From the pass tag system in German Southwest Africa and discussions within the colonial society about tattooing the colonized to numbering and classifying refugee bodies in European hotspots and beyond, I discuss how colonial ordering as a racialized and racist technology facilitates (post) colonial governance over time. This chapter further involves scholarship tackling the colonial context of German Southwest Africa to sketch a genealogical line from Windhoek, the capital of present-day Namibia, to Lesvos.

There is an ongoing discussion debating the historical links between German colonialism and European fascism. While the continuity "from Windhoek to Auschwitz" in terms of violence, ideology, economics, and social and racial relations remains contested within the discipline of history, my chapter follows a genealogical approach to the practice of colonial ordering between the German colony and the present border crisis. Far from eclipsing fascism on the European continent or substituting the legacy of the Third Reich with colonial racism, this chapter instead firmly interlinks colonialism, fascism, and the present border regime by discussing Residenzpflicht, a law stipulating the containment of abject mobilities in the German colony, the Third Reich, as well as asylum politics in contemporary Germany.

The chapter, "Bodies of Data," traces the colonial origins of biometrics from British India and German Southwest Africa to the filing cabinets of nineteenth-century criminology and police work and the databases of the current European border regime. Biometric technologies were invented and applied during the age of European imperialism in the disciplines of Anthropometry, Phrenology, and Craniology. While these fields have been rejected as unscientific due to their racism-inflected assumptions and methods, their technologies have, to some extent, survived and continue to inform current biometric practices. My analysis is concerned with understanding biometrics not as a smooth, efficient, and clean mode of identification but a set of necropolitical technologies that target bodies in visceral ways. The entanglement of biometrics and torture at European borders reveals a sovereignty underpinning modes of biometric governance that subjects bodies to physical violence and death with impunity. Refugees and migrants have, however, appropriated biometric technologies for their pursuits and tell their stories to counter death and political erasure. The refugee selfie emerges in a context characterized by imperial faciality and machine readability—both practices used in today's border regime to determine eligibility for citizenship and asylum. These technologies of the self go beyond surveillance and biometric capture to become a powerful intervention into postvisual borderlands.

Since the Cold War, many states of the Global North have developed a range of policies to deter and prevent migrants and refugees from arriving at their territory and accessing their asylum system. Deterrence has not only accelerated deportations but effectively created a climate of fear shaping border regimes around the world. Commonly understood as a policy designed to discourage future actions, deterrence also works beyond operational strategies and policy making. The chapter "Viral Deterrence" frames the Cologne 2015–2016 event as a landmark of political deterrence that used images and numbers to create a politico-affective landscape in which fear of invasion and contagion thrives. Cologne's moral panic created and reiterated the refugee-as-rapist figure to mobilize feelings of insecurity, fear of transgression, and other liberal anxieties that rendered the integrity of the national body under attack. The event had both symbolic and institutional repercussions. It reterriorialized Europe on the sentiment of Western civilizational progress and achievements while introducing a stricter legal framework to deport migrants. My chapter reads Cologne against its (post)colonial precursor: the "Black Shame" campaign of the interbellum period that accused Black colonial troops of raping white German women during the Weimar Republic. Both the "Shame of Cologne" and the "Black Shame" campaign deployed a racialized and sexualized notion of invasion to defame and delegitimize non-white and postcolonial presence in Germany. Moreover, both discourses conflated the body natural and the body politic to cast invasion in viral terms. These discourses presented invasive others as transgressing an already too permeable border, ranging from the contamination of the purity of blood to the undermining of Western cultural accomplishments.

In the coda, I open with a critical reflection on the notion of the state of exception and the crisis. Crisis talk and crisis-mongering have put forth the idea that the transformations we are witnessing today disrupt a state of stability and unfold as a singular event. They tend to conceal the violence and permanent exception that are the norm under global capitalism and our global geopolitics by singling out moments of presumed emergency and crisis from an already crisis-driven status quo. I unpack the colonial genealogy of the state of exception and situate the current complex of multiple crises as racial/colonial instruments that are part of a more extensive arsenal of raciality. EU state violence organizes and technocratically camouflages extrajudicial murder as collateral damage and organizes its politics of killing in a manner that makes it increasingly difficult for the (supra)state to be held accountable. The EU has liquefied many of its institutional bodies by means of postcolonial extraterritorialization and privatization and is applying, perhaps mimicking, the nonstate tactics of those it seeks to target.

## NOTES

1. WHO, "WHO Recommendations for International Traffic in Relation to COVID-19 Outbreak."

2. Crawley, "How COVID-19 Became a Cover to Reduce Refugee Rights."

3. Litzkow, "The Impact of COVID-19 on Refugees and Migrants on the Move in North and West Africa."

4. Todo, "Revealed."

5. In a May 2020 press release, Frontex stated that "if we cannot control the external borders, we cannot control the spread of pandemics in Europe. Frontex plays a key role in ensuring effective protection of the external borders of the European Union

not only against cross-border crime but also against health threats. Frontex, "Europe Day—United against Corona Virus with Eyes on the Future."

6. Monroy, "Frontex and the Use of Force."

7. Michel Foucault prominently began his explorations on the shift in power formations by describing how societies deal with the management of disease with leprosy standing for social exclusion, the administering of the Plague bringing the disciplinary apparatus to the fore, and vaccination against smallpox representing normalization within a biopolitical framework.

8. During the course of the seventeenth century, when the Plague ravaged Europe, the police began to play an increasingly important role, gradually developing into a governmental instrument to help secure the new secular sovereignty of the monarchy while setting the police as the promise of salvation, the counterpart of contagion. Lorey, "Der Traum von der Regierbaren Stadt."

9. Palmer, *The Control of Plague in Venice and Northern Italy*, 54.

10. Winkle, *Geisseln der Menschheit*, 491f.

11. McCormick, *William Petty*.

12. Goodacre, "Economics, Geography and Colonialism in the Writings of William Petty."

13. Foucault and Ewald, *Society Must Be Defended*, 103.

14. Césaire, *Discourse on Colonialism*, 36; Fanon, *The Wretched of the Earth*.

15. Cooper and Stoler, *Tensions of Empire*, 4.

16. Park, "Money, Mortgages, and the Conquest of America."

17. McCoy, *Policing America's Empire*.

18. Schneider, "Smallpox in Africa during Colonial Rule."

19. Rosman, "Racism Row as French Doctors Suggest Virus Vaccine Test in Africa."

20. Garcia, "How the Pandemic Turned Refugees into 'Guinea Pigs' for Surveillance Tech."

21. GIZ, "The Coronavirus Pandemic."

22. Black, "Monitoring Being Pitched to Fight Covid-19 Was Tested on Refugees."

23. Dijstelbloem, "The Migration Machine"; Molnar, "Technology on the Margins." In the first year of the global health crisis, philosopher Paul Preciado suggested that the Covid-19 pandemic transposed control measures previously targeting the non-white and formerly colonized population onto the white social body, bringing home those technologies of confinement, control, and surveillance to make "your body . . . the new territory where the violent border politics that we have been designing and testing for years on 'others' are now . . . taking the form of containment measures and of a war against the virus." In declaring that surveillance protocols and containment measures have boomeranged back onto "your body," which now manifests as "Lampedusa on your skin," Preciado, however, fails to account for the uneven distribution of pandemic control, surveillance, and enclosure procedures across the social spectrum. Preciado, "Learning from the Virus."

24. Venetian authorities considered contagion as coming from outside their city's territory by associating the Plague with sea trading routes, which prompted them to close off their borders by forcing ships into quarantines onto islands off the city for

forty days (*quaranta*). Although the spiritual number forty was taken from the Bible, where it is associated with times of purification, the cordon sanitaire drawn around cities proved to some extent effective even four hundred years prior to the development of the germ theory of disease because it exceeded the two-week incubation period for the Plague bacteria.

25. Chew, Phillips, and Yamada Park, "COVID-19 Impacts on Immigration Detention."

26. Mitropoulos, "Invisible Hand(s): Hidden Labor, AI-Driven Capitalism and the COVID-19 Pandemic," 26.

27. Derrida, *Schurken*.

28. Headrick, *The Tools of Empire*.

29. Wood, "The 'Surveillance Society.'"

30. Ibid.

31. Fiske, "Surveilling the City."

32. Browne, *Dark Matters*, 17.

33. The authors see the surveillance and security landscape entangled with a neoliberalism that has put forth and legitimized racialized notions of security that offer a new "psychological wage" as a compensation for the decline of the social wage, following W. E. B. Du Bois, who has described the public deference and titles of courtesy endowed to nonelite whites in the U.S. antebellum South, which offered entitlement in the form of racial privileges. "Security," they conclude, "has become one of the primary means through which racism is ideologically reproduced in the 'post-racial,' neoliberal era." Kundnani and Kumar, "Race, Surveillance, and Empire."

34. Bhambra, "Whither Europe?"; Saucier and Woods, "Ex Aqua"; Broeck and Saucier, "A Dialogue: On European Borders, Black Movement, and the History of Social Death."

35. Heynen and Meulen, "Unpacking State Surveillance: Histories, Theories, and Global Contexts," 4.

36. Lyon, *Surveillance as Social Sorting*.

37. Cooper and Frederick, *Decolonization and African Society*, 334.

38. Heynen and Meulen, "Unpacking State Surveillance: Histories, Theories, and Global Contexts," 20.

# Chapter 1

# The European Border Regime

## *Conditions of Emergence in a Mediated World*

In 1891, French economist Paul Beaulieu fiercely defended European colonialism in Africa, stating that "this state of the world implies for the civilized people a right of intervention . . . in the affairs of the [barbarian tribes and savages]."[1] His defense came amid the carve-up of Africa by European colonial powers, an act cemented in the 1885 Berlin agreement and vested in the desire to civilize, extract resources, and shape the continent in a manner most beneficial for Europeans. Leroy-Beaulieu's proclaimed "right of intervention" resurfaces again in the externalization of the European Union (EU) border apparatus, a system premised on postcolonial exploits, or, as the European Commission noted, in "the *special relationships* that EU member states may have with third countries, reflecting political, historic and cultural ties fostered through decades of contact [that should be] exploited to the full benefit of the EU."[2] Reverberating through this account is the unbroken claim and entitlement to put African land and resources into the service of European objectives, a process also identified by Peo Hansen and Stefan Jonsson, who have challenged the myth that postwar European integration marked a break with Europe's colonial past. They show that the origins of the EU are inextricably bound up with imperial politics and the "perceived necessity to preserve and prolong the colonial system."[3] From the beginning of the Pan-European movement in the 1920s to its institutionalization in the European Economic Community (today's EU), European integration and the formation of Europe as a political subject were inextricably entangled with the effort to maintain Europe's continued dominance over Africa. Indeed, "a unification of Europe and a unified European effort to colonize Africa were two processes that presupposed one another."[4]

If the EU's political and intellectual forerunner, Eurafrica, was predicated on the very idea of bringing Africa as a "dowry to Europe" and demanded the continent's incorporation into the European enterprise, including its resources of land, labor, and markets,[5] it is most starkly in today's EU border externalization that we see a continuation of these demands, as border externalization is best understood as the EU's ongoing imperial effort to spatially expand its border sovereignty and jurisdiction over neighboring countries. Since 1992 and even more extensively since 2005, the EU has developed a policy of externalizing borders so that displaced people never get to Europe in the first place. Border externalization has created a shift from governing migration on a national level to a shared European migration politics. The system is premised on European intervention abroad as EU border politics depend on the maintenance and financing of a border regime extending far beyond the supranation. This produces a de facto postcolonial border regime stretching as far as North Africa, the Middle East, and sub-Saharan African countries.[6]

Since the first stages of the so-called joint Euro-African strategy on migration with conferences held by EU representatives in Cairo (2000), Rabat (2006), Tripoli (2006), Lisbon (2007), and Valetta (2015), the EU has entered partnerships with thirty-five countries, most of them former European colonies, including Libya, Egypt, Sudan, Niger, and Chad.[7] These partnerships include collaborating with third countries in terms of accepting deported persons, training their police and border officials, developing extensive biometric systems, and donating equipment including helicopters, patrol ships, vehicles, and surveillance and monitoring equipment. One detrimental effect of these partnerships is that they do not externalize the asylum process to non-European territory, as is often claimed,[8] but rather retract the right to asylum,[9] which increases the illegalization of people's movements while substantially expanding the conditions for deportation.[10] The agreements with third countries are further bound in colonial matter as they inherently depend on the former colonies' subjection to European terms of agreement, which reconfigures colonial legacy in terms of a political memory discourse. The agreement between Italy and its former colony Libya, for example, included payment for increased border control along with an apology by Italy for the crimes committed during colonial rule.[11]

For Ann Stoler, contemporary global inequalities present "refashioned and sometimes opaque reworkings . . . of colonial histories."[12] The "debris" and "ruins" that empires leave behind are enduring and can be reworked and reactivated under current conditions—often by mistakenly assuming them to be new. These durable and hardened ruins of the colonial past, Stoler makes clear, produce "imperial formations,"[13] which are distinct from the fixed and readily recognizable sovereignty of past empires. The postcolonial European border regime, with its many flexible entities such as changing geopolitical locations, the multiplication of border checks, local best practices of member states and (sub)contracts with the private industry, constitutes precisely such an imperial formation that might be dismissed as not belonging to the more manifest project of empire. The EU's abdication of migration responsibilities to former colonies (as seen in the many partnerships with third countries), however, constitutes a pivotal moment in which the debris empires leave behind surfaces in a manifest way: border externalization is reminiscent of the strategy of indirect rule employed by European powers during their colonization of Africa, Asia, and the Middle East. Used by the British and French to control parts of their colonial empires, remote governance of colonies or protectorates was inspired by the idea that African and European people were culturally distinct and that local institutions were necessary for colonial governance. European nations sent small military units and white settlers to their colonies to impose a top-down colonial apparatus that would eventually pass on authority from European administrators to existing power structures.[14] Relying on African rulers and collaborators, European authorities invented tribal authority where none existed and co-opted the local leaders' inherited legitimacy to implement cost-efficient control measures. Rather than preserving the precolonial polity, indirect rule modified the public authority of traditional chiefs to ensure the exploitation of the country through taxes, forced labor, and the modification of customary law that allowed European empires to dominate economic and military interests in the colonies without having a large on-the-ground presence.

Colonies have long served as the "preeminent loci of exception" where the controls and guarantees of judicial order can be suspended, and the zones where the violent technologies of the state of exception are deemed to operate in the service of civilization.[15] Today, the legitimizing context for the application of border and surveillance technologies is the proclaimed crisis and the exceptionality ascribed to the European refugee crisis rooted in the unacknowledged colonial legacies that inform today's migration to Europe, including the routes migrants take and the technological apparatuses they encounter on the way. While the 2015 migration event has been repetitively named a crisis and a rupture in the status quo of the political order, some scholars insisted that what we are witnessing today is less a moment of exception but the continuation of racialized violence and part of Europe's ongoing encounter with the world that it created through more than five hundred years of empire, colonial conquest, and enslavement.[16] The root causes of the European refugee crisis are often attributed to events befalling the territory outside of Europe. This assumption severs contemporary migration from Europe's colonial past while presenting the continent as historically sanitized of colonial legacies.[17] Disconnecting contemporary migration from Europe's colonial history necessarily means neglecting the fact that migration and displacement are the historical products of the aftermath of European colonialism and that the majority of migrants seeking asylum in Europe are coming from countries that until recently were under colonial rule.[18] From the days of colonial conquest to the economic exploitation under the Mandate System and recent years' interventions in Afghanistan, Iraq, and Libya, any serious consideration of what lies behind migratory movements toward Europe must account for this colonial history and the way in which it continues to structure the present. The persistent refusal to acknowledge the colonial past has further led to the silencing of alternative histories and, therefore, the silencing of others considered not belonging to Europe.[19]

## ON POSTVISUALITY AS METHOD

Such as the "post" in postcolonial does not denote the end of colonial power, but a rearrangement of power formations after (some) of the colonies formerly ended and nations gained structural independence from empires, I use the term *postvisual* to denote a power formation that was put into play as an answer and effect to the contestations of the ordering power of visuality. With the panopticon as the archetype of surveillance culture, a disciplinary mode of power derived from the optical tradition of visual inspection that instilled a gaze directed against the other and, by way of incorporation, also against oneself, Surveillance Studies has been necessarily entangled with inquiries into visuality, visual culture, and vision. Conversely, the study of *visuality*,[20] a term much in currency during the postmodern 1980s and associated with Visual Culture Studies, where it provided the scholarly framework to scrutinize the ocularcentrism of post-Enlightenment societies—the privilege of vision in the hierarchy of the senses—could not do without considering its complicity with projects of political and social control, including its implications in surveillance assemblages. Vision and visuality are always mediated, and the study of surveillance apparatuses must consider technology as the dominant mode of mediation.

The image, whether produced by a machine autonomously or with the help of a human hand, was always accompanied and complemented by a system that sought to circulate, categorize, or classify the visual by means of numbers. Martin Jay observes that throughout the history of visual discourse, the concept of vision has been extended to cover the eye and the technological apparatuses that augment the eye.[21] The shift from analog to digital technologies and forms of media over the past fifty years has fundamentally altered visual truth production with new technologies provoking a crisis in optical vision that for some Visual Culture theorists reflected an overall decline in the epitome inherited from the Enlightenment where the notion of seeing serves as knowledge acquisition. One of the most significant technological transformations is the increasing predominance of interfaces and the hyperinflation of images it brought along. The replacement of command-line interfaces by graphical user interfaces from the middle of the 1960s led to a new ubiquity of visual interfaces. In his discussion of contemporary visual media, Mark Poster argues that what we are witnessing today does not present an increase of visuality compared to the history of visual media but rather a visual regime distinct from the scopic regimes identified by Jay.[22] Nowadays, the visual world is in the first instance determined by the technological setting that allows employing calculating machines to generate images by binary coding and algorithms. The difference between earlier and present visual regimes is the current use of information machines to create an image and to see, the analysis of visuality must thus always situate the visual in the broader domain of information machines. Postvisuality complicates the neat distinction between images and numbers and conceptualizes these distinct fields according to their malleability rather than mutual exclusivity. The focus on technologies and infrastructure that produce and host the images surrounding us enables to situate postvisuality as a mode of power that creates and depends on technological infrastructure: the sovereign gaze used in population oversight, media representations, panoptic surveillance, and identification technologies are frequently transformed into and exist along streams of data, numbers, and statistics. In turn, these sets of data become again part of the terrain of visuality, not merely by means of data visualization, but the visual objectivity ascribed to them.

As borders have been understood as a method for reproducing racialized distinctions,[23] I argue that postvisuality is also a method of bordering and illustrate how it works as a key strategy for the capture, containment, and regulation of mobility and movement. Postvisuality is an attempt to recuperate the numerical within the visual and grasp the mathematical fundament of visualizing border practices. This numerico-visual gaze resurfaces in assemblages of coloniality and crisis where it seeks to meticulously frame, objectify, and measure subjects and their lifeworlds onto the calculating plane of postvisuality. From the actuarial gaze in media infrastructures to the panoptic gaze of border and surveillance technologies, postvisuality situates the gaze within a regime that is both concerned with the optics of a catastrophic event as well as the numerical patterns put into play to tackle it. Postvisuality is at the same time methodology and object of investigation and reverberates with an approach that Elsbeth Probyn formulated with regards to affects, presenting both an "idea and effect"[24] of sociopolitical situations. As a methodological perspective, it defines, structures, and mediates research objects in the process of interrogation, data retrieval, analysis, and selection of research material. It figures as a technology of power that has morphed into racial/colonial formations underpinning and sustaining the border and surveillance apparatuses between colony and crisis. It interrogates claims of newness ascribed to current technologies: the notion that technologies are unprecedented and developed in a sociopolitical vacuum, clean and shorn of the messy realities of gender, race, class, and geopolitical location that work to maintain global inequalities. It further serves as a methodological tool to question what is usually perceived as succeeding the regime of visuality: the algorithms, metrics, and numbers that increasingly define and organize the visual world, forming its mediological and technological backbone.

In *Into the Universe of Technical Images,* Vilém Flusser attended to what he perceived as a shift occurring in the quality of images by making a distinction between traditional and technical images. Flusser provided a genealogical reconstruction of the various phases of the history of the image that he saw marked by increasing abstraction. Technical images that, for him, include predigital images such as photographs and television, differ from traditional images (Flusser gives the example of cave painting) in that they rely and owe their existence to technical apparatuses. Technical images are "calculated concepts that explain visualizations"[25] and are produced through computation, while traditional images arise through the observation of objects and their depiction. Flusser asserts that "all technical images are visualizations,"[26] and they increasingly become conceptual and are reproduced and distributed on a global scale. Notably, it was in the pre-Internet era or before the Internet became a mass commodity when Flusser proclaimed the ubiquity of technical images and their immersive character. "We live in an illusionary world of technical images," he wrote in 1985, "and we increasingly experience, recognize, evaluate and act as a function of these images."[27]

Since Flusser declared the shift from traditional to technical images in the mid-eighties, Media Studies scholars have made similar observations concerning the qualitative distinctions of images. Carolyn Kane[28] explicitly relates to Flusser's distinction between traditional and technical images when analyzing the intimate alliance between the history of color in information technologies and modes of surveillance and control. For Kane, the use of color in these systems is indicative of the transformation from the use of optics and vision in the disciplinary society to the use of information systems and algorithms in the control society. Kane declares a paradigm shift from optical and visual epistemology into what she terms a "post-optic" and algorithmic lifeworld. According to her, we no longer use color or sight as an end in itself but as a means to another end for "optical vision is also always already subject to technical enframing, calculation and math."[29] Images and color are increasingly generated and manipulated—not by optics or natural vision—but mathematics and electronic media such as television, video, and computer, that are, on a material level, primarily concerned with code, signals, and algorithms and only secondarily with visual expression. In Kane's analysis, the co-emergence of color and surveillance is aided by optical prosthetics, and she understands digital images as, from the start, produced by information technologies—algorithms—and not optics. Here, the image is always an adjunct to the algorithm, and the shift to our post-optic society is marked by a decline in the optical image in exchange for a rise in algorithmic visualization.

It is noteworthy that for Kane, the difference between the optical and the algorithmic image—the former pertaining to disciplinary modes of capture and the latter to the control era—"is analogous to the difference between Flusser's traditional and technical image": "In contrast to an optical image like a photograph or a film, an algorithmic image is a *system* operating through the post-optic principles of informatic reduction, predictive scanning, and the allegorical representation of data."[30] Such as Kane's concept of the algorithmic image consists of a set of algorithms executed to produce a visual result, Flusser's technical image transcodes symptoms (data captured from the world) using the programs and rubrics of cybernetics and information theory. If the technical image is a mosaic assembled from particles,[31] we clearly see the reference Kane relies upon: the millions of electronic bits that obey an algorithmic input and eventually create an optical product in the form of the illusion of a coherent image.

Flusser's and—working in his spirit—Kane's distinction between traditional/technical and optical/algorithmic images may not altogether be convincing. The paradigmatic example of a traditional image that Flusser gives, the cave painting, has been fundamentally reassessed by historians of Paleolithic art, at the latest since the discovery of the *Grotte Chauvet-Pont d'Arc*, one of the best-preserved sites for prehistoric art in the south of France.[32] The cave's different motifs far from merely depict life in a mimetic or indexical mode (Flusser's criteria for traditional images) but instead qualify as technical images, "concepts made into visualizations." This will serve to caution against conceiving the changing fabric of images within a narrative of Western progress—cast in the increasing abstraction of images and technologies of visualization. Postvisuality assumes that both in the metrics and the algorithms lies a visuality that has fundamentally transformed itself for the sake of accumulating power that might otherwise be contested. The perspective acknowledges the transformation of images over time without placing their qualitative shifts on the chronological timeline of technological modernity. It further recognizes the codependence of optical and algorithmic images without hierarchizing them temporally. Hence, the "post" in postvisual does not evoke a hierarchical order that refers to a moment after visuality but acknowledges that it is inflected by anachronism.

Akin to the existence of race in post-Holocaust Europe, colonial remnants are often seen as anachronistic and a relic of the past. Anachronism has been mobilized for different ends, often denouncing the existence of present (post)colonial tangents as untimely, such as when Spain's King Felipe VI called on Britain to "end the colonial anachronism of Gibraltar" to reiterate Spanish claims over the Rock.[33] The longue durée of the racio-technological formations analyzed in this book invoke anachronistic postcolonial time. Anachronism, understood as chronological inconsistency in some arrangement, especially a juxtaposition of persons, events, objects, or customs from different periods, was long recognized as a methodological error to avoid. Postcolonial and queer theory, however, celebrate anachronism as a visible site of dislocation that calls into question what counts as timely and what constitutes history.[34] For both fields, embracing anachronism becomes a way to rethink contemporaneity as untimely coexistence and to claim lived relationships to the past that dominant forms of historicism obscure. The postvisual and postcolonial condition of the European border regime must be placed against this chronopolitical backdrop. Postcolonial time consigns colonial experience simultaneously to the past and the center of contemporary sociopolitical experience.[35] It locates both the entire burden of enduring colonial domination but also the capacity for insubordination, on a single plane, in what might be considered an anachronist architecture. This trans-historical perspective bears some potential pitfalls. Sandro Mezzadra and Federico Rahola caution against positing a logic of absolute continuity from the colonial past to the postcolonial present as this might end up perpetuating a "redemptive mechanism" that dispenses with "anti-colonial struggles as a mere inconvenience . . . along the linear and uninterrupted thread of the history of domination and exploitation."[36] According to them, the danger lies in depriving the colonial subject of all forms of agency and eliminating any revolutionary act not pertaining to the West to a point where action is shifted from the colonized subject to the eternal (neo)colonial subject. By conflating regimes of power that have emerged under specific historical conditions, we not only risk neglecting the transformationalist character of these systems––their flexibility and adaptability—but the very effects that acts of resistance against these regimes have. Migration movements, labor protests, abolitionist thought, anticolonial struggles, feminist critique, queer uprisings, student protests, and Indigenous resistance all have contested and challenged these regimes and forced them to fundamentally alter their mode of operation. How can we grapple, then, with the postcolonial time of the European border regime? How can we foster an analysis where the postcolonial present is not sucked inevitably back into the vortex of the colonial past and, by doing so, absolves the neocolonial present of all responsibility?

This book attempts to recuperate moments of upheaval between colony and crisis that have, if only temporarily, radically altered the path of empire, exploitation, and conquest. It assembles and archives the struggles that went alongside racial technological formations and points to the ruptures in post-colonial governing and the many moments of failure that have led, if only sometimes, to the breaking of (post)colonial machines. At the same time, it narrates the moments of persistence of these regimes that often, like the moments of rupture, remain untold in public discourse and history-making. In other words, it recounts the messy actualities of racial governmentality between colony and crisis in a complex of contradictions, anachronisms, and moments of regime triumph and failure. What we might gain from such an analysis are the incoherent contours of shadow archives that have accompanied empire, and fractions of empire, into the present moment of investigation.

## NOTES

1. Pollard and Holmes, *Documents of European Economic History*, 165.
2. "Communication from the Commission to the European Parliament, the European Council, the Council and the European Investment Bank on Establishing a New Partnership Framework with Third Countries under the European Agenda on Migration," 8; my emphasis.
3. Hansen and Jonsson, "Bringing Africa as a 'Dowry to Europe,'" 461; Hansen and Jonsson, *Eurafrica*.
4. Hansen and Jonsson, "Bringing Africa as a 'Dowry to Europe,'" 449.
5. Besides Eurafrica, there existed yet another intellectual project fundamentally premised on Europe's exploitation of African resources. In the 1920s, German architect Herman Sörgel presented a gigantic engineering and colonization scheme named Atlantropa or Panropa, a technological utopia that envisioned building a giant dam across the Strait of Gibraltar to create the world's largest hydroelectric facility. Gall, *Das Atlantropa-Projekt*.
6. Gaibazzi, Dünnwald, and Bellagamba, *EurAfrican Borders and Migration Management*.
7. The main outcome of the Valetta Conference was the European Trust Fund in Africa (EUTF), a policy document that seeks to address the root causes of migration and displacement on the African continent. The legal document supporting the implementation of the fund stipulated that the countries covered by the EUTF "are considered to be in crisis . . . for the duration of the Trust Fund." European Commission, "Commission Decision on the Establishment of a European Union Emergency Trust Fund for Stability and Addressing Root Causes of Irregular Migration and Displaced Persons in Africa," 8–9; Article 3. The crisis-narrative accompanying the encroachment of the European border apparatus into its former colonies allowed the EU to forego public procurement law and, by declaring half of the African continent in

crisis, permitted the EU to grant the vast majority of the fund not to NGOs or African organizations, but to agencies run by EU member states. The majority of the EUTF fund was granted to IOM, UNHCR, the German development agency GIZ, the Italian government, and the French organization Civipol. Together, these organizations implement 74 percent of the migration management projects funded through the three migration funds, resulting in the establishment of a de facto "European migration management cartel." Spijkerboer and Steyger, "European External Migration Funds and Public Procurement Law," 507; footnote 91.

8. Hamood, *African Transit Migration through Libya to Europe: The Human Cost.*

9. Andrijasevic, "Deported."

10. Ibid.; Genova and Peutz, *The Deportation Regime*; Fekete, "The Deportation Machine."

11. De Cesari, "The Paradoxes of Colonial Reparation."

12. Stoler, *Duress*, 5.

13. Ibid., 56.

14. Korieh, "Hegemonic and Negotiated Encounters: Reflections on Indirect Rule and Protest in Colonial Eastern Nigeria."

15. Mbembe, "Necropolitics," 24.

16. Broeck and Saucier, "A Dialogue: On European Borders, Black Movement, and the History of Social Death"; Saucier and Woods, "Ex Aqua"; Danewid, "White Innocence in the Black Mediterranean."

17. De Genova, *The Borders of "Europe,"* 18.

18. Bhambra, "The Current Crisis of Europe"; Hegde, *Mediating Migration*; Khiabany, "Refugee Crisis, Imperialism and Pitiless Wars on the Poor"; Ponzanesi and Blaagaard, "In the Name of Europe"; Zaccaria, "(Trans)MediterrAtlantic Embodied Archives."

19. Bhambra, "Whither Europe?"

20. Haraway, "Situated Knowledges"; hooks, *Black Looks*; Mulvey, *Visual Pleasure and Narrative Cinema.* The term *visuality* was developed in contrast to *vision,* understood as the physical process of seeing, and widely taken to mean the sociopolitical process of producing, circulating, and consuming images. In *Situated Knowledges,* however, Donna Haraway crucially politicized vision and visual perception, which, she argues, is mediated and embedded in power formations as vision depends on technologies of seeing, both hard (e.g., camera and scanners) and soft, such as discursive practices and the clinical or technocratic gaze.

21. Jay, *Downcast Eyes.*

22. Poster, *What's the Matter with the Internet?*

23. Mezzadra and Neilson, *Border as Method.*

24. Probyn, "Writing Shame," 23.

25. Flusser, *Into the Universe of Technical Images*, 43.

26. Ibid., 44.

27. Ibid., 10.

28. Kane, *Chromatic Algorithms.*

29. Ibid., 215.

30. Ibid., 18; original emphasis. Similarly, the authors of the anthology *Technovisuality* understand their concept as "an extension of Flusser's concept of the technical image." Grace, Kit-Sze, and Yuen, *Technovisuality*, 3.

31. Flusser, *Into the Universe of Technical Images*, 10.

32. In the view of archaeologist and filmmaker Marc Azéma, the cave's sophisticated depictions of space, line, and movement that prehistoric people drew some thirty thousand years ago present an early form of cinema, foreshadowing its temporal logic and immersive quality. Azéma, *La Grotte Chauvet-Pont d'Arc*.

33. Govan, "King Felipe Urges UK End 'Colonial Anachronism' of Gibraltar."

34. Espousing what Bliss Cua Lim terms "temporal critique," postcolonial theorists have shown that the homogenous, empty time upon which Western history depends, relegates non-Western people and practices to a previous historical moment. Lim, *Translating Time*. In turn, queer theorists question the "straight time" of history—the way linear time reinforces heteronormative patterns of development and depends upon reproductive futurity. Edelman, *No Future*; Halberstam, *In a Queer Time and Place*.

35. Mezzadra and Rahola, "The Postcolonial Condition."

36. Ibid., 44.

## Chapter 2

# The View From Above

## *The Traffic of Non-White Bodies in the Mediterranean World*

In 2014, photographer Massimo Sestini was aboard the *Bergamini* frigate to follow the rescue operation Mare Nostrum off the Libyan coast. After twelve stormy days on the boat, Sestini and the crew spotted a boat carrying migrants and flew above it with a helicopter, taking the picture that would become emblematic of the European migrant crisis and extensively circulate in newspapers, magazines, and websites, including humanitarian campaigns. The photographer's elevated viewpoint from the helicopter documents the tightly packed refugee boat and the many faces looking back and returning his gaze from above. It sheds a documentarist gaze upon a precarious moment of illegalized flight across the Mediterranean Sea, captured and witnessed from a safe distance. The widely circulated media photograph provides the entry point to this chapter's analysis of racial surveillance at Europe's maritime borders and is read against another iconic image that documents the tragedy and system behind a tightly packed ship: the diagram of the slave ship *Brooks* (also known as *Brookes*), which became widely known after prints of her were published in 1788 that became iconic for the slave trade's inhumanity. Built by Liverpool-based slave merchant Joseph Brooks Jr. in 1781, the *Brooks* ship was the object of critique of the London Committee, a British abolitionist group that depicted the gruesome conditions on board the slave ship by showing slaves arranged in accordance with the Regulated Slave Trade Act of 1788. The diagram, Simone Browne[1] observes, is filled with miniature Black figures dressed in loincloths who are not replicas of each other but have distinct gestures while some seem to look back at the view from above capturing them. The sketch is "clinical in its architectural logic and provides an almost aerial viewpoint," namely that of predominantly white and male abolitionist lawmakers.[2] In both the photograph of the migrant ship and the slave ship, the view from above is returned by those depicted, but the vertical gaze shed onto the migrant ship is welcomed euphorically with outstretched arms, waving hands, laughter, and victory signs. Not unlike the abolitionist white men who produced the *Brooks* sketch to provoke "an instantaneous impression of horror upon all who saw it,"[3] the capturing of the migrant ship from above documents the horrific conditions of migrant journeys and might also interpellate us, the spectators, to witness and abolish the system enabling the violence portrayed.

The entanglement of the contemporary border regime with the Atlantic world is an intricate affair, as slavery has been mobilized as both a trope and historical background by critics as well as defendants of Mediterranean migrant policies. Politicians, journalists, and antislavery campaigners frequently link migrant journeys in the Mediterranean to the coerced necrotransport of the Atlantic slave trade, a historical template that enabled some to demand the abolition of trafficking networks as if it were a moral necessity. When in 2015 Matteo Renzi titled traffickers the "slave traders of the 21st century,"[4] the Italian prime minister presented the trafficking complex as the real danger for migrant journeys, an informal sector that has, on the contrary, grown in response to the illegalization of flight. Renzi used the figure of the slave trader to legitimize policies that would eventually make migrants' journeys across the sea more dangerous, so substantially increasing the fatality of migrant journeys ascribed to the smuggling networks in the Mediterranean basin. The statement mirrors a disturbing coalition in public discourse on sea-bound migration that, in using the terms *trafficking* and *smuggling* interchangeably, aligns people advocating for military force with slavery abolitionists by presenting all illegalized movements as potentially involving coercion. While both terms criminalize irregular migration, the act of smuggling involves, contrary to trafficking, voluntary and consensual agreements between migrants and those who help to navigate borderlands. The history ostensibly thwarted in Renzi's narrative is the fact that it were the slave states of the eighteenth and nineteenth centuries that used an abolitionist logic to legitimize the carving up of Africa during one of colonialism's most notorious moments, the Berlin Conference of 1885.[5] While the 1885 Berlin Agreement stipulated that Africa "may not serve as a market or means of transit for the trade in slaves, of whatever race they may be,"[6] today, it is in Libya where a present-day slave trade emerged,[7] targeting Europe-bound refugees and migrants that became immobilized and contained by EU border politics in Libyan detention centers. With over 4,000 km of land borders, each of the six countries bordering Libya on its south, east, and western frontiers acts as an often-used point of entry for refugees and migrants on their way to Europe. During the medieval Trans-Saharan Slave Trade, Tripoli became the primary outlet for trading slaves across the desert.[8] The current routes refugees take toward Europe strongly resonate with those that once determined the ancient trade relations between Europe and North African countries. These routes were used to connect Europe to the "Orient" and Africa to trade spices, silk, and gold and went along Baghdad, Aleppo, Damascus, Cairo, Al Mahdiyya, and Côte d'Ivoire, Fez, and Pantelleria to Palermo. Today's people on the move have adopted existing trans-Saharan trade routes that have operated for centuries in transporting goods between Libya and neighboring African countries but that frequently change according to political circumstances.[9] Just as the "Scramble for Africa" legitimized its colonizing mission based on a civilizational discourse promoting the stamping out of slavery, EU officials apply a paternalistic discourse against illegalized migration that sanctions state violence in the disguise of a protective and humanitarian politics. If the trope of slavery is used to condemn trafficking and smuggling networks and to sanction restrictive access to Europe, the question remains how to grapple with the border crisis as a complex defined by (post)colonial governance, maritime power, and racial capitalist surplus production—features that were defining for the Middle Passage.

The abolitionist gaze from above, as captured in the *Brooks* sketch and the migrant boat image, is also a panoptic one, one that registers—in line with the meaning of the Greek prefix *pan*—"all members of a group" while exerting, like the Greek god of the shepherds, pastoral or well-meaning power over those subjected to its gaze. If, as David Lyon suggested, "the disciplinary gaze of the Panopticon is the archetypical power of modernity,"[10] in *Dark Matters*, Simone Browne contends that the slave ship, too, must be viewed as an essential operation of modernity as it presents a mobile, seagoing prison at a time when the modern prison had not yet been established on land.[11] Recounting Jeremy Bentham's departure from Brighton to Krichev in imperial Russia where the English social reformer conceived of the panopticon for the first time,[12] Browne remarks that at one point during his journey to Constantinople, Bentham traveled on a cramped Turkish *caïque* that held, as he noted in his journal, "18 young Negresses (slaves) under the hatches."[13] The fact that the history of the panopticon's formation is marked by the experience of chattel slavery prompts Browne to situate the ur-model of surveillance in "strategies that first accompanied European colonial expansion and transatlantic slavery that sought to structure social relations and institutions in ways that privilege whiteness."[14]

Since Foucault wrote his elaborations on panopticism in the mid-seventies, scholars have criticized the Eurocentric premises of panopticism and suggested alternative genealogies by situating the emblem of modern disciplinary power not in European penal institutions but the laboratories of modernity: the colonies. Although Foucault acknowledged the experimental character of colonies in his boomerang thesis and asserted that the panopticon "was also a laboratory," insofar as "it could be used as a machine to carry out experiments, to alter behavior, to train or correct individuals," he never connected the panoptic modality of power to the imperial setting.[15] Timothy Mitchell has incisively shown how the colonial mapping of space and its underlying cartographic reason produced a detachment from the world and the viewing subject from its object. This allowed seeing the world as if it were an exhibition and this "exhibitionary order," in turn, innately depended on elevated viewpoints such as viewing platforms, rendering colonized space visible and governable.[16] Colonizers, among them Western tourists and artists visiting the Middle East, used mounds of rubbish, military observation towers, or the Great Pyramid of Giza to sneak a view from above. At the top of the renowned pyramid, teams of Bedouin were organized to heave and push the traveler to the top and "would carry the European on their shoulders to all four corners, to observe the view."[17] Striking in Mitchell's example of the colonial view from above is the labor on which the gaze depends—the "labor of surveillance"[18]—and the blatant visual description it offers, for here, the view from above is literally enacted on the back of the other.

It was also Jeremy Bentham who, during a trip to the Middle East, aspired a panoptic gaze over a Muslim town "from a thing they call a *minaret*,"[19] allowing him to appropriate the holy tower as a viewing platform to inhabit a position from where, "like the authorities in the panopticon, one could see and yet not be seen."[20] The view from above here figures as an Orientalizing tool for strategic military observation in the colony, while also foreshadowing its use in the form of weaponized airpower that rendered legible Oriental cities and villages to colonial air policing in the 1920s and 1930s,[21] including the more recent history of warfare in the Orient in which "elevation secures the higher truth."[22]

The view from above has gradually distanced itself from the subject being viewed and progressed from the top of the hill, the mountain, or the height of the horse cavalry overseeing the battlefield into the air to produce sky-situated knowledge.[23] The First World War was the first conflict in which aircraft-borne cameras enabled widespread photoreconnaissance. Since then, satellite imagery presents a powerful resource for international security and geopolitical aspirations, governing the below through map-making, aerial survey, and photogrammetry. Seeing like a state, whether militarily, cartographically, or administratively, is akin to airborne and synoptic superiority, implementing what Donna Haraway termed "the view from above," a view "from nowhere, from simplicity," which aims to play the "god trick" in science/technology and militarism.[24] The illusion of being able to see everywhere from a disembodied position of nowhere is an integral component of histories of capitalism, colonialism, and male supremacy.[25] The immunized eye in the sky is a patriarchal and colonial tool, an "avatar" of capital, masculinity, and whiteness.[26] The distant view is credited with being more rational and unambiguous than any other perspective. It accounts for the aerial position as an imagined rational, scientific, and epistemological space that facilitates testing, analysis, experimentation, and exploration. Situated at the interface of science, ways of seeing, and militarism, "there are few perspectives more culpable in their enlistment into practices of war, violence and security than the aerial one."[27] Although from above, "everything seems ordered and organized, calculated and rendered unambiguous,"[28] the aerial view, as this chapter will make clear, pertains to a system of domination rather than the perfected final step in the history of visualizing technologies.

## BLACK DATA: DRONES IN THE MEDITERRANEAN SEA

Since the EU started funding drones under the Preparatory Action for Security Research (2004–2006), border control drones have received more research and development (R&D) funding than any other kind of drones.[29] Although current EU laws prohibit fully unmanned drones from flying in commercial airspace, the funding for joint European dronification continues unchecked with the EU investing research and development funds in unmanned aerial vehicles (UAVs), optionally piloted aircraft, remotely piloted aircraft, and balloon aerostats. EU dronification is marked by corporate lobbyism as Europe's new but essential role in the drone business is set by board members of the leading European defense companies such as BAE Systems, Airbus, Leonardo, and Thales.[30] The European military and security industry profits on both sides of the refugee tragedy: it delivers arms and other equipment that fuel conflicts and repression in parts of the world where most refugees originate and is not, as Mark Akkerman observes, a passive beneficiary of EU largesse but instead actively encourages the growing securitization of Europe's borders to benefit the security and defense sector.[31] While the money trail of the emerging European drone business has been documented,[32] information about the actual deployment of drones in the Mediterranean region is still scarce.[33] At the moment of writing, Europe is testing border drones in a wide range of contexts[34] while still relying on U.S. and Israeli drone technology, with the latter tested on Palestinians living in the occupied territories.[35]

As for drones in the Mediterranean basin, the EU has launched a military operation known as Operation Sophia (formerly European Union Naval Force Mediterranean, or EUNAVFOR MED) to disrupt established refugee routes in the Mediterranean region. Operation Sophia was the EU's answer to the Libya migrant shipwrecks of April 2015—one of the most fatal disasters yet produced by the border regime, which left over four hundred people dead. The mission presents a turn in border policing for it enlists military and defense assets against the logistics of migrant journeys, placing the destruction of smuggler and trafficker networks front and center. The operation's core mandate is documented in an EU classified report[36] providing insight into six months of EUNAVFOR MED's operations and states its preemptive mission to "identify, capture and destroy" vessels on Libyan territory before they enter EU waters. The operation's technical equipment includes "nine surface units, a submarine, three fixed-wing maritime patrol aircraft, five helicopters and one tactical UAV"[37] for surveillance, reconnaissance, and interference.

Operation Sophia was named after a baby born to a Somali woman on the German frigate *Schleswig Holstein* in August 2015 and, with this, evokes the operation's life-saving capacities by suggesting that it works in the biopolitical framework of making life. This stands, however, in stark contrast to the surge in fatalities it produced.[38] The operation's preemptive and proto-territorial approach—destroying vessels on Libyan territory before they are used to cross waters—resulted in illegalized migration networks no longer sending larger vessels with five hundred or six hundred people. Instead, 70 percent of all boats leaving the Libyan coast are rubber dinghies, which are then picked up twelve miles off the coast, a change that made the crossing more dangerous for migrants and led to a surge of deaths at sea.[39] The precarious shift toward unseaworthy vessels brought about a radical change in visibility-making in the Mediterranean Sea. Up to this date, state-of-the-art technology cannot detect small boats such as rubber dinghies on satellite radars,[40] and while these remain invisible to detection, drones promise to deliver the signal intelligence needed to generate an effective maritime overview. By pushing migrants to use smaller vessels, Operation Sophia effectively makes them disappear under the current view from above while at the same time providing a rhetorical basis for the further technological enhancement of aerial surveillance. To be undetectable under satellite radars can indeed be a desirable effect and guarantee the success of clandestine border crossings. Yet, at the same time, the production of invisibility must be read as a necropolitical effort depriving illegalized migrants of the possibility to appear in the systems for SAR.[41] Operation Sophia creates the conditions under which refugees disappear in monitoring systems only to use this same deficiency to legitimize the further fortification of the electronic curtain. This creates a closed circuit of technological solutions in which the security and defense industry takes on the role of both demand and supply.

As the 2015 Libya migrants' shipwrecks were used to implement and legitimize the border Operation Sophia, the adoption of Eurosur, the European Border Surveillance System, was framed as a consequence of the 2013 Lampedusa tragedy, where 360 deaths at sea were reported. Designed for the surveillance of land and external sea borders to "ensure the safety of the

Schengen area,"[42] Eurosur uses drones, reconnaissance aircraft, ship reporting systems, offshore sensors, and satellite remote sensing to track migratory movements. It is conceived as a "system of systems"[43] as it interlinks intelligence gathered from the European situational picture and the common pre-frontier intelligence picture (CPIP, managed by Frontex), which focuses on areas beyond Schengen. Data shared within the Eurosur network consist of information related to incidents at the EU's external land and sea borders, the status and position of patrols, small vessels, and analytical reports and intelligence. These data are then used to establish situational pictures at the national and European levels, along with the pre-frontier situational sketch. According to the regulation introducing Eurosur, a "situational picture means a graphical interface to present near-real-time data and information received from different authorities, sensors, platforms, and other sources" and is deployed to "achieve situational awareness" as well as to "support the reaction capability along the external borders."[44] A technical feasibility study carried out by large defense companies gives an example of its modus operandi:

> 5th May 20XY: According to satellite imagery provided by XY, this morning around 5am 7 wooden boats (length 12–15m) with about 250 illegal migrants departed from the coast of the African country Z next to the village K (coordinates xz East yw West) in harsh weather conditions (wind level 5 increasing). The type of boats used has typical speed of 7–8 knots. Due to the current migration trends, it is expected that the boats will head for MS A (70% probability) or for MS B (30% probability). The authorities of country Z have been contacted by NCC A, which, despite the recently delivered patrol boats, is not expected to take any action. NCC A is currently coordinating with NCC B and FRONTEX (joint operation Karies) their patrolling activities for SAR and interception. FRONTEX is currently redirecting satellites and two surveillance planes over the area TOMATO (route to MS A).[45]

Although situational awareness and reaction capability are put forth as a key focus in policy documents, it is far from clear from this example that the goal of the alert and subsequent surveillance measures is a priori to save lives. Despite the "harsh weather conditions" and the likelihood of overcrowding in the boats, life-saving measures do not appear as an operational priority. Instead, the migratory event is orbited by sophisticated border technologies and assessed from a distance, a technique Andrew Herscher termed "surveillant witnessing."[46] If panoptic technologies permit "proactive approaches of control at a distance"[47] and do not instantly lead to SAR, it is vital to ask what Eurosur in effect enables.

According to Martina Tazzioli, the near-real-time data provided by the multilayered situational pictures are not used for real-time interventions but work as a continuously updated map that locates migratory events.[48]

Eurosur's key function, the pooling of information, is a process of mediation "as the information is often partially processed before dissemination."[49] The life-threatening event of the boat in distress is a mediated event, albeit one that is actively geared toward a specific trajectory. The size of a dot on the Eurosur map indicating an illegal border crossing is not given by the number of people on the boat, but "the entity of the dots marked on the map depends on the risk factor associated with that migration phenomenon and its manageability— namely the estimated costs and the feasibility of tackling it."[50] Tazzioli concludes that Eurosur, far from being a tool for SAR, uses migrants' visibilities as a pretext to generate future visibility and data. The example above shows how Eurosur operationalizes intelligence in a preemptive and risk assessment–driven mode: the situational picture generated from aerial surveillance and other sources is made up of past probability calculations as data generated from risk calculations feed into the image and calculate a (probable) future trajectory that then becomes the basis for operational measures. The functioning of Eurosur's locating and tracking devices demonstrates that an always already digitalized calculus of handling the visual is determining the military visibility at work in the agencies' border technologies. This type of seeing enabled by border surveillance technology creates a "statist regime of visuality" that effectively abstracts its human targets and reduces them to a "calculable formula of risk factors" as it "enables the effective liquidation of the subject in instrumentalizing life in terms of an algebraic formula."[51] Not geared as a tool for SAR, visibility is built and sustained for industry purposes and functions within a closed circuit where security and defense companies stipulate both demand and supply.

Notably, it is precisely the reduction of those captured on the Eurosur screens to risk factors that generates value. For Jonathan Beller, the entanglement of visuality and digitality is materialized in what he terms the "screen/ image," an effect of the "re-organization of the life world by that interface called the screen along with the calculus of the image."[52] The screen/image is both the interface that displays and creates images and that which produces data and meta-data, presenting images as fundamentally composed of informatics and information. Beller describes the informationalization of our social practices regarding images with the sequence "Image-Code-Financialization." The process produces images as valuable through codification and facilitates that images eventually emerge as "image-commodities."[53] Following the Marxist interpretation of value generation, Beller states that "workers put more value into the creation of commodities than they receive in their wages; with spectatorship, spectators do more to valorize and legitimate images, media platforms and the *status quo* than they receive in pleasure or social currency."[54] While this account at first reads like pertaining to a cycle of value extraction from and within the Global North, Beller makes sure to locate the (neo)colonial underpinning of value generation through screen/ images in the colonial enterprise and the notorious slave ship records:

> Like the ledgers of slave ships, the East India Company, and monopoly cartels, the metrics of dataveillance are precisely the metrics of valuation. They measure the very metabolism of a society organized by screens in a way that suggests that computational capital is also computational colonialism. These screens interface the dynamic data-visualizations of computational capital and convert the general population into content providers. They are also worksites—points where attention is required to valorize capital through the production of new information.[55]

Screen/images work as interface and conjuncture of the visual and the digital and mark the transmutation from visuality to postvisuality. An effect of this formation is that refugees' movements appear as commodities, statistical probabilities, deviations, and vectors of risk as they become content providers for an expanded European surveillance and security apparatus. The generation of surplus through the screen/image is congruent with the colonial extrapolation of resource extraction from the Global South. While the "dispossessed" have always been content providers for a (scientific) surplus-driven white male and sexualized gaze,[56] Beller suggests that "[p]eoples of the Global South were the first 'content providers.' Now the situation is generalized."[57] From collecting anthropological data to using Black and colonized bodies for Western scientific projects, what the reorientation of Beller's remarks toward the migrant ship elucidates is less the generalization of data harvested from everyone equally—suggesting a boomerang effect that levels the data collection of contemporary surveillance capitalism with the alleged "raw data"[58] violently subtracted during the colonial period—but the persistent mode of generating "black data"[59] in the context of European migration. If migrants' appearance on the screen/images of Eurosur becomes an essential locus for financialization in Europe's enhanced border-security complex, the effects of the entanglement of image and code—screen/images—become salient as they reveal a financialization directly connected to border security. Signal intelligence is not mounted into humanitarian action but used to increase the preemptive capacities of the border regime, thus creating further demand for the security and defense industry. This scope of activity continues beyond Europe's outer borders where it fortifies its early warning and deterrence capacities and increases refugees' and would-be migrants' reliance on trafficking networks.

The assigning of numerical value to non-white and particularly Black bodies and the simultaneous process of harvesting data from these bodies is caught up in the history of enslavement and colonialism that transforms bodies into value via risk cost and assessment. As if to rehearse the signature moment of risk capitalism's Atlantic genealogy, when Captain Luke Collingwood threw sick, dying, and healthy slaves off the slave ship *Zong* (1781), which enabled the shipowner to file an insurance claim for his lost "cargo," the view from above in the Mediterranean is—like the historic homicidal moment—facilitated by a system in place that transformed "the slaves from bearers of personhood into bearers of an abstract quantum of value."[60]

Returning to the diagram of the *Brooks* slave ship, we see that well before the panoptic gaze of EU border surveillance turned the emergence of migrant ships on their screens into surplus for the European defense industries, the panoptic sketch illustrated a moment of "computational colonialism."[61] Beller remarks that seen against the white background of the slave ship floor, the Black bodies captured in the *Brooks* sketch present an early version of digital measurement: the zeroes and ones from the binary code assigning a pattern of binary digits, or bits, to each character, instruction, or rule. These classificatory mathematics were one of the logics accompanying the Middle Passage as it stripped the enslaved of their individuality and singularity and reduced them to specimens within the transatlantic economy. Computational rationality prominently materialized in the system of cybernetics, and the model fundamentally depended on the trope of slavery to introduce and proliferate its techno-rational episteme. Modern technics, as Bernard Stiegler remarked, is dominated by cybernetics as the science of organization,[62] and it was also with the notion of cybernetic science in mind that Martin Heidegger delivered his critique of technological modernity. Not coincidentally, it was the explicit racial and slave analogies the Father of Cybernetics, Norbert Wiener, used in his book *The Human Use of Human Beings* (1950) that accompanied the introduction of the cybernetics discourse and made the logic behind the system readily available by using slavery metaphors. Wiener's abundant use of slave analogies reflected "a growing concern for the ethics of a technological notion of otherness that can be traced back to the historical ground of the analogy itself: slavery."[63] The question posed in Wiener's book—whether machines have feelings or not—is, of course, a racialized one, and Wiener explicitly stated that "the automatic machine, whatever we think of any feelings it may have, is the precise economic equivalent of slave labor."[64]

By using the ship, icon of slavery, for introducing cybernetics theory, Wiener not only foreshadowed the racial structure undergirding later digital technologies[65] but, surely unbeknownst to him, launched an early lexicon in which to make sense of today's Black sea-bound movements that are again put into the service of resource extraction and capital accumulation. Coerced movement and containerization were part and condition of the dehumanizing project of chattel slavery that objectified people to goods to trade them between imperial European powers. The numerical logic underlying the slavocratic infrastructure in the Mediterranean historically enchains precarious migrant journeys and off-shore detention to a six-hundred-year sequence of extraordinary renditions of people of color, as alien, chattel, and movable property. The surplus-oriented economies of border and surveillance technologies are inherently dependent on the movements of non-white sea traffic in the Mediterranean, bringing into stark relief the important locus of the waters surrounding Europe, for the resources that would later empower the racial capitalism of the Atlantic enterprise, as remarked by Cedric Robinson, were accumulated in the Mediterranean world. For the context of present migration in the Mediterranean, this historical backdrop elucidates some of the persisting factors surrounding migrant journeys, among them Italian ports as relevant loci for both present and historical capital accumulation[66] and the ongoing struggle over ports as open and safe points of entry for migrants. At the same time, the agency of migratory movements renders these historic routes complex up to the point where they fundamentally undermine the notion that the "slave past provides a ready prism for apprehending the black political present."[67]

## THE HORIZONTAL GAZE

When the Romans christened the Mediterranean Sea *Mare Nostrum*, Our Sea, and when Italian nationalists reclaimed the term during the "Scramble for Africa" to call for the establishment of an Italian colonial empire, the "our" did not include Black, non-white, and non-European bodies. *Mare Nostrum* recalls the violent history of conceiving the sea, as Carl Schmitt[68] did, as the ideal route for globalization and capital accumulation, and the moment when the sea that formed part of the commons was transformed into the property of the Western state.[69] Édouard Glissant[70] notes that for many, the history and collective memory of the sea is marked by the violence of colonial expansion, chattel slavery, loss, and grief. In foundational colonial narratives, such as *Robinson Crusoe,* the ocean, Suvendrini Perera writes, signifies a borderless domain "wherein the castaway and the sailor, cast as white heroic, masculinised figures, exemplify and assert the moral attributes of imperial racial virtue, to end by making for themselves new homes and new worlds at the end of their voyaging."[71] The sea provides the backdrop for unfettered white masculinity in search of adventures, wealth, and new worlds. This project is premised on the back of racialized others, a fact also underlined by Peter Hulme,[72] who understands the counter figures of the heroic white explorer as the countless non-white bodies that were charged with carrying the weight of imperial projects across the sea. Vertical visualities in the Mediterranean—and foremost the drone, avatar of capital,

masculinity, and whiteness—assert claims of controlling migratory movements, a project that is, however, refuted by many other movements in the
Mediterranean Sea that run counter to and alongside the view from above
observing the waters around Europe. Humanitarian organizations such as
*Migrant Offshore Aid Station* and *Drones for Refugees* have appropriated the
vertical gaze and launched drone monitoring systems to conduct SAR. Their
drones surveil common migratory routes in the Mediterranean basin, identify
people in distress, and send the geolocation, camera footage, and infrared
sensor data to websites and cell phones used by coastguards, SAR teams,
and merchant ships. Between November 2015 and April 2016, the *Maritime
Organisation for Following up and Rescue* (MOFR) helped around thirty-five
thousand refugees to cross the eastern Mediterranean by giving directions via
Whatsapp. Cofounded by Ahmad Terkawi, a pharmacist from Homs in Syria,
who, together with his family, made the perilous sea crossing, MOFR is one
among many organizations that contribute to a network of shared resources
helping people to travel alongside the legally accessible routes. In the below
communication, MOFR's remote guides attempt to direct a group of migrants
leaving the Greek coast across the sea via GPS:

9:58pm steer to the right very quickly

9:58pm to the right god have mercy on your grandparent who told you to go left

9:58pm (angry emoji) or would you like to sail few more kilometers in the water

9:58pm steer to the right quickly

9:59pm after two minutes give me a location

9:59pm (photo)

Okay, that's cool[73]

With maps shared in private communications and on social media, these
informal resources direct people across the Mediterranean and the Aegean
Sea, around the view from above, and inform travelers about transport fares
and stationed police and border patrols. Besides informing about the scope
and length of the journey, its risks and dangers, they communicate that
there is a network of migrant support in place, one that operates alongside
states, NGOs, and human rights activists. These messages and maps are not
merely the resources to create a "parallel system of movement";[74] they at the
same time form the testament and elusive archive documenting that people–
–despite the dangerous restrictions of safe travel routes—make use of their

right to move in the aspiration for a better home, a safer life, and a more secure horizon.

Under the search term *harraga*, YouTube presents an archive of short mobile phone films produced by young men who are crossing the Mediterranean Sea in makeshift boats for Europe's southern shores, most of them leaving from the Mediterranean coasts of North Africa, Algeria, Tunisia, or Morocco and crossing the Strait of Gibraltar for Spain, Malta, or Lampedusa. Translated from Arabic, the self-chosen term *harraga* means "those who burn," whereas in French, *brûler* colloquially means to "leave" or "to burn," referring to the moment the harraga have left their homes, burnt their identification papers, sometimes burnt their fingertips to avoid biometric tracking, and have, by the very act of crossing the sea, burnt the border.[75] In the video footage, the harraga often speak, wave, and sing directly into the camera. They give each other hugs, help to trim each other's beards while pointing us, the spectators, to the objects accompanying their journey: the boat engine, food and water supplies, mobile phones, and at times dolphins following the boat. Here, the sea—usually cast as a backdrop—often gets a long shot from their cameras and becomes a crucial protagonist. While their travelogues might be too easily read as either imitating the white heroic seafarer project or pertaining to the shadow traffic of non-white bodies moving, at times involuntarily, across oceans, the videos boldly reference another trajectory. The camera, often circulating within the boat, captures an intimate and heterotopic place where proximity to and solidarity with fellow travelers is documented in a joyful way. Spectators encounter the adventurous life of seafarers while their shared vulnerabilities and the portrayed homosocial intimacies run counter to the narrative of the white male explorer who conquers the sea in an imaginary solo effort.[76] By hoisting the pirate flag, the harraga suggest that the sea, presented through a horizontal gaze captured shakily with a mobile phone camera, now belongs to them, and despite the precarity and uncertainty that characterizes it, they claim it for better or worse. Being neither refugees because not having laid down their claims to asylum, illegal because of not having had the right to defense nor legal because they have not entered national-territorial law, this liminal space offers a horizontal gaze between the not-there (from where they departed) and not-(yet)-here. Running counter to the panoptic view from above, cast as the all-seeing eye that is immune to its environment and contained in technology, the horizontal gaze in the harraga videos is a testimony of solidarity and hope for a better future. These visual testimonies communicate signs of life and the triumph of a dangerous journey undertaken. Some harraga even trick the view from above by using a *gris-gris*, an amulet made out of the skin of a black cat or a goat that makes boats disappear on the Frontex radar.[77] Such as the maroons remapped colonial space and created zones of exception in which slavery was not permitted, the trickster practices of the harraga create alternative channels of movement that run counter and alongside EU border operations forestalling flight toward Europe. Together with the practice of burning the fingertips in order not to be recorded by biometric machines, the *gris-gris* skewing Frontex radars pertains to the long history of breaking colonial and capitalist machines, including its Luddite antecedent, when Maschinenstürmer destroyed textile machinery as a form of protest against new modes of capital accumulation.

## NOTES

1. Browne, *Dark Matters*, 49.

2. Ibid.

3. Clarkson, *The History of the Abolition of the African Slave-Trade*, 216.

4. Adler, "Migrant Deaths Renew Pressure on EU."

5. Convened by Otto von Bismarck to discuss the "future of Africa," the conference had *The Berlin Act of 1885* as its outcome, a treaty signed by the thirteen European powers attending the conference. In the two decades that followed, millions of Africans lost their lives, including vast numbers of Congolese under the tutelage of the great "philanthropist" himself, King Leopold II of Belgium: "All the Powers exercising sovereign rights or influence in the aforesaid territories bind themselves to watch over the preservation of the native tribes, and to care for the improvement of the conditions of their moral and material well-being, and *to help in suppressing slavery, and especially the slave trade.* They shall, without distinction of creed or nation, protect and favour all religious, scientific or charitable institutions and undertakings created and organized for the above ends, or which aim at instructing the natives and bringing home to them the blessings of civilization." The General Act of the Berlin Conference on West Africa, "The General Act of the Berlin Conference on West Africa," Article 6; my emphasis.

6. Ibid., Article 9.

7. Baker, "'It Was As If We Weren't Human.' Inside the Modern Slave Trade Trapping African Migrants."

8. Slaves were captured from mostly interior African lands, as well as Southern and Eastern Europe, the Caucasus, and Central Asia. Wright, *The Trans-Saharan Slave Trade*, 114.

9. Hamood, *African Transit Migration through Libya to Europe: The Human Cost*, 43.

10. Lyon, *Surveillance Studies*, 57.

11. Rediker, *The Slave Ship*.

12. Jeremy Bentham visited his brother, Samuel, in imperial Russia, and it was there where the English social reformer conceived of the panopticon for the first time. Samuel was commissioned by Prince Potemkin to improve naval manufacturing in Krichev and, in the process, conceived of an "inspection house," a structure that would, by its very nature, facilitate the observation of working processes and mediate

problems between imported English experts and local Russian peasants. The inspection house was never built but, according to Peter Redfield, inspired Bentham, who was already concerned with thinking about penal reform and learned about the model while visiting his brother in 1786. Redfield, "Foucault in the Tropics," 53.

13. Bentham, *Correspondence of Jeremy Bentham, Volume 3*, 387.

14. Browne, *Dark Matters*, 17.

15. Foucault, *Discipline and Punish*, 203. For Alexander Barder, the panopticon was "innovated, experimented, and actualized to a far greater degree in imperial spaces over the course of the nineteenth and twentieth centuries than in Northern Europe." Barder, *Empire Within*, 86. Colonies presented privileged sites for empires to model and experiment with carceral structures, so for Peter Redfield, it was also at "the margins of Europe" in which the panoptic model emerged, namely the penal colonies of Australia, New Caledonia, and French Guinea. Redfield, "Foucault in the Tropics." Also, Martha Kaplan situates an early moment of panoptic power in British-occupied Maharashtra, India. There, panopticism materialized in the construction of panoptic prisons in early-nineteenth-century Poona and Bombay. Besides building penal institutions, British colonizers sought to make the surveillance over the colonized population more efficient by inquiring into "local customs" with questionnaires. Per Kaplan, these registration efforts provide examples for the fusing of power and knowledge and turned "the people of Maharashtra into objects of scrutiny, like inmates of a panopticon." Situating panopticism in the colony enables Kaplan to complicate Foucault's European trajectory that proclaims a shift from a power fostering death to one centering on life—as instantiated by the shift from public executions to school and prison timetables. Kaplan is right to doubt whether Foucault's claim took place historically, or if he merely followed conventional European historiography that characterizes present governmental technologies and punishment as more benevolent than those of the past and the non-European outside. Kaplan, "Panopticon in Poona," 88–90. Prisons and criminal reform have indeed formed part of the civilizing mission. And colonizers often condemned penal practices that included physical punishment as barbaric and uncivilized, an attempt to strengthen and legitimize their imperial hold onto occupied territories. Dikötter and Brown, *Cultures of Confinement*.

16. Mitchell, *Colonising Egypt*.

17. Ibid., 24.

18. Asaro, "The Labor of Surveillance and Bureaucratized Killing."

19. Bentham, *Panopticon; Or, the Inspection House (Volume 2)*, 136; original emphasis.

20. Mitchell, *Colonising Egypt*, 24.

21. Neocleous, "Air Power as Police Power."

22. Airpower in the "Orient" retained its penal quality as enacted during colonial times, as seen in the 2003 invasion of Iraq, where the tactic of *shock and awe* aimed at displaying overwhelming airpower that sought to paralyze and punish the Oriental enemy. Gregory, *The Colonial Present*, 54.

23. Cameras were attached to tethered balloons as early as 1858 and widely used in Europe's and America's wars of the nineteenth century. Adey, Whitehead, and Williams, *From Above*. Aerial knowledge further enabled the bombing of Guernica and,

according to Graham Swift, today's Predator drones are the direct descendants of the Heinkels and Lancaster bombings of the Second World War. Swift, *Out of This World*.

24. Haraway, "Situated Knowledges," 589.

25. Wilcox, "Embodying Algorithmic War," 13.

26. Beller, *The Message Is Murder*, 144.

27. Adey, Whitehead, and Williams, *From Above*, 6.

28. Mitchell, *Colonising Egypt*, 13. Adey also notes that the view from above is structurally intertwined with failure, ambiguity, and invisibility. Auschwitz, for example, had been photographed more than thirty times by Allied aircraft before Soviet forces liberated it in 1945. Still, nobody had connected the images to the Final Solution until former CIA photo interpreters retrospectively analyzed the files over thirty years later. Adey, Whitehead, and Williams, *From Above*, 292.

29. Hayes, Jones, and Töpfer, "Eurodrones Inc."

30. Hayes, "NeoConOpticon."

31. Akkerman, "Border Wars," 33.

32. Jones, "Market Forces: The Development of the EU Security-Industrial Complex."

33. Marin, "The Deployment of Drone Technology in Border Surveillance, between Techno-Securitization and Challenges to Privacy and Data Protection."

34. Drones for documentation and surveillance purposes observed thousands of people walking to Austria after trains stopped coming from Hungary. Finland tested drones on its border with Russia to keep track of the number of migrants. Greece is buying drones from Israel that tested on Palestinians, and Switzerland operated Aerospace Ranger Su-27 drones (developed in collaboration with Israel) on its border with Italy to identify illegalized immigrants.

35. Italy, France, and Germany have created a plan for a European-based drone development program (MALE 2020) for reconnaissance that would reduce their countries' reliance on foreign technology.

36. Operation Commander Op Sophia, "EUNAVFOR MED–Operation SOPHIA: Six Monthly Report: June, 22nd to December, 31st 2015." The report was released by Wikileaks.

37. Ibid.

38. Notably, the number of deaths has continued to drop after the deadliest year in 2017 due to the EU's externalization policies. At the same time, the death rate has doubled, meaning that fewer migrants take the risk of traveling via the Med, but the route has become more dangerous *because of* the surge in surveillance apparatuses. "Missing Migrants Project."

39. Travis, "EU–UK Naval Mission on People-Smuggling Led to More Deaths, Report Says."

40. Stupp, "EU Maritime Agency Gets Ready to Use Drones to Monitor Refugee Boats."

41. Migrants have frequently used this strategy in the wake of the Mare Nostrum operation. Tazzioli, "EUROSUR, Humanitarian Visibility and (Nearly) Real-Time Mapping in the Mediterranean."

42. Frontex, "EUROSUR."

43. European Commission, "Examining the Creation of a European Border Surveillance System (EUROSUR)."

44. European Parliament and European Council, "Regulation Establishing the European Border Surveillance System (EUROSUR)."

45. Quoted from Hayes and Vermeulen, "Borderline," 45.

46. Herscher, "Surveillant Witnessing."

47. Bigo and Guild, "Policing at a Distance," 3.

48. Tazzioli, "EUROSUR, Humanitarian Visibility and (Nearly) Real-Time Mapping in the Mediterranean."

49. Bellanova and Duez, "The Making (Sense) of EUROSUR," 32.

50. Tazzioli, "EUROSUR, Humanitarian Visibility and (Nearly) Real-Time Mapping in the Mediterranean," 566.

51. Pugliese, *State Violence and the Execution of Law*, 208.

52. Beller, "Informatic Labor in the Age of Computational Capital."

53. Beller, *The Cinematic Mode of Production*, 245.

54. Beller, "Informatic Labor in the Age of Computational Capital"; original emphasis.

55. Ibid.

56. The incomplete list includes Black enslaved women providing nonanesthetized bodies for the "Father of Gynecology," James Marion Sims; the case of Henrietta Lacks; the experiments of Joseph Mengele on Jewish people; Jean-Martin Charcot, the founder of modern neurology and his fellow doctors writing on the skin-surface of their female hysteria patients at the Salpêtrière; and the medical experimentations on colonized and imprisoned Herero and Nama of the German concentration camps in Southwest Africa.

57. Beller, "Informatic Labor in the Age of Computational Capital."

58. Rosenberg and Williams, *Raw Data Is an Oxymoron*.

59. McGlotten, "Black Data."

60. Baucom, *Specters of the Atlantic*, 150.

61. Beller, "Informatic Labor in the Age of Computational Capital."

62. Stiegler, *Technics and Time*.

63. Chude-Sokei, *The Sound of Culture*, 84–85.

64. Wiener, *The Human Use of Human Beings*, 152. The slave ship does not merely haunt the panoptic model, but, if we trace Wiener's race analogies further, Foucault's thinking on governmentality. For Wiener, it was the image of steering a ship that could best illustrate cybernetics as a self-regulatory system. The choice of the field's name reflects cybernetics' emphasis on *feedback*, a general term for the processes by which information is used to keep a system functioning smoothly. The circulatory system of a living being is an example of such a self-regulating system, as is an intelligent robot that learns from and responds to the information it receives from the environment. In *The Cybernetic Hypothesis*, the French collective Tiqqun connects Wiener's reflections on cybernetics in the 1940s ("numerical information as medium of power") to the work of Foucault's biopolitics in the 1970s ("institutional knowledge as medium of power"). They attend to what they understand as the incredible similarity between Foucault's 1982 lecture on the art of government

as piloting ("pilotage") and cybernetics' meaning as the "act of piloting a vessel" (from the Greek term *kubernèsis*), which, in the figurative sense, meant the "act of directing, governing." In his 1981–1982 classes, Foucault insisted on working out the meaning of "piloting" in the Greek and Roman world, suggesting that it could have a more contemporary scope. In *The Nerves of Government* (1963), a book written by Karl Deutsch, Wiener's friend and colleague, Deutsch reflected on the political possibilities of cybernetics by recommending the abandonment of the old sovereign concept of power, which, according to him, had too long been the core of politics. A new understanding of government would be the rational coordinating of the flows of information and decisions that circulate through the social body, a concept much resonating with the one presented by Foucault. Tiqqun, *The Cybernetic Hypothesis*, 7.

65. Chun, "Introduction: Race and/as Technology; or, How to Do Things with Race."

66. The Italian financiers and merchants whose capital subtended Iberian exploration of the Atlantic and Indian Oceans were also masters of European slave colonies in the Mediterranean. With slaves and cloth as the most precious cargo of European trade, Mediterranean traders established ports and merchant colonies along the coast that founded the medieval cities of Europe's hinterland. By the middle of the fifteenth century, it was their capital that determined the direction and pace of the "discovery" and would eventually bring forward Columbus as "bourgeois creation of Genoese capital." Robinson, *Black Marxism*, 106.

67. Best, "On Failing to Make the Past Present," 453.

68. Schmitt, *Land und Meer*.

69. In the seventeenth century, the sovereign state inaugurated property rights over water adjacent to its land boundaries, despite its assertion that the sea was nothing (*res nullius*) and common to all. Yet the understanding of the high seas (*mare liberum*) as common and free to all was subject to one major contradiction: the "free" oceanic trade was used to transport people as unfree property. Mirzoeff, "The Sea and the Land."

70. Glissant, *Poetics of Relation*.

71. Perera, "Oceanic Corpo-Graphies, Refugee Bodies and the Making and Unmaking of Waters," 60.

72. Hulme, "Cast Away."

73. Quoted from Keenan and Mohebbi, "It Is Obvious from the Map," 121.

74. Ibid., 126.

75. Kuster, *Grenze filmen*, 261.

76. Heidrun Friese noted the dominant absence of women in the harraga videos and suggested that the success of their voyage is based on enacting a masculine subjectivity that includes the blanking out of vulnerability, failure, or death. Friese, *Grenzen der Gastfreundschaft*, 53.

77. The practice was mentioned by a fisher from the urban periphery of Dakar to Brigitta Kuster. Kuster, *Grenze filmen*, 273–272.

## Chapter 3

# Data on Bodies

## *Colonial Ordering from Windhoek to Lesbos*

When in 2015 Syrian refugees stranded at Břeclav railway station in the Czech Republic, a junction close to the borders of Austria and Slovakia, authorities numbered the incoming people with a felt-tip pen, a practice that was rapidly condemned as resonating with the infamous tattooing of concentration camp victims in Nazi Germany.[1] Also in Catania on Sicily's east coast, border guards numbered migrants on their hands and shoulders, again replicating, as some remarked, the fascist aesthetics associated with 1930s Germany.[2] Nazi analogies present a pervasive everyday expedient in media and serve as an available framework to denounce atrocities committed against refugees in the European border regime. The parallels are indeed uncanny, such as when in 2016, Denmark and Switzerland seized incoming people's assets and possessions at the border, a practice conducted by Germany since the 1990s and firmly grounded in federal asylum law.[3] Links were drawn to the expropriation of Jewish property, and the outrage surfaced again when in the same year, authorities accommodated refugees in an outpost of Buchenwald,[4] a site that hosted hundreds of Polish and French forced laborers from the concentration camp in Thuringia at the end of World War II. Pushback operations turning away refugee ships before European shores have been compared to the warding off of Jewish refugees during the Second World War, a comparison drawn most notoriously when the UK government intercepted migrants with British ships, which was paralleled to the treatment of the Jewish refugee ship *SS Exodus* by the British navy in 1947.[5]

When around 1990 Godwin's Law demonstrated the ubiquity of Nazi analogies in early Internet culture and marked the inevitable point where, as Leo Strauss noted in 1951, "the scene is darkened by the shadow of Hitler,"[6] Strauss made clear that *reductio ad Hitlerum* necessarily rests on the premise

31

that a view is refuted by the fact it was shared by Hitler, a fallacy that shortens arguments into the Nazi analogy as argumentative endgame. If it is unclear whether the above performed indignation concerned the fact that migrants were numbered as an act of dehumanization, presenting them as a mass without identity and a name, or lamented the recurrence of fascist aesthetics believed to be banned from political life in post-Holocaust Europe, it is precisely this ambiguity that hampers the genealogical quest for the transfer of technologies from one historical context to another, as Hitler's shadow looms both over the colonial past that provided the conditions of emergence for European fascism and the postcolonial present. This chapter moves beyond the framework of analogy to provide a genealogical map for the recurrence of technologies of colonial ordering that reach back to the eras of fascism and colonialism. While the numbering and inscribing of migrant bodies at Břeclav railway station and Catania sparked outcry, tagging, labeling, numbering, and inscribing the refugee body is a widespread practice in the European border regime and includes material body inscriptions and labeling with wristbands, tags, pens, along with the bureaucratic ordering of individuals into ethnic and racial categories.

The marking of migrants presents the starting point from which to think colonial ordering as the process by which imperial regimes group, classify, and segregate bodies by means of counting, registering, tagging, and labeling. Numbering and classifying bodies via colonial ordering has long accompanied colonial projects and made its way from the colony of German Southwest Africa (GSWA) to the postcolonial metropole where it facilitates containment and control. From the pass tag system in GSWA and discussions within the colonial society about tattooing the colonized to numbering and classifying refugee bodies in European hotspots and beyond, I discuss how colonial ordering as a racialized and racist technology facilitates postcolonial governance over time. By centering moments of colonial ordering that put information—data—onto migrants' and colonized people's bodies, I link the racial infrastructure of surveillance and control between the colonial era and today's border regime. The genealogical take displays the coloniality underpinning the current border crisis's technological rationality and highlights moments of translatability of white supremacist infrastructure. Far from eclipsing fascism on the European continent or substituting the legacy of the Third Reich with colonial racism, what this genealogical take instead unveils are the moments of co-emergence of these systems and their repercussions in today's political context.

Historian Jürgen Zimmerer has prominently shown that the transfer of ideas, people, practices, research methods, and ideologies migrated from Windhoek to Auschwitz, revealing at once a historical continuity and the constitutive role of the colony for European technologies of violence.[7] The colony of German Southwest Africa, which is today's Namibia, served as a laboratory for technologies of surveillance, totalitarian governance, and mass destruction that would eventually be applied to those persecuted during the Third Reich, namely the Jews, Roma, communist militants, and LGBTQ people. The Germans' warfare in Southwest Africa was realized only decades later in Europe, making the extinction campaign against the Herero paradigmatic for the Nazi war of extermination. German colonial wars presented a decisive link to the Nazis' crimes and were an essential source of ideas for Germany's war of annihilation in eastern Europe after 1939–1941. Nazi leaders such as Hermann Göring, Franz Ritter von Epp, and Eugen Fischer served as "human conduits" who enabled the flow of ideas and methods from GSWA to the leadership of the Third Reich.[8] In 1927, Eugen Fischer became the first director of the Kaiser-Wilhelm-Institute for Anthropology, Human Heredity and Eugenics (KWI-A) in Berlin. Fischer earned his scientific merits in genetics and racial science in GSWA, where he conducted his infamous "Bastard Studies" and used the skulls of dead prisoners from the concentration camps on Shark Island. The KWI-A connects the origins of racial science with the Nazi atrocities of the 1940s as the institute was centrally involved in applying race-based laws to exclude Jewish people from the German population. Fischer later became chancellor of the University of Berlin, where he taught medicine to Nazi physicians; among his students was Josef Mengele, who would continue his infamous anthropological studies and heredity research in Auschwitz.

While the continuity between Windhoek and Auschwitz in terms of violence, ideology, economics, and social and racial relations remains contested within the discipline of history,[9] a range of Black intellectuals have long argued that the Shoah did not present a slip in an otherwise democratic and enlightened path of Western history, an unexpected totalitarian turn, but rather the logical continuity of the Western civilizational project.[10] In *The Wretched of the Earth*, Frantz Fanon[11] declared that it was "not long ago Nazism transformed the whole of Europe into a veritable colony." And in *Discourse on Colonialism*, Aimé Césaire[12] wrote that in the 1940s, the Nazis "applied to Europe colonialist procedures which until then had been reserved exclusively for the Arabs of Algeria, the 'coolies' of India, and the [N-word] of Africa." Césaire suggested that the real "taboo" shuttered by Nazi fascism consisted in the very fact of applying directly to European subjects what was conceivable only in the colonial world.[13] He understood European fascism as a kind of European imperialism turned inwards, a dynamic he termed the "boomerang effect of colonization": "And then one fine day the bourgeoisie is awakened by the terrific boomerang effect [*choc en retour*]: the gestapos are busy, the prisons fill up, the torturers are standing around the racks, invent, refine, discuss."[14]

Also, Hannah Arendt understood the genocide of the European Jews as a boomerang effect of European imperialism. For her, the rise of the methods and mentalities of totalitarianism were enabled by the period of imperialism and the "Scramble for Africa" that ensued after the Berlin Conference. The ideas pioneering in the totalitarian project at home—"race as a principle of the body politic" and "bureaucracy as a principle of foreign domination"– –were both discovered on the "Dark Continent."[15] Race was an "emergency explanation," or a response to the encounter between colonizers and colonized "whom no European or civilized man could understand."[16] Writing about the "traumatic" encounter between colonizers and Blackness, or, in Arendt's terms, the contact with the "overwhelming monstrosity of Africa," Arendt reinforces the Eurocentric conception of colonies as a "dark" space marked by historic and physic regression.[17] Opposed to Césaire's and Fanon's boomerang thinking that underlines the transposability and, indeed, ubiquity of racial violence, Arendt's shift of imperial strategies back to the imperial homeland institutes the notion that totalitarianism's colonial conditions of emergence were born under the "merciless sun"[18] of tropical imperial spaces, presenting the boomerang effect as contamination and kaffirization[19] of white rational faculties in spaces considered shorn of historicity and rationality. Notably, the notion of colonizers' kaffirization in the tropics, their "going native," and ultimate adaption to a life posited outside of any civilizational framework, is a profoundly gendered narrative, as for perceived less-rational femininity, there was less at stake in the colonies, casting narratives of kaffirization as almost exclusively disintegrating white masculinity.

Boomerang thinking exposes the sinister valence of postcolonialism that reveals itself in postcolonial time or the very moment when the dispositifs of domination initially forged in the context of the colonial experience filter into metropolitan spaces. If fascism can be situated a South–North flow of colonial politics, as in Franco's use of Moroccan armies in Spain, and the installation of a German police state with members of the colonial elite, then the central question for European postcolonial border politics concerns the transfer of colonial warfare and ideology to the fascist metropoles, and their recurrent activation for a border regime both shaped by the inequalities of the South/North divide, and the fascist efficiency of a disciplinary and bureaucratic apparatus born in imperial Germany.

## COLONIAL PASS LAWS

Germany is the only former colonial state to continue the legal requirement of mandatory residence (*Residenzpflicht*),[20] a law affecting asylum applicants and those given a temporary stay (*Geduldete*). Established with the 1982

Asylum Procedure Law, the obligation lays down that, for the duration of the asylum procedure, applicants are required to live within the boundaries defined by the applicants' local foreigners' office (*Ausländerbehörde*) and are not allowed to leave the district without written permission. While in 2015 Germany expanded the law to include state-level territory, Bavaria remains one of only two states in which mandatory residence is restricted by the local municipality and, thereby, allows for racial profiling by police. Authorities justify the measure by pointing to applicants' availability during their asylum cases and frequently employ monetary and jail sanctions in case of failure to comply with the measures. The law enforces a restriction of movement on the refugee who, in order to move freely, must enter the bureaucratic apparatus and is under constant surveillance. Mandatory residence has a long history in Germany, reaching from the colonies to the First World War up to Nazi Germany and today's Aliens Act, where it was frequently applied to curb mobilities and prevent those affected from organizing resistance, such as when in 2005, Hyacienth Nguh Tebie from Cameroon, who applied for asylum in Brandenburg's Bahnsdorf, had to pay a fine for breaching the Residenzpflicht because he attended an "anticolonial conference" in Berlin.[21]

During the early years of the First World War, the law targeted forced laborers from foreign countries and mandated their relocation from private to collective accommodations to prevent scattered housing and facilitate increased control. The Weimar era continued the obligation without the tight spatial regulations as the weak economy relied on foreign labor. This changed again with the economic boom in armaments and capital goods during the Nazi era. The employment rate of foreign workers increased significantly in 1938, and it was during that same year when spatial restrictions were again introduced. In August 1938, the Nazi party introduced the law via the ordinance for the police in charge of foreigners (*Ausländerpolizeiverordnung*, or APVO), stipulating that "if the alien applies for a residence permit . . . his stay is permitted in the area of the district police to which the application was made."[22] Besides foreigners, the law targeted Jewish people along with Sinti and Roma,[23] and like the mandatory residence in place in today's Aliens Act, it imposed fines in case of noncompliance.[24] The Nazi-era law remained valid until 1965, when a new foreigner's law was enacted that extended discretionary powers on the part of the authorities. The 1982 Asylum Procedure Act again referred to the Aliens Police Ordinance of 1938, and in this version, the linguistic similarities are uncanny for the legal text merely replaced "applying for a residence permit" with "seeking asylum." Residenzpflicht demonstrates how regimes delegitimize racialized bodies in space and demand a supplemental crutch (e.g., written permission) requiring that bodies carry data with them—in the colony as well as in the "colony within the metropole."[25]

Activists and refugee advocacy groups have long pointed to the law's colonial history and denounced mandatory residence as a form of "modern colonialism."[26] Ahmed Sameer, a Palestinian human rights activist who was on trial for breaching the obligation, sees the law "in the same light as the then apartheid pass law in South Africa": "Then, Blacks and other non-whites were required to obtain written permission before they could go outside their immediate habitations. Today, I and all asylum seekers are required to do the same before we can leave our districts. It is a means of repression and an avenue for police brutality and racial profiling."[27] Also for Sunny Omwenyeke, who launched the anti-Residenzpflicht campaign in 2000 and was imprisoned for fifteen days for his protest, the law provides the legal basis and "the most effective means to criminalize refugees" as it hampers refugee activism and organization across federal states.[28] According to Omwenyeke, the colonial model of this policy was first applied in the German colonies of Southwest Africa, Togo, and Cameroon, where the colonized were barred from attending meetings without permission from the German state, which aimed to prevent "any sort of unrest against their colonial masters."[29] When in 1907, the colonial state of German Southwest Africa introduced the "Pass Ordinances" to stipulate the compulsion to work and to make identification mandatory for the colonized population, colonizers indeed regarded the ordinances as an answer to the "incalculable threat"[30] of unrestrained African movement, which, they feared, may lead to anticolonial resistance. Similar to the introduction of fingerprinting in British India, which was a response to an uprising by Indian conscripts against British colonizers, control measures in GSWA were legitimized by a discourse lamenting the ungovernability of the colonized. A German engineer who was hired by the state to solve the colony's drought problem portrays Africans'[31] unruliness as hampering the colonial project in GSWA:

> It is evident that the great shortage of workers is due to the many lazy black men and women who feed themselves at the expense of their working comrades. This cannot be dealt with other than by effective control measures and a reasonable compulsion to work. Without these two preconditions, neither the German colonists nor the Natives will emerge from stagnation.[32]

The Native Ordinances were officially introduced in 1907 and consisted of three parts: the "Control Ordinance," the "Pass Ordinance," and the "Master and Servant Ordinance," each addressing the way the German colonial state envisaged African people's subjection under colonial rule.[33] Before the official introduction, almost all local districts already had some degree of passport obligation for Africans. Yet it was only after the genocidal war (1904–1907) when the pass obligations were centralized and legally enforced. Policies and infrastructure of surveillance and control are often a leftover of war—also of contemporary warfare—and profoundly change social infrastructure. Whereas the prototype of settler violence in the history of modern colonialism was the near-extinction of Native Americans in the New World, in the African colonies, it was the German annihilation of thousands of the Herero in a single year. Other colonial powers indeed perpetrated similar acts of violence, unique about the German brutality was that it aspired to exterminate an entire people in 1904—the nation of the Herero (also known as Ovaherero).[34]

In 1904, the Herero, a Bantu ethnic group living in parts of Southern Africa, organized armed resistance against land appropriation and cattle theft by German colonizers and led, along with the Nama, the largest group of the Khoikhoi people, a guerilla war against Germany's primitive accumulation in the settler colony. Under General Lothar von Trotha, who took over military command when General Leutwein failed to put down anticolonial resistance, the German colonial state answered with a racial extermination campaign and collective punishment that killed around 80 percent of the Herero and 50 percent of the Nama population.[35] The colonial war, which presents the first genocide of the twentieth century, lasted from 1904 to 1907 and left the defeated Hereros and Namas internalized in concentration camps, where the majority died of disease, abuse, and exhaustion.[36] At the German Reich's colonial periphery, the concentration camp found one of its first large-scale applications, a violent architecture not pioneered by the Nazis but the colonial generals of GSWA who would eventually become part of the Nazi elite.[37]

Von Trotha's race war profoundly deranged civilian structures and prepared the necessary conditions to implement a German colonial surveillance apparatus. From the beginning, and unlike in other settler colonies, policies of "total control over Africans"[38] were at the very heart of colonial rule, and the German state sought to firmly establish the rule of the few over the many.[39] As the youngest of European nation-states, established in 1871 after the Franco-Prussian War, Germany was still in the process of state consolidation when it formed its first protectorates. Chiefly by military force, it took possession of territories in Africa and the South Seas, territorial claims later confirmed in the Berlin Conference of 1884–1885. Reichskommissar Heinrich Göring began the official establishment of the colonial administration in 1885 to build a colonial bureaucracy that would mirror the Prussian bureaucratic apparatus of the imperial homeland.

The German colonial project was as much state-driven as it was privately organized by industrials and merchants of the German Colonial Society for Southwest Africa (Deutsche Kolonialgesellschaft für Südwest-Afrika; known as DKGSWA). This multistakeholder society was a trade and management company in charge of the mining industry and was granted monopoly rights to exploit mineral deposits in the newly acquired territory. Besides plundering natural resources, Europeans claimed valuable land and livestock from African communities and displaced their seminomadic economy and usufruct claims to territory with a wage and forced-labor agricultural and mining economy. The accumulation by dispossession was legally confirmed in 1905, when acting governor Lindequist barred Africans from owning land and cattle and legally claimed tribal communities' possessions. Only one year after the enclosure of African commons, the protectorate's entire ownership structure radically changed and the majority of the country's raw materials were considered to belong to the German colonial state. As a consequence, African communities were increasingly unable to organize life in the forms that existed prior to German intrusion. Both the desire for capital accumulation and white settler supremacy drove the enclosure of African commons in this "racist interventionist state,"[40] for colonizers rationalized taking African land and resources by claiming German superiority and the need for *Lebensraum*. The term later became synonymous with Nazi Germany's territorial expansion into Central and Eastern Europe but was first coined by Friedrich Ratzel with GSWA in mind.[41] Compared to other European colonial powers, the German colonial project was relatively short in time (1884–1915). Still, almost thirty years were sufficient to destroy African communal structures, disown people of their land, and build the foundations of a settler society.

The Native Ordinances were part of a more extensive racial surveillance complex in the German colony, ranging from the division of the protectorate into zones of governance to panoptic housing and labor architecture. In 1908, district official Schenke of Swakopmund reflected on the benefit that Africans would eventually internalize the surveillant gaze—a key feature of panopticism for it translates arbitrary and selective monitoring into the feeling of permanent surveillance:

> Due to constant police surveillance and the frequent and unexpected inspections of the shipyards, the Natives of Swakopmund *believe that they are watched continuously* as soon as they violate the well-known ordinances. For this reason, it is not uncommon for the Natives to demand from their masters immediate registration with the police and to only start work once they are in possession of the passport stamp or the service book.[42]

In Lüderitzbucht, a mining site that formed the economic nucleus of the German colony, some three thousand African families were subjected to forced labor in the mines and surveilled by a system of oversight. The labor facility "New Camp" was overseen by a policeman who lived "in a stone house built in a strategically arranged location near the shipyard,"[43] an elevated position that shed a view from above onto the racial capitalist economy, recalling Nicholas Mirzoeff's description of the overseer in plantation slavery who stands at the beginning of the view from above's colonial and slavo-cratic genealogy.[44] The system of oversight was further institutionalized in the *Landespolizei* who used camels and horses to patrol the colonial terri-tory. Like the nearest high-point of a hill or a mountain, the slightly elevated position used by the horse cavalry was, according to Peter Adey,[45] an early military strategic position prefiguring remote sensing capabilities that would gradually develop into a more distanced view onto the battlefield.

In *The Wretched of the Earth*, Frantz Fanon[46] attended to the spatializa-tion of colonial occupation and the categorization of space according to race. For Fanon, colonial rule entails first and foremost a division of space into compartments and involves the setting of boundaries and internal frontiers. In GSWA, it was within the demarcations drawn by the colonial state that the Native Ordinances stipulated the compulsion to work and to carry a passport. To recover the colony-in-crisis, colonizers sought to control movements across the protectorate by dividing the territory into zones of governance or districts, which introduced a spatial fragmentation of African tribes and communal living. As the ordinances prohibited more than ten families or individual laborers on a single plot or shipyard,[47] the colonial administra-tion expected the decrees to work as a biopolitical tool that would guarantee the even distribution of the colonized over territory as well as to provide an overview of how many Africans lived in a particular district. The approach mirrors General Leutwein's prewar military strategy of *divide et impera*, which aimed at destroying African social structures, sowing discord among communities, and preventing anticolonial sentiment, an approach also used by the British Empire in India and elsewhere.

The colonial tactic uncannily reverberates through the contemporary border regime, as besides being spatially restricted on the basis of the Residenzpflicht, refugees have no right to choose their place of residence. A quota system called Königsteiner Schlüssel determines the reception capaci-ties of the sixteen German federal states by taking into account tax revenue and population size. The rationale of the practice is grounded in a 1949 state treaty known as Königsteiner Staatsabkommen and was activated in 1991 when the country enacted laws enabling Jewish people from the Soviet Union and later the CIS countries to move to Germany as so-called contingent refugees on the legal basis of the Geneva Refugee Convention. Originally intended to regulate the funding of academic institutions that exceed the funding potentials of the separate provincial states, the key has been steadily expanded to other areas and, since 2004, also applies to the distribution of asylum seekers. A recent discussion on the replacement of the Königstein Key with a digitized algorithm[48] elucidates the economic rationale behind the scheme, for it not merely continues the racial/colonial history of spatial ordering and containment but distributes refugees according to the most probable chance of work employment and not to reunite with family and community. If in GSWA, the justification for surveillance and control measures was driven by the need to contain African labor, along with the legal and ideological apparatus of white German settler supremacy, resurfacing in today's imperial German homeland is again the matrix that links racist spatial segregation and the unabashed desire for capital accumulation. Postvisual governance is the underlying fundament of this matrix, for it relies on the visibility of the racial subject for racial profiling and subjugates refugees' life worlds onto the calculating plane of the algorithm, in both its analog and digital version.

## TAGGING BODIES

In Athens and Thessaloniki, the United Nations High Commissioner for Refugees (UNHCR) and the European Support Office on Asylum (EASO) set up preregistration hubs to identify migrants before they lay down claims to asylum. Athens' former airport, Ellinikon International, serves as a temporary preregistration hub providing the initial registration procedure that includes tagging refugees with wristbands marking the hour and the date of registration. Once the application is registered, refugees receive asylum-seekers cards barring them from leaving the Greek mainland, so spatially restricting their movements to remain on the Greek border archipelago. Also in Passau, a reception facility in Southern Germany that has served as a laboratory for refugee politics (dubbed the "German Lampedusa"),[49] staff distinguish refugees by colored wristbands into a "normal person," a "young person traveling by themselves," and a "trafficker."[50] The practice continues in the Welsh port city of Cardiff, where Clearsprings Ready Homes, one of the largest private contractors facilitating accommodation refugees, ordered incoming people to wear "visible" and "brightly colored" wristbands, which lead to their harassment and abuse in public space.[51]

The colonial technology preceding these and similar efforts to identify and spatially contain refugees are the metal discs or pass tags that German colonial officials introduced as a response to the failure of the paper pass system in GSWA. In today's Swakopmund, a coastal city in Western Namibia, the remains of this German colonial surveillance apparatus are still stored in a large, square-shaped block sitting at a site where, during colonial times, people disposed of waste, including metal pieces such as dismembered railway tracks, jewelry, flatware, and weapons. When these pieces were deposited in the landfill a century ago, the electrolytes of the saltwater initiated a slow chemical process in combination with the metal, known as electrolyte corrosion, which led to the fusing of these pieces into one single block with several meters of height. Still today, the old landfill attracts people who retrieve these memorabilia and other valuables by pounding and hammering the block to pieces. Stuck among this tangible colonial archive are the palm-sized metal discs or pass tags that the German colony produced to tag and number Africans living in the protectorate.

Soon after the colonial state began using paper passes in the colony as part of the Pass Ordinances, the documents were tattered illegible and effectively put the system of paper identification out of order.[52] The subsequent pass system introduced in the colony was seen as a more permanent way to identify and control the African population: a pass tag (*Blechmarke* or *Paßmarke*), which had to be worn around the neck or attached to the clothes "in a visible manner."[53] The Leipzig-based company Beck & Co. provided the majority of the pass tags handed out in almost every district of the German protectorate.[54] In a communiqué to each district office of the protectorate, Deputy Governor Hintertrager conceived of a perfected surveillance system through pass tag control, noting that each police force is assigned a numerical sequence of pass tags that would help to instantly identify the person's appropriate police district.[55] Without a pass tag or the required service book (*Dienstbuch*) indicating their place of employment, Africans were allowed to obtain neither work nor accommodation and could be charged with vagabondage.[56]

The Pass Ordinance required Africans to carry a registration mark to be stored in the tag, a system that allowed, as the colonial legislation noted, any European or police officer to stop and demand immediate identification.[57] The pass tag rule fundamentally differed from the paper pass system as it introduced the instant visibility of an identification medium that served to delegitimize African presence in public space. "Surveillance," Patricia Hill Collins writes, "highlights individuality by making the individual hyper-visible and on display."[58] With the pass tag, colonizers sought to establish the compulsory visibility of the racial subject by governing who was authorized to move. German colonial law did not subject all African people living in the colony to the pass tag obligation, only those considered "full-blood Africans"[59]—thus producing the tag as a tangible extension of the abstract legal codex of the settler colony's blood and race doctrine. If implemented successfully, colonial law and its technological limb, the pass tag, would create a stratified society neatly separating the population on a scale of race and achieving surveillance as social sorting. The marker attached to bodies was an attempt to instill a geography of containment well before the badge system was exported to Europe two decades later as the yellow David Star.

By replacing paper with metal, Germans aspired to create a more permanent link between Africans' bodies and the colonial bureaucracy. Each tag bore the brand of the imperial crown, the district in which the tag owner is registered along with the consecutive number corresponding with the owners' number in the Native Register. The register was seen as a biopolitical tool that should enable the bookkeeping of the colonized population by requiring personal data such as gender, tribal affiliation, age, family relationships, place of origin, and residence.[60] As the division tables of ethnic, caste, and tribal counts were essential to the surveillance technology and governmental imagination of imperial administration in general,[61] in GSWA, the government's totalitarian fantasy was that eventually, every African living in the colony would be tagged and registered, allowing "a more precise surveillance of their activities,"[62] as the acting governor wrote in 1905. Here again, colonizers hoped for Africans to collaborate with the colonial surveillance measures by reporting "deaths, births, as well as their immigration or expatriation . . . without delay to the competent authority."[63] By imposing an apparatus of indexicality linking the tag to population statistics, the tag regime facilitated postvisual governance by establishing racial visibility and the mathematical structure of personalized data in the Native Register.

The pass tag resembles in its handy shape the many data storage devices we use today, and, not unlike current devices that link us to vast information repositories such as the Internet, the tag is linked to the information system of the Native Register. Before a technology or a "machine" is technological, "[t]here is always a social machine which selects and assigns the technical elements used."[64] What emerges from this line of reasoning is the social apriori of racial/colonial violence along with the pass tag as the technological antecedent of present tracking devices: a technological formation surfacing in moments when empire is contested or in crisis. Katherine Hayles[65] has argued for over a decade against the assumption that electronic texts are immaterial and that inscription, storage, retrieval, and transmission of information—all key aspects to data processing of electronic texts—are freed from all kinds of fixed form. Also, in his theory of the materiality of electronic writing, Matthew Kirschenbaum[66] centers on the materiality of storage media and the multitude of inscribed surfaces surrounding data processing that he considers as inherent to computation as such. Kirschenbaum situates electronic textuality amid other technologies and practices of writing such as indexing, cataloging, longhand, adhesives, and the felt tip pen, and advocates to understand these "textual and technical primitives of electronic writing"[67] as generative for electronic writing. Inherent in the logic of electronic writing is what he terms "forensic materiality," a process defining computation and its constitutive hardware:

> [Data inscription] rests upon the principle of individualization (basic to modern forensic science and criminalistics), the idea that no two things in the physical world are ever exactly alike. . . . Less exotically perhaps, we find forensic

materiality revealed in the amazing variety of surfaces, substrates, sealants, and other materiel that have been used over the years as computational storage media.[68]

Forensic materiality is inherent in the logic of electronic writing as the process produces and depends on trace evidence. Electronic writing is marked by forensics, creating a chain of contacts that are never materially lost. In this understanding, electronic writing, the material inscription of material surfaces, is much more than the sequencing of inscriptions. Undergirded by forensic materiality, the operational mode that enables it is based on the forensic idea that every individual bit can be identified, located, and (re) traced. In the case of the colonial pass tag system, forensic materiality transcends the materiality of the tag medium to become the sociopolitical reality of tracking individual bodies for census-taking and containment—instances of colonial ordering that are put into the service of racial/colonial governance. To include this social moment into the machine—or, conversely, to acknowledge the social moment as an inherent part of the tag medium—allows to understand data inscription as even more closely entangled with mechanisms of forensic tracking as perhaps envisioned by Kirschenbaum.

In a most reductive understanding of law and technology, the surveillance technology of the pass tag simply executes the legal framework of the Native Ordinances. But the prosthetic relationship between (colonial) law, its technologies, and the bodies it targets is much more complex. Technology, as noted by Kieran Tranter,[69] is often considered external to law and the body. The predominant theory conceives of law as a process that can be deployed—similar to a machine. It posits both law and technology vis-à-vis and in opposition to the physis of a subject. As opposed to this relationship of exteriority, Derrida articulates the co-implication of the natural (*physis*) and the synthetic (*techne*) by understanding life as "always already inhabited by technization."[70] Recognizing the relationship between technologies and bodies not as instrumental but codependent, he understands life as instrumentalized by technology from the very first.[71] Technology haunts life from the very beginning, and a prosthetic strategy of repetition marks its relationship to the body. Taking this cue from Derrida, Joseph Pugliese[72] comprehends law and technology as in a prosthetic relationship with the body: law is "inextricably entwined with technology from its originary enunciation through the technology of language." The entanglement of technology and law is not separated from the human but rather the "human agent [is] always-already inscribed by the technics of the law."[73] In other words, law as technology, is embodied, making the dichotomy between the human and technics untenable. Viewed from this account, the pass tag emerges, in the words of Bernard Stiegler, as "indissociably prosthetic"—a prosthesis that is "not a mere extension of the human body; it is the constitution of this body qua 'human.'"[74] Notably, Stiegler casts the prosthetic relationship between the body and technology as a general phenomenon. What can be gained from situating this nexus in the colony is the insight that it was perhaps precisely the forceful colonial use of technology that provided the conditions for this general relationship to emerge. Technology always depends on an "impaired body that needs to be supplemented by a techno-conceptual 'crutch,'"[75] only in the colonial context, this precondition is overtly racialized. Colonizers produced the African body as less-than-human, an episteme bolstered by the tag for it dehumanized by both numbering and evoking the structure of ownership, not unlike in chattel domestication where possession was indicated by branding and tagging livestock. In GSWA, colonizers attached data onto the other's body, allowing them to emerge as inhuman precisely because they have visually marked the other through their imperial prosthetics. If surveillance systems, as Simone Browne[76] remarked, are linked to the tracking of escaped slaves and coded the Black escaping body as findable and searchable, the forensic materiality of data inscription—the undergirding logic of today's tracking systems—emerges as the historical precondition to mean nothing less than the intrinsic entanglement of data infrastructure with the racialized motif of forensic tracking.

## SKIN INSCRIPTIONS

Already in autumn 1907, there was a shortage of pass tags, registers, travel passports, and service books, and the colonial law and order measures were far from working. Although the Landespolizei of GSWA targeted "vagrants" by "continuously patrolling the bush" and "arresting Blacks without a master . . . who indulge in sweet idleness,"[77] colonizers still deemed the control system insufficient. "The most challenging question for the aspiring farmer," a colonial commentator claims, "is neither to buy land, negotiate livestock, nor to build a house or a yard, not even the water supply, but to recruit workers. Everything else is relatively easy to obtain."[78] As maroonage was a constant threat to New World plantation societies, runaways and truants caused a persistent problem to contain the colonized in GSWA. Similar to the resistant practices of slaves in the United States, colonial Southwest Africa saw frequent truancy and arbitrary name changes rupturing colonial dominance. Africans made use of the protectorate's division by changing the district in case of prosecution[79] but also forged personal data:

> The Black man, however, has every intention to break his contract. He runs off and sells his numbered pass tag, throwing away the only legitimacy that might

betray him. He then goes on and presents himself in another district as a hitherto free bushman who suddenly felt the need to work. It is, of course, impossible to control this. On the contrary: the bailiff, police and farmers of the fortunate district are pleased they gained a new workforce, and the Black man is happy that the Dütschmann is so stupid. There are hundreds of such runaways occurring every year.[80]

The failure of the pass tag regime led to different reactions from the colonial society. Some suggested making Africans "more comfortable to be sedentary"[81] by rewarding them with food and tobacco;[82] others spoke out to further tighten the bond between the colonized body and the imperial bureaucracy by the "coercive tattooing with numbers or license plates"[83]:

> Therefore, in Southwest African newspapers, it has been suggested to tattoo the district letter and the district number onto the [natives'] forearm, as has been done by most of our German workers voluntarily. Should the case occur that [a native] is stopped with a cut out tattoo—as is well known, the Black's nervous system reacts much less to pain and the like than the one of whites—then one would know that this happened for a more substantial reason than because of escape.[84]

Not missing the opportunity to mention the racist notion of disparities in pain perception—a belief still in place today that discriminates against people of color in medical pain assessment and treatment[85]—the German engineer presents tattooing as a forensic tool that would unveil the body's criminological background. The government, however, was reluctant to comply for it dreaded anticolonial agitation and, instead, introduced harsher biometric identification measures for Africans, including the obligation to provide fingerprints and body descriptions in the manner of Bertillonage.[86]

Although coercive tattooing was never implemented in GSWA and would only be practiced decades later in Nazi concentration camps, the conditions that led to the surfacing of these requests form part of an episteme that sought to permanently link the body with the imperial apparatus in general and the German-colonial bureaucracy in particular. When considering skin inscription over time, it is crucial to foreground the volatility of the practice as meanings of body markings shift depending on the context. From ancient Greece and Rome to medieval Europe, tattooing and branding were widespread to mark slaves, prisoners of war, convicted criminals, heretics, and saints.[87] The Greek term *stigma* referred to the prick or mark of a pointed instrument used for branding that would let the practice shift between punishment such as the branding of heretics and religious self-stigmatization to express being among the chosen. Still, the Atlantic world brought forward the most ill-famed body inscriptions in the widespread practice of branding slaves. These modes of denoting possession in slavery and serfdom were transposed from animal husbandry such as the branding of cattle, rendering racialized methods of control and containment as caught with the speciecist project.[88] Branding slaves worked both as an individualizing and massifying method for it, first, enabled the tracking of individual slaves (by searing "hot irons on skin") and, second, classified people according to color by branding Blackness as a sellable commodity, thus combining literal inscription of skin with the racist branding of a group of people defined by the one-drop rule that maintained the enslaved body as Black.[89] Branding before embarkation onto slave ships was akin to marking resources to be extracted; hence, in the "naturalized extreme, racially identified groups are treated much like the natural resources found in the environment."[90]

If through data inscription the power relation between state and subject is written into the epidermis, or, as Foucault would say, "into the very grain of individuals,"[91] skin inscriptions at the same time present moments of self-actualization that bind surface to depth and serve as an interface between the outside world and the inside of the body. In 2015, photographer Ricci Shryock met Eritrean migrants in the Porta Venezia area of Milan. Almost all the people that Shryock interviewed had decided to get tattoos before embarking on the perilous journey that would take them through the Sahara desert to Libya and across the Mediterranean Sea to Europe. Many of these tattoos reference their reasons for leaving home ("Rule of Law"; "everything will pass away"), others inscribed that which they were forced to leave behind ("home is desert without mother"; "I love Mum") or transmitted hope for a safe crossing by inking the archangel Michael, Jesus, and phrases such as "rely on the cross." If crosses were used centuries ago in the Mediterranean slave trade to denote serfdom and property, here in Sicily, at the gates of Europe's Southern border, they emerge yet again, only in this case, crosses are inscribed into the skin to protect the body during precarious and unsettling circumstances. Similar to historical seafarer tattoos, these protective symbols present at once a mode of memory-making, evidence, and testimony for a perilous journey undertaken.

Yet another example of a tattoo shows that migrants inscribe the skin-surface to pronounce agency and self-determination and reclaim skin inscription as a way of reassigning control back onto their past, present, and future. The Syrian activist newspaper *Enab Baladi*, launched during the Arab Spring uprisings, dedicated a report to the challenges Syrian refugees face in Germany.[92] The article features a photograph of an unnamed Syrian refugee in Germany who holds his tattooed forearm into the camera. The tattoo depicts two hands holding a camera and is subtitled by the capitalized dictum: "HEY YOU . . . DONT [*sic*] TELL ME THERE IS NO HOPE AT ALL." The inked camera lens is directed at the spectator looking at the tattoo as if to take a photograph, thus returning the frequent gaze onto the refugee body. The analog camera of the tattoo recalls, perhaps even more than the smartphone used as a camera, one of the essential accessories of the tourist. Evoking the figure of the tourist on the refugee body recollects border zones as a locus where "two absolutely dichotomous figures—the wealthy tourist from the Global North and the utterly disenfranchised refugee from the Global South—[emerge] within the same geographical space."[93] Carceral islands such as Lampedusa in the Mediterranean Sea and Christmas Island in the Indian Ocean constitute "crisis heterotopias"[94] that bring these two distinctive figures into geographical proximity. If the tourist is also the figure that, by having generated wealth in the Global North from the Global South, travels to the South to reify this object-status by looking through the camera with "imperial eyes,"[95] then rejecting the gaze includes the defying of this unequal geopolitical setting. It inscribes into the body the desire for mobility and unimpeded travel and repudiates the immunity of the tourist—the figure who is merely watching and observing the crisis from a safe distance. This last point may well be a moment of reclaiming "the right to look back," a right to see, to identify, and dismantle the visuality that constructs its objects, as well as "the claim to a subjectivity that has the autonomy to arrange the relations of the visible and the sayable."[96] The right to look is not only about interfering in visual power practices but the assuming of autonomy and the claiming of political subjectivity and collectivity. It not merely questions what can be seen but constitutes the very right to see of the one being looked at, or what Derrida termed "the right to look, or the invention of the other."[97] The tattooed camera at once returns the gaze and claims the right to invent the other, only in this case, the other is "us" or "me," or those consuming the European border spectacle. Here, the skin emerges as an interface of protest; it rejects the narratives of violence commonly associated with the inked body as forcefully inscribed by state violence and institutes a moment where the gaze of the spectacle is turned around. If writing on the body produces this body as a vessel and medium for an entire history of violence written on the skin, the tattoo gives way to another trajectory. It literally flattens the camera onto the skin-surface. The camera-apparatus is now devoid of its visual technology; it merely exists in the ink and epithelial cells of the epidermis and the underlying connective tissue of the dermis, presenting at once the destruction and transformation of this visual machine.

## NOTES

1. Krüger, "Ehemaliges KZ als Flüchtlingsunterkunft."
2. Brigida, "Blog | Migranti."

3. Shields, "Swiss, Like Danes, Seize Assets from Refugees to Recoup Costs."

4. Krüger, "Ehemaliges KZ als Flüchtlingsunterkunft."

5. Head, "The Failure of Empathy." Also David Cameron, during his time as prime minister, described the admitting of mostly Syrian refugee children into the UK as the modern equivalent of the Kindertransport. Friedman, "Learning the Lessons of the Kindertransport." In a different manner, UKIP leader Nigel Farage made use of the Nazi visual archive when he produced a poster showing refugees marching along a highway in 2015 with the call to "take back our borders." The poster bore an uncanny resemblance to a 1941 Nazi newsreel depicting the forced march of Bessarabian Jews in Romania.

6. Quoted from Behnegar, *Leo Strauss, Max Weber, and the Scientific Study of Politics*, 77.

7. Zimmerer, *Deutsche Herrschaft über Afrikaner, Von Windhuk nach Auschwitz?*; "Annihilation in Africa."

8. Madley, "From Africa to Auschwitz."

9. Since the mid-2000s, historians on both sides of the Atlantic gave considerable attention to the relationship between German colonialism and Nazism. They debated how to conceptualize, if at all, the link between genocidal politics in German Southwest Africa and the Third Reich. Those wary of the connection between the colonial and fascist regimes argue, for example, against using the term *genocide* in the German colonial context because it presents an anachronism as the United Nations General Assembly only mandated the term in 1946. Gerwarth and Malinowski, "Hannah Arendt's Ghosts." Historian Dan Diner, for example, emphasized the status of the Holocaust as a breach of civilization by distinguishing it from colonial genocides and considers the continuity-debate as a flattening out of Nazi events. Diner, *Gegenläufige Gedächtnisse*. Others agree that the German colonial experience provided a blueprint for the imperial project at home in the form of chains of influence, transfers, and situational parallels. Kundrus, "Kontinuitäten, Parallelen, Rezeptionen Überlegungen Zur 'Kolonialisierung' Des Nationalsozialismus." Some highlight the continuity of race and the "racial order" between the regimes but deny any structural continuity. Grosse, "What Does German Colonialism Have to Do with National Socialism? A Conceptual Framework."

10. Césaire, *Discourse on Colonialism*; DuBois, *The World and Africa*; Fanon, *The Wretched of the Earth*.

11. Fanon, *The Wretched of the Earth*, 57.

12. Césaire, *Discourse on Colonialism*, 36.

13. For Césaire, the boomerang effect not merely operates on a macro scale but entails subjective dimensions as he remarks that the colonizer "gets into the habit of seeing the other man as *an animal*," which provokes the colonizer to "transform himself into an animal." Ibid., 41; original emphasis.

14. Ibid., 36.

15. Arendt, *The Origins of Totalitarianism*, 185.

16. Ibid., 190.

17. Ibid., 185. For a critique of Arendt see Dhawan and do Mar Castro Varela, "Human Rights and Its Discontents: Postkoloniale Interventionen."

18. Arendt, *The Origins of Totalitarianism*, 185.

19. The notion of *Verkafferung* or *kaffirization* described the bourgeois fear of German colonialists to "degenerate" and become indistinguishable from the colonized. The German Colonial Encyclopedia (*Deutsches Koloniallexikon*) describes the process of Verkafferung in the following terms: "In GSWA the term '*Verkafferung*' is understood as the sinking of a European to the cultural level of the native [by means of] continual contact with Africans, but more especially mixed marriage—these things encourage the regrettable degeneration of the white settler. Despite his occasionally active personal intelligence, the *verkafferte* European is always a lost member of the white population." Alterated from Schnee, *Deutsches Koloniallexikon: Vol III*, 606.

20. The term originated in the law of the Roman Catholic Church, where it referred to the obligation of spiritual dignitaries to be permanently present at the place of office and emphasized the importance of those subjected to the law. Stoffels, "Residenzpflicht," 69.

21. Fritsche, "Strafe für antikoloniale Aktivität (neues Deutschland)."

22. Quoted from Stoffels, "Residenzpflicht," 73. Original: "Beantragt der Ausländer die Aufenthaltserlaubnis . . . , so gilt sein Aufenthalt im Bereich der Kreispolizeibehörde, bei der der Antrag gestellt ist, als erlaubt."

23. Hilberg, *Die Vernichtung der europäischen Juden*.

24. Stoffels mentions a police document from 1944 containing a list of names of Polish and Russian forced laborers who were fined 15 or 20 Reichsmark for having been found in the Neuss city area without the written permission of their local police authorities. Stoffels, "Residenzpflicht," 70.

25. Gueye, "The Colony within the Metropole."

26. Gronenberg, "Asylpolitik ist moderner Kolonialismus."

27. Sameer, "Why I Fight against the Residence Obligation Law."

28. Omwenyeke, "The 'Fortress Within.'"

29. Ibid.

30. Quoted from Zimmerer, *Von Windhuk nach Auschwitz?*, 101; my translation.

31. I use the term *African* as the historical context is before nationalization.

32. Ingenieur von Zwergern, "Zur Eingeborenenfrage in Deutsch-Südwestafrika," 790; my translation. Original: "Man sieht also, daß man dem großen Arbeitermangel, der herrührt von den vielen faulenzenden schwarzen Männern und Weibern, die sich auf Kosten ihrer arbeitenden Genoßen durchfüttern, nicht anders beikommen kann, als durch eine wirksame Kontrolle und einen angemessenen Zwang zur Arbeit. Ohne diese zwei Vorbedingungen kommen weder die deutschen Kolonisten, noch die Eingeborenen aus der Stagnation heraus."

33. Deutsche Kolonialgesetzgebung, *Die Deutsche Kolonial-Gesetzgebung. Sammlung Der Auf Die Deutschen Schutzgebiete Bezüglichen Gesetze, Verordnungen, Erlasse Und Internationale Vereinbarungen*, 345–57. Germans were by no means the first to introduce pass laws to govern colonized people; neither was their idea original. In the South African context, pass documents restricting the movement of non-white Africans date back to 1760, when slaves were required to authorize their travel to move between urban and rural areas. During the first British occupation of the southern tip of Africa in 1795, farmers regulated and contained slave labor

through a pass system. Pass laws entitled police to stop Africans for identification at any time and stipulated residence, which tied them to their white employers. Almost a century later, in 1896, the South African Republic brought in two pass laws requiring Africans to carry a metal badge or pass tag. Pass laws would further become one of the dominant features imposed on the Black population under South African Apartheid and would only be abolished when Apartheid formally ended in 1986. Also in the antebellum United States, slave owners adopted pass laws to control the mobility of Black enslaved bodies and to monitor Blackness as property. Christian Parenti maintains that the slave pass system was one of the first surveillance and identification systems in the United States that allowed whites to instill a geography of containment by stipulating the specific times and locations for slaves to leave the plantation. The first pass laws were introduced in Virginia and targeted white indentured servants who ventured to escape serfdom. By 1656, the law required Native Americans entering the colony to carry passes or "tickets" issued by the colonial authorities. Some of these earlier regulations mentioned slaves, but it was only in 1680 that an exclusive slave pass law was enacted in Virginia. As the passes initially did not contain personal descriptions, naming became a site of resistance and allowed slaves to pretend to be someone they were not; enabling some literate slaves to forge passes to liberate themselves and others. Parenti, *The Soft Cage*.

34. The massacres by Spain and the United States in the Americas, the British in Tasmania and Kenya, the Belgians in the Congo, the Italians in Libya, and the French in Madagascar and Algeria permit the notion of a particularly brutal German colonialism, as was often claimed. For a critical discussion see Callahan, *Mandates and Empire*. The historical discourse of German colonial brutalism as exceptional was motivated by the desire to justify the takeover of German colonies by the British in the post–World War I moment—above all Southwest Africa. Steinmetz, *The Devil's Handwriting*, 69.

35. Zimmerer, "Annihilation in Africa."

36. In 2007, the Namibian government planted a memorial stone in the cemetery of Swakopmund, a coastal city located in the former territory of GSWA. Commemorating the fate of the Herero community, the stone inscription reads that the Herero "perished under mysterious circumstances at the realm of their German colonial masters in concentration camps . . . during 1904–1908." Not mentioning the extinction campaign conducted by German colonial officer Lothar von Trotha, the memorial tacitly acquits the German state of all culpability and bars the Herero and Nama from redress for the colonial genocide. Both in Namibia and Germany, the struggle to consolidate memory on German colonial history is ongoing, and public monuments, along with street names, and university and school curricula, have become vital battlegrounds to push the nation to face its postcolonial obligations.

37. Chancellor von Bülow commanded von Trotha to "establish Konzentrationslager for the temporary housing and sustenance of the Herero people." Quoted from Madley, "From Africa to Auschwitz," 446. Mahmood Mamdani traces concentration camps back to U.S. settler colonialism, where, under President Lincoln, reservation camps were established as part of a campaign for Indian removal. Mamdani, "Settler Colonialism." John Toland remarks in this regards that Hitler studied the camps for

Boer prisoners in South Africa and Native Americans in the United States, and often praised America's extermination campaign. Toland, *Adolf Hitler*.

38. Zimmerer, *Von Windhuk nach Auschwitz?*, 63.

39. Bley, *Namibia Under German Rule*. Regarding German colonialism, there is an ongoing debate on how to conceptualize the reach of colonial governance. Historian Tilman Dedering mentions a new generation of historians of colonial Namibia who tend to question the German colonial hegemony in GSWA. Dedering, "War and Mobility in the Borderlands of South Western Africa in the Early Twentieth Century." According to George Steinmetz, historians who have focused on specific German colonies (post-1904 Southwest Africa, Qingdao before 1904, New Guinea in the first several years of German rule, or the Marshall Islands) have overestimated the military and capitalist character of German colonialism. He describes colonial states, including its German versions, as extremely weak in terms of their material "apparatus." Steinmetz, *The Devil's Handwriting*, 31 and 68.

40. Shahabuddin, "The Colonial 'Other' in the Nineteenth Century German Colonization of Africa, and International Law," 31.

41. Madley, "From Africa to Auschwitz," 432–35.

42. Quoted from Zimmerer, *Deutsche Herrschaft über Afrikaner*, 129; my translation and emphasis. Original: "Die Eingeborenen in Swakopmund selbst werden durch die ständige polizeiliche Aufsicht und häufige unvermutete Kontrolle der Werften dauernd unter dem Eindruck gehalten, dass sie stets beobachtet werden, sobald sie gegen die ihnen bekannten Verordnungen verstossen. Es kommt aus diesem Grund auch nicht selten vor, dass Eingeborene von ihren Dienstherrschaften selbst [die] sofortige Registrierung bei der Polizei verlangen und den Dienst erst aufnehmen, wenn sie im Besitz der Passmarke oder des Dienstbuches sind."

43. Quoted from ibid., 130; my translation. The stone house is described as being in a "clearly arranged location" ("übersichtliche Lage"); the German terminology thus directly refers to the system of oversight.

44. Mirzoeff, *The Right to Look*.

45. Adey, Whitehead, and Williams, *From Above*, 2.

46. Fanon, *The Wretched of the Earth*.

47. The shipyard was considered an integral part of the colonial surveillance apparatus with regular controls conducted by either a European employer, an appointed "native commissioner," or a "native headman" assigned by the government. Steinmetz, *The Devil's Handwriting*, 171.

48. Schwenkenbecher, "Ein Algorithmus, der Flüchtlinge über ein Land verteilt."

49. Connolly, "A Laboratory for Refugee Politics."

50. Datta, "A Town at Its Limits."

51. Taylor, "Refugees in One of Britain's Poorest Towns Say the Red Doors on Their Housing Make Them Targets." Further north in Middlesbrough, *Jomast*, a private firm contracted by the UK government to accommodate refugees, provided housing to refugees with red doors, which made their domiciles easily identifiable. The "red door controversy" only became known to the public after refugees repeated their complaints of being targets of abuse and harassment. In both of the UK cases, media drew links to "Nazi Germany" and "Apartheid," and in some cases, created the

image of class-driven racism in British working-class towns, thus shifting the focus away from the state-sanctioned violence of the private contractors. Araujo, "'It's Like Nazi Germany' Fury as Asylum Seekers Forced to Live behind Red Doors"; Hartley-Brewer, "Red Doors and Wristbands."

52. While neither sources nor historians give a reason for the blatantly short half-life of the paper pass in the German colony, it might as well be speculated, considering the cases discussed above, that the first version of identification systems in GSWA was subject to resistant practices through the making-unintelligible of personal data.

53. Deutsche Kolonialgesetzgebung, *Die Deutsche Kolonial-Gesetzgebung. Sammlung Der Auf Die Deutschen Schutzgebiete Bezüglichen Gesetze, Verordnungen, Erlasse Und Internationalen Vereinbarungen*, 348; my translation. See also Zimmerer, *Von Windhuk nach Auschwitz?*, 95.

54. McGregor, *Die eingeborenen Passmarken von Deutsch Südwest Afrika*, 78.

55. Zimmerer, *Deutsche Herrschaft über Afrikaner*, 127.

56. Steinmetz, *The Devil's Handwriting*, 171.

57. Deutsche Kolonialgesetzgebung, *Die Deutsche Kolonial-Gesetzgebung. Sammlung Der Auf Die Deutschen Schutzgebiete Bezüglichen Gesetze, Verordnungen, Erlasse Und Internationalen Vereinbarungen*, 348.

58. Hill Collins, "Controlling Images and Black Women's Oppression," 20.

59. In a letter to the district office, the imperial governor advocates to subject those "Basterds" to the ordinances, in whom the "colored blood evidently predominates" and who are "not on the same level as Europeans" regarding their "habits and levels of education." Quoted from Lerp, Imperiale Grenzräume, 107; my translation. Original: "bei denen das farbige Blut offenbar überwiegt und die nach ihren Lebensgewohnheiten und Bildungsgrade nicht auf gleicher Stufe mit Europäern stehen."

60. Zimmerer, *Deutsche Herrschaft über Afrikaner*, 127.

61. Appadurai, *Modernity Al Large*.

62. Quoted from Steinmetz, *The Devil's Handwriting*, 171.

63. Quoted from Zimmerer, *Deutsche Herrschaft über Afrikaner*, 127.

64. Deleuze and Parnet, *Dialogues II*, 70.

65. Hayles, *Writing Machines*.

66. Kirschenbaum, *Mechanisms*.

67. Ibid., xiii.

68. Ibid., 10.

69. Tranter, "The Laws of Technology and the Technology of Law."

70. Derrida and Rottenberg, *Negotiations*, 202.

71. Ibid., 244.

72. Pugliese, *State Violence and the Execution of Law*, 184.

73. Ibid., 202.

74. Stiegler, *Technics and Time*, 1:152–53.

75. Pugliese, *State Violence and the Execution of Law*, 202.

76. Browne, *Dark Matters*.

77. Spectator Germanicus, "Eingeborenensorgen in Deutschsüdwest," 250; my translation.

78. Ibid., 249; my translation. Original: "Die schwierigste Frage für den angehenden Farmer ist nicht, den Grund und Boden zu kaufen, das Vieh zu erhandln, nicht der Bau von Haus und Hof, ja nicht einmal die Wassererschliessung, sondern die Gewinnung von Arbeitern. Alles andere ist verhältnismässig einfach zu beschaffen."

79. Zimmerer, *Deutsche Herrschaft über Afrikaner*, 115 and 145.

80. Ingenieur von Zwergern, "Zur Eingeborenenfrage in Deutsch-Südwestafrika," 789; my translation. Original: "Dagegen liegt dem Schwarzen gar nichts daran, seinen Vertrag zu brechen. Er reißt einfach aus, wirft seine einzige Legitimation, die ihn verraten könnte, fort und verkauft diese enumerierte Blechmarke. Dann geht er in einen anderen Bezirk, stellt sich dort vor, als bisher freier Buschmann, den plötzlich die Lust nach Arbeit gepackt hat. Eine Kontrolle ist selbstverständlich unmöglich, Amtmann, Polizei, Farmer des beglückten Bezirkes freuen sich im Gegenteil der neu gewonnenen Kraft; und der Schwarze freut sich, daß der Dütschmann so dumm ist. Solche Ausreißereien kommen jährlich zu hunderten vor."

81. Spectator Germanicus, "Eingeborenensorgen in Deutschsüdwest," 251; my translation.

82. Zimmerer, *Deutsche Herrschaft über Afrikaner*, 144.

83. Spectator Germanicus, "Eingeborenensorgen in Deutschsüdwest," 251; my translation.

84. Ingenieur von Zwergern, "Zur Eingeborenenfrage in Deutsch-Südwestafrika," 790, my translation. Original: "In südwestafrikanischen Zeitungen ist deshalb die Eintätowierung des Bezirksbuchstabens und der Bezirksnummer in den Vorderarm vorgeschlagen worden; wie ja die meisten unserer deutschen Arbeiter solche Tätowierungen sich freiwillig verschafft haben. Sollte der Fall vorkommen, daß eine Person angehalten wird mit herausgeschnittener Tätowierung—bekanntlich haben die Schwarzen ein auf Schmerzgefühle u. dergl. viel weniger reagierendes Nervensystem als die Weißen—so wüßte man, daß dies aus einer erheblicheren Ursache geschehen ist, als wegen bloßen Ausreißens."

85. For a study on the racial bias in medical pain assessment and treatment see Hoffman et al., "Racial Bias in Pain Assessment and Treatment."

86. Zimmerer, *Deutsche Herrschaft über Afrikaner*, 147.

87. Before Christ, skin markings etched with a hot iron or a knife were regarded as a clear sign of infamy and impurity. Goffman, *Stigma*. The Greeks, Romans, and Celts, including the slaveholders of ancient Greece and Rome, used tattooing "for penal and property purposes." After the spread of Christianity, body markings took on a new meaning, when Christian pilgrims received tattoos as signs of religious observance and as souvenirs of pilgrimages to the Holy Land. Caplan, *Written on the Body*, 106.

88. Charles Patterson notes in this regard: "Not only did the domestication of animals provide the model and inspiration for human slavery and tyrannical government but it laid the groundwork for western hierarchical thinking and European and American racial theories that called for conquest and exploitation of 'lower races,' while at the same time vilifying them as animals so as to encourage and justify their subjugation." Patterson, *Eternal Treblinka*, 27. The etymology of the term *colony* is a point in case here: the Latin word *colonia* for settlement, or farm and from *colere*, "to

cultivate," emphasizes how the colonial, in the name of exploitation as improvement, links back to both the enclosure of land and the utilization and killing of animals. Pugliese, *State Violence and the Execution of Law*, 39.

89. Browne, *Dark Matters*, 92.

90. Goldberg, *The Racial State*, 110–11.

91. Foucault, *Power/Knowledge*, 39.

92. Ziada, "Where Did the Syrian 'Ya Batel' Tattoo Disappear in Europe?"

93. Pugliese, "Crisis Heterotopias and Border Zones of the Dead," 664.

94. Pugliese, "Crisis Heterotopias and Border Zones of the Dead."

95. Pratt, *Imperial Eyes*.

96. Mirzoeff, *The Right to Look*, 1.

97. Derrida and Plissart, *Droit de Regards*, 85, xxxvi.

## Chapter 4

# Bodies of Data

## *(Early) Biometrics from the Colony to the Border*

Biometric technologies have become the global standard operating procedure for regulating the entry and exit flows in most of the world's countries, a development taking place against the backdrop of a growing biometric industry that offers technological solutions to manage borders, citizenship, and national security. Also, in EU migration management, "smart borders" based on biometric technology have become the leading border technology since the European Commission adopted the Smart Border Package in 2013.[1] The contract preceding this development was the 1985 Schengen Agreement, which, although often hailed as fostering the freedom of movement, substantially hardened the EU's external frontiers as the treaty extended policing and biometric data collection, enabling the wide-ranging registration and surveillance of large population groups in the countries concerned.[2] But these biometric data collection efforts, as I will show in this chapter, have a much longer history that still reverberates through biometric data collection in EU border landscapes. Biometric technologies were invented during the age of European imperialism, where they were born in a matrix intersected by colonial rule, biological racism, and the suppression of anticolonial resistance. More specifically, they arose out of the ideological backdrop of scientific racism in the now denounced disciplines of Anthropometry, Phrenology, and Craniology that were predicated on the assumed objectivity of geometry and the hierarchic classification of human bodies. While these disciplines have been rejected as unscientific due to their racism-inflected assumptions and methods, their technologies have, to some extent, survived and continue to inform current biometric practices.

Biometrics are often seen as offering a clean and smooth way of establishing someone's identity. Derived from the Greek terms *bios* (life) and *metron* (measure), in the most general understanding, the term refers to the measurement of the human body by applying statistical analysis to biological and physiological data. Biometric technology collects, synthesizes, and analyses human characteristics and traits such as palm or fingerprints, facial structure, iris patterns, and gait. Through biometric enrollment, bodily traits are turned into patterns of data, which then can be used to recognize a person by either verification or identification. Through a fingerprint, for example, the subject gives a biometric template that serves as a proxy for each subsequent time she registers with the system. While verification matches up the body presented at the border with identity documents stored in a system, identification is a more targeted approach and identifies someone from a broader system of records, such as people apprehended while crossing a border to determine their migrant status. The durable marks that the racial sciences have left on modern biometrics are revealed in the multiple moments where biometrics, as Amade M'charek has it, do not "solve problems of identification" but present practical solutions that redefine "human life itself."[3] Far from merely establishing someone's identity at the border, biometrics must instead be understood as tackling the problem of life itself: they define the faculties that count as human and they make sovereign decisions over life and (social) death, thereby determining "the break between what must live and what must die," which, for Foucault,[4] is the key mechanism of racism in liberal societies.

Toward the end of the eighteenth century, a profound epistemological change took place in Europe, producing new scientific representations of race and thereby triggering "a radical transformation in the European (and later Western) visual economy relating to race and its inscription in the body."[5] This historical moment brought forward a canon of racial taxonomies resulting from naturalist models—most prominently developed by the work of Buffon and Linnaeus—allowing for the differentiation between human groups according to somatic characteristics.[6] Racist disciplines were concerned with anthropological typologies that supported classifying human populations into physically discrete human races with the primary goal of asserting white supremacy. At the moment when racial science insisted that racial groups were constituted by distinct physiological and anatomical differences, the visual representation of the (racialized) body enabled an "increasingly consolidated article of faith that racial characteristics were irrevocably inscribed through the measurable size and shape of the human body."[7]

A key figure of scientific racism who sought to visualize racial differences was Johann Friedrich Blumenbach (1752–1840), whose craniometric experiments in racial anthropology ordered and ranked humans into different racial groups according to skin color and aesthetic judgment (the "Caucasian," "Mongolian," "Malayan," "Ethiopian," and "American"). Blumenbach's typology is considered the starting point of Anthropology and articulated a taxonomy that would form the basis for the increasingly rigid racial classifications of the nineteenth century. His chronometric schema of five races reinforced the superior position of the white European male over all other races. It led Blumenbach to conclude that "the white or Caucasian was the first and the most beautiful and talented race, from which all other races had degenerated to become Chinese, Negroes, etc."[8]

By the mid-nineteenth century, a hermeneutic paradigm had gained widespread prestige, manifesting in two tightly entwined disciplines: Physiognomy and Phrenology. Both shared the belief that what is located on the outside or surface of the body, especially on the face and head, "bore the outward signs of inner character."[9] Phrenology emerged in the first decade of the nineteenth century in the research of Franz Joseph Gall and was later modified and expanded by his apprentice Spurzheim. The new discipline proposed a map of the brain by measuring the shapes and bumps of the skull and sought to discern correspondences between the topography of the skull and what were thought to be specific, localized faculties seated within the brain. Besides Blumenbach's "cranial volumetrics" and Gall's *Schädellehre*, other indicators to separate races were the classification of facial features devised by the Dutch anatomist Petrus Camper (1722–1789). The widely popular discipline of Physiognomy isolated the profile of the head and the anatomic features of the head and face, assigning a characterological significance to each element such as the forehead, eyes, ears, nose, and chin. Camper's so-called facial angle theory intended to provide a sound criterion to distinguish and hierarchize races by measuring the profile of humans and animals. In his grid-like scheme, Camper placed the European skull next to a Greek statue and the Angolan skull next to an Orangutan, aiming to prove that African facial features differ the most from his favored Greco-Roman aesthetics. Camper's cranial sequence influenced an embryonic science of morphology (such as conducted by Goethe) to eventually become, in the words of Londa Schiebinger, the "central visual icon of all subsequent racism."[10]

In the late eighteenth century, the Physiognomy of Johann Lavater attempted to identify character traits from facial features by pictorially imaging people in silhouettes. The practice was dedicated to detecting hidden causes legible only to specialized interpreters. Lavater understood that "reasoning from the exterior to the interior" would enable one to "discover solid and fixed principles by which to settle what the Man really is,"[11] an approach firmly entrenched in the optical fundamentalism of the Enlightenment, where seeing and knowing are inextricably bound. German physiognomics established a "panoptic schema for cataloging the racial body"[12] as both systems— Lavater's physiognomic gaze and Jeremy Bentham's panopticon—construct a monologic structure of observation where the human object is exposed to constant surveillance and rendered transparent while the position of the one observing remains hidden. With the resurgence of Physiognomy during the Weimar era, the discipline eventually became a weapon of mass destruction: Lavater's Physiognomy served as a foundation for racial-genetic biology and anthropology and proved crucial for the construction of racial ideologies in general and Nazi racial theories in particular.

Taking biometrics' history in the racial sciences as a starting point, this chapter traces biometrics' origins from their invention in the colonial period to the filing cabinets of nineteenth-century criminology and police work, and further to the biometric databases of the European border regime. I identify three strands that closely link biometrics' colonial applications to the present European border regime: physical violence, identification, and evidence. The first link treats the relationship between biometrics and the infliction of physical pain as the often-violent biometric data retrieval can be traced back to the colonial terror inherent in early biometric projects. Second, biometrics' common understanding of identifying individual subjects must be reviewed in the light of past and present biometric practices. These technologies are frequently used to identify not an individual body, but its fitting to a particular group or category. Third, I trace the notion of biometrics as truth apparatuses from British India to the present EU fingerprinting database, which elucidates the usage of biometrics as evidentiary technologies that habitually supersede the subject's claims: machinic truth about the body is brought in opposition to self-narrated biographies and testimonies. Although biometrics are often put in the service of state violence, refugees have appropriated biometric technologies for their pursuits and tell their stories to counter death and political erasure. This chapter ends by situating the refugee selfie as born in a context characterized by imperial faciality and machine readability—both practices used in today's border regime to determine eligibility for citizenship and asylum. The refugee selfie, however, goes beyond surveillance and biometric capture to become a powerful intervention into postvisual borderlands.

## THE VISCERAL ARCHIVE OF BIOMETRICS

Biometric technologies are often seen as transforming the body into "pure information" and producing a "data double" that results in a "decorporealized body . . . of pure virtuality."[13] The production of a data double is the moment of abstraction when data have left the body to henceforth exist within the realm of digitality, on the screens of border agency headquarters, in the biometric databases that, by capturing the data double, facilitate its spatio-temporal tracking. In creating a data double of the person through biometric enrollment, the biometric double is conceived as transcending human corporeality and reducing flesh to pure information, thus producing a digital entity that exists separate from the body, guiding the research's focus[14] to the tracking of the data double rather than the body that is conceived as holding it. As I will show in this section, the violence attached to border biometrics is not only due to enhanced tracking but involves the very moment the body is conceived as holding data and forcefully subjected to subtracting it. The entanglement of biometrics and torture at European borders reveals a sovereignty underpinning modes of biometric governance that subjects bodies to physical violence and death with impunity, so the centering on harmful data extraction shifts the focus away from tracing "data doubles" to the production of "bodies of data."

Identification practices are based on the notion that human beings have consistent, heritable characteristics that can be discovered, aggregated, and acted upon. Biometrics presupposes the body as a "stable, unchanging repository of personal information from which we can collect data."[15] To measure and identify an individual, to make the body machine-readable, biometric technology necessitates a body that is coherent over time and space, a body that, rephrasing Haraway, ends at the skin. Although the emergence of an identifiable self is a complex historical formation also rooted in the shaping of the humanist subject as the bearer of rights and liberties, the history relevant for understanding the extrajudicial violence committed under the sign of biometric data retrieval must center on the enclosure of the individual in her own body as a process achieved by violence. The creation of a coherent body and self, a self that can be identified over time and place, pertains to the process of primitive accumulation. Silvia Federici has shown that the rise of capitalism was coeval with a war against women and fortified violence and terror against those bodies needed in the transition to industrial capitalism.[16] This early capitalist moment brought forward a new paradigm of conceiving the body and the self, which located responsibility and agency not in nature, prophecy, or magic, but the rational subject. For the identifiable subject to emerge, "the bourgeoisie had to combat the assumption that it is possible to be in two places at the same time, for the fixation of the body in space and time, that is, the individual's spatio-temporal identification, is an essential condition for the regularity of the work-process."[17] Indeed, the production of an identifiable self was an epistemological shift, but the dissemination of the epistemology depended on the extermination of large groups of people—namely, the poor women persecuted during the witch hunt and the near-extinction of Indigenous peoples in the New World and elsewhere. Both the violent underhistory of body contours in biometrics and current attempts to define what is enclosed in the skin and, thus, worth measuring, challenge not only the demarcation between the material and immaterial body but the self-evident body as such.

In early modern Europe, sorcery and magic had to be extorted for the coherent and identifiable self to emerge, but British India, the colonial context that birthed the biometric fingerprint, depended on these systems' (discursive) existence to govern via biometrics. For Michael Taussig, the "decisive ingredient" in discovering the scientific value of the fingerprint was the use of the hand and thumb "as a type of modernizing sorcery by the colonial bureaucracy."[18] Fingerprinting continued the ritualistic procedure of mimesis by connecting the sorcerer's use of the footprint to the state practice of taking fingerprints. Also, M'charek[19] notes that there was something "fetishistic" about the British faith in fingerprinting, and, in colonized India, biometrics "became signatures and fetishes, used to make people legible and to scare them with the power of mysterious signs."[20] If primitive accumulation enclosed the body into fixed contours, biometric data extraction at the border presents another moment where the undergirding physical violence of biometrics resurfaces in manifest ways.

In December 2015, around two hundred Eritrean migrants who had arrived in Lampedusa refused to be fingerprinted by the Italian police. The silent dissent soon became a loud collective refusal and was heard across Europe when migrants organized a march and sit-in in Lampedusa chanting, "We are human beings! No fingerprints! We want freedom! We want to move out of the camp!"[21] This collective moment of organizing arose from the many moments of dispersed resistance against biometric data collection as migrants have long physically resisted the fingerprinting process, escaped the procedure after arrival on EU hotspots, or tampered with the machine-readability of their fingertips by using glue, acid, or burning them with hot irons.[22] These resistant acts have provoked violent responses on both an institutional level and in encounters with European border guards. In 2015, the European Commission allowed Italian authorities the use force and long-term detention to make migrants comply with Dublin (II) regulations to achieve the target of a "100% fingerprinting rate."[23] But even before physical force was EU-sanctioned, the Italian Ministry of Interior circulated a flyer among migrants who had arrived on Italian shores, informing them that facial portraits and biometrics would be collected "even with the use of force, if necessary."[24] The self-mutilation of fingertips and coerced biometric data collection are but two examples revealing the intimate relationship between physical harm and biometric body inspection. Also, the court hearing of Frontex Coordinating Officer Miguel Ângelo Nunes Nicolau confirms that physical violence in biometric encounters does not depart from an otherwise nonviolent and nonintrusive data collection project but is an inherent part of biometric data collection and state-sanctioned:

Many people think that forced fingerprinting includes, for example, the breaking of the fingers, but this is not the case. The forced acquisition of fingerprints for digital processing consists of several phases: a phase of advice, a phase of attempt, and, if the person does not cooperate, the relocation into another center to try another attempt until you reach the goal. The use of force is, of course, the last resort, but in the meantime, all conditions must be met so that the person cannot proceed with his trip out of the hotspot.[25]

The gradual transgression of bodily integrity in Nicolau's account demonstrates that biometric violence is presented as an answer to resistant practices. It seems to respond to refugees' perceived transgressive acts—that is, their noncompliance with border security measures. However, racial border policing, including harmful biometric data collection, must be understood as gratuitous violence and not contingent upon refugees' behavior. Amnesty International[26] documented that the systematic use of "unnecessary" and "excessive force" in the form of cruel, inhuman, and degrading treatment or torture by border guards to force "uncooperative individuals" to provide their fingerprints had become the rule on the Lampedusa hotspot. In one testimony, Ishaq recounts the gruesome story of torture and sexual humiliation occurring within the framework of biometric data retrieval by police officers inside the Turin train station. His testimony is accessible in the third-person, which distances us, the readers, further away from his account of evidence:

First, [Ishaq] said, police officers took the group to a room. "They made us undress, all naked. The policemen started laughing." Then, as he still resisted fingerprinting, police officers resorted to a different tactic: "They held me by my four limbs, one person for each. The fifth pulled my penis down until she got me seated. At that point one took a photo of me, while another one was turning my head towards the camera. And they managed to put my hands on the fingerprinting machine. . . . For two days I bled every time I peed."[27]

There is a persistent belief that torture is instrumental, designed, that is, to extract information from an enemy or suspect who would not otherwise disclose it.[28] Torture is seen to come with exchange value: by physically harming and invading the body, the data believed to be stored in the body will eventually be subtracted and put into the service of (supra)national security. The case of abuse in the Turin train station, along with other testimonies of border violence, reveals "the intimate link between moral order and body inspection"[29] in biometrics, as well as the innumerable physical and mental injuries attached to the process.

While Ishaq's testimony is accessible to us in written form, the account is reminiscent of the pornotropic pictures taken of Abu Ghraib detainees during the U.S. occupation of Iraq, which scholars refused to understand as the work of a few "aberrant" individuals but the systematic terror that neocolonial and imperial settings are infused with.[30] Although there is no visual testimony portraying the acts of violence committed against Ishaq, still, the camera is present in his account. When the border agents took a picture of him and turned his head toward the camera, we cannot tell whether the photo taken during the abuse is captured as a mugshot-like facial portrait for biometric purposes or if it frames the entire scene of abuse. Regardless of the intention, here, the "photographer becomes part of the apparatus of intimidation and exposure,"[31] as Allen Feldman remarked considering the Abu Ghraib pictures, for it captures the abused in a moment where state violence consolidates in the most humiliating and cruel way. Not unlike the trophy pictures taken in the U.S. Black site that have been understood as demonstrating how empire visually comes into existence through racialized and sexualized violence, aiming at restoring a form of power that seemed lost on the battleground,[32] the blending of Ishaq's testimony and the Abu Ghraib photographs, although it has its limitations indeed, reveals how exceptional spaces such as neocolonial warzones and porous borders interrupt regulatory frameworks as part of state power's normative procedure.

Writing on the terror of colonialism, Taussig ventured that neither the political economy of rubber nor that of labor accounts for the violence perpetrated against the Indians of the Putumayo in Peru during the rubber boom. Taussig reminds us that terror is an essential mediator of colonial hegemony, and he understands the infliction of physical pain as first and foremost a "memorializing"[33] or imprinting of power on the bodies of the colonized. In the War on Terror, torture was legitimized with the "prevention of prospective violence and terror,"[34] while at the European border, torture and physical harm are used to extract the truth about someone's identity in the name of border security. The violence committed under the sign of EU border biometrics, however, cannot be justified or subsumed under a securitization narrative; the use of torture pertains to the border regime structurally, not collaterally. Gratuitous violence is a systematic part of a geopolitics of conquest, reaffirming hegemony over postcolonial border territories. Torture is invariably situated as productive of truth and knowledge. Like the War on Terror, Europe-in-crisis de facto suspends the Geneva Convention prohibiting torture, defined as the intentional infliction of severe pain or suffering. The entanglement of physical violence and biometrics at the European border challenges not the informatization of the body as such but the notion of biometric technologies as a set of noninvasive practices that leave the body intact. It reveals the viscerality inherent to biometric archives, the flesh underlying the biometric records, and the pain, suffering, and violence that the biometric archive is constituted upon.

## COLONIAL SORTING IN EU HOTSPOTS

Biometrics are often presented as fueling the transition from border control to body control. They apprehend and identify individuals at the border and follow the body by continually tracking and fracturing the individual for surveillance purposes. This shifts the understanding from borders as normative "lines in the sand"[35] to their multiplication and dispersal over territories and creates a scenario in which the body becomes coextensive with the technologies that target it. The body becomes "(re)searchable at a distance [because it] can be transported to places far removed, both in time and space, from the person belonging to the body concerned."[36] While biometrics have certainly contributed to borders' modified character, producing borders as delocalized entities that track bodies by establishing physical and virtual locations of control and capture, it is crucial to keep in mind that also during the colonial era, the identification of bodies via pass tags, branding, and coercive tattooing was predicated on the fact that bodies move through space and that, by disclosing the data attached to them, they could be definitely identified and (re)captured. The architecture of European hotspots complicates the relationship between the refugee and her biometric data double for the logic of carcerality inherent to Mediterranean detention archipelagos presents biometrics not as identification technologies but as technologies of capture: they are fundamentally predicated on storing "fractured body parts"[37] and are used to contain subjects.

When in January 2016, hundreds of people stood in line in front of Berlin's office for health and social affairs or *Lageso*, the first contact point for newly arrived refugees that facilitates asylum applications in the German capital, volunteers stepped in to provide some of the basic needs lacking on its property. People often waited for days outside the German reception facility with no food, shelter, or medical care with temperatures below freezing. The images of an understaffed and unprepared bureaucracy circulating in media swiftly became the epitome of Berlin's failure to accommodate migrants in the early days of the European refugee crisis. To ameliorate the optics of this desperate spectacle unfolding in the heart of the EU, the German state hired the New York–based multinational consulting firm McKinsey & Company to "streamline asylum procedures" in collaboration with the Federal Office for Migration and Refugees (BAMF).[38] The selection of the company is not coincidental, for McKinsey presents a crucial pillar in European and German neoliberal history. After the Second World War, the company advised corporate executives in Europe on how to rebuild the war-torn economy in the image of American business under the auspices of the Marshall Plan.[39] Later in 1990s Germany, when the state-owned companies of the former GDR were gradually privatized, McKinsey was a member of the Hartz commission that initiated the Hartz laws deregulating employment relationships in Germany.[40] For its efforts to streamline asylum procedures with BAMF, McKinsey alone will have received around 47 million euros until the end of 2020—funds that were never put out to public tender.[41]

Among McKinsey's projects[42] has been developing fast-track arrival centers with the capacity to process asylum claims within days. The firm proposed a strategic framework for swift and cost-efficient mass deportations and the substantial expansion of the German border–industrial complex. To accelerate the pace in deportations, the company advocated for a data-driven approach to tackle migration, including the long-term data collection from refugees to measure "integration outcomes," which translates into the surveillance of refugees long after they have arrived in Europe.[43] One of McKinsey's first measures was to shift away from approaching asylum claims as individual cases to dividing them into clusters or groups based on the applicant's country of origin, an approach at odds with international human rights as it effectively undermines the individual's right to have their asylum case considered singularly.

If the hiring of McKinsey may be dismissed as an unprompted crisis response by the German government, the departure from considering asylum cases singularly to adherence of predefined classifications of those coming to Europe is, however, firmly institutionalized in the strategic architecture of European hotspots that serves as the first point for biometric data collection for those traveling irregularly to Europe. Developed by the European Commission to "strengthen" the border function of frontline states such as Italy and Greece, the official rationale accompanying the policy was to set up a border architecture to tackle "exceptional migratory flows"[44] and capable of the filtering out of "those who need international protection and those who do not."[45] Hotspots are set up to separate so-called economic migrants from refugees, a distinction that disregards Western states' obligation toward migrants, which results from the connected histories of states and their (former) colonies but, instead, classifies those coming to Europe into worthy and unworthy of European protection, a practice similar, as Gurminder Bhambra remarked, to attempts at distinguishing the deserving from the undeserving poor.[46]

Upon arriving at the EU border archipelago in Greek (Lesbos, Chios, Samos, Leros, and Kos) or Italian (Taranto, Messina, Pozallo, Lampedusa, and Trapani) hotspots, authorities attempt to determine migrants' nationality or ethnicity via ethnic and racial profiling[47] by taking their fingerprints and assigning them to preexisting migrant profiles based on nationality and some scant biographical information gathered during swift identification procedures. These profiles then serve as templates that effectively sideline refugee testimonies in favor of classifications defined by national and racial parameters. People from West African countries, for example, are precluded both from claiming asylum and the relocation program, while Eritreans, Syrians, and Iraqis are allowed to start the asylum procedure.[48] Hotspots thus effectively serve as a bulwark from the European mainland, restrict the freedom of movement of the people contained in these spaces, and serve as de facto detention spaces[49] by creating what Foucault termed the *carceral archipelago*: "the way in which a form of punitive system is physically dispersed yet at the same time covers the entirety of a society."[50] If the criteria for asylum are not met, migrants are illegalized on the spot and determined for deportation, creating a "migration frontline archipelago"[51] in the Central and Eastern Mediterranean.

According to Foucault,[52] the emergence of the biopolitical state shifted its penal practices toward the veridictional question, asking criminals no longer "What have you done?" but "Who are you?" To ask for someone's identity is the biopolitical question par excellence because it assumes that who you are fundamentally determines not only what you have done but what you are capable of doing. By identifying someone via biometrics and racial profiling, EU bordering practices not only define a person's identity but, at the same time, answer the persecutional question: what have you done? Contrary to international law that anchors the right to seek asylum, both detention and deportation from European hotspots frequently occur without habeas corpus. The biometric apprehension of refugees at the fringes of the European border regime presents less a moment of identification but the sovereign labeling of persons into preexisting profiles and racial groups. Identifying people corresponds with identifying a type, and this process is encoded into the term *identity*. In its etymological history, the term not only referred to the individual as such but to the sameness with another group, presenting the history of identification as not so much "a history . . . of individuality as of *categories* and their *indicators*."[53] In Foucault's terms, the background against which individuals are measured is called the *metabody*, a term he used when studying nineteenth-century psychiatry to argue that in order to accommodate the physical absence of a sick body in which to locate pathology, psychiatrists generated a kind of fantastical metabody that incorporated a congeries of symptoms suffered by the patient's ancestors.[54] The metabody defines and overdetermines individuals by evoking their ancestors' presumed criminal attitude, which essentially presents a typification to provide specimens in the process of "serialization."[55]

"Racism," abolitionist Ruth Wilson Gilmore writes, "is the ordinary means through which dehumanization achieves ideological normality," while at the same time, the practice of dehumanizing people "produces racial categories."[56] In today's border context, the alien other is not cast through individual depiction but the exaggeration and serialization of individualistic traits as markers of a type or species. Current biometric efforts to distinguish people at the border continue this legacy as they target and supersede the bodies they put under scrutiny by privileging biological properties, behavioral aspects, and physiological characteristics.

In German Southwest Africa, the gradual implementation of the Native Ordinances impelled colonizers to discuss whom to target with the legal restrictions. Along with other texts of the colonial judiciary, the decrees introduced the sociolegal category of *Eingeborener,* a term designating that someone was born in the colony but that was used by colonizers in a particular racialized and racist way.[57] Attempts to neatly define a blood and race doctrine were shaped by both biological and cultural racism as they discussed blood, habits, and levels of education given not by physicality but cultural context.[58] The administering of the African population into different racial groups emerges again in the hotspots of the European border regime where migrant profiles introduce "a hierarchical order, a nomenclature reminiscent of the Orientalist and racialized practices of European colonialism and imperialism."[59] Regarding hotspot procedures, Claudia Aradau[60] has further noted that migrants' swift segregation into different categories prevents the forming of a collective political subject, a practice reminiscent of the colonial–military strategy of *divide et impera* that segmented Africans' social and communal spaces into zones of governance.

The desire to classify and order according to race was the guiding principle in early attempts to establish typologies of the (sub)human, as conducted in biometrics' early application in the disciplines of Anthropometry, Craniology, and Physiognomy. According to Alana Lentin,[61] racial science still exists today and maintains some of the most potent stereotypes attributed to "old-fashioned racism," yet it paradoxically claims to be postrace as racial science is located in the past, which is the "consequence of failing to deal with the political, social, and cultural legacies of racism on our societies." As long as biometrics are still used to create racist typologies, it is crucial to evoke the history of disciplines created to aid and abet white supremacy.

The legacy of biometrics' early application in the racial sciences further manifests in the uncanny history of the Italian carceral archipelago that is closely entangled with what Antonio Gramsci[62] termed the "Southern question." Soon after national unification in 1861, Italy's government established the policy of *domicilio coatto* (forced exile) to crush the political opponents of unification. The internal exile policy to stamp out political dissent primarily targeted Southerners and banned insurgents to penal colonies dispersed across the South's islands, including Lampedusa, Favignano, Lipari, Tremiti, Ustica, Pantelleria, Ventotene, and Ponza.[63] The system allowed officials to resettle and rehabilitate hundreds—and sometimes thousands—of "dangerous criminal suspects" in police camps each year. Like the migrants contained in EU hotspots, suspects sent to domicilio coatto found themselves in an ambiguous legal position: not only had many of them committed no crime, but they also could not appeal their assignments before a judge.

Once Italy began to acquire colonies, it started to build police camps in Libya, with the first agricultural penitentiary colonies established in 1915 when some convicts were sent to the experimental field in Sidi Mesri in the neighborhood of Tripoli, and some North African prisoners were returned from the colony to Sardinia.[64] Colonial expansion had opened up a vast terrain for examination, classification, and investigation by criminal anthropologists and Italy's Southern carceral archipelago, with its internal criminals and deported colonized prisoners, aroused the interest of physicians, criminologists, and anthropologists who were keen to study the "characteristics" of the Libyan population and the supposed inclination to crime of anarchists and the many other detained insurgents. So, in the Libyan colony in 1912, a service for the identification and registration of detainees employing photographs and biometric fingerprint identification was established with the purpose to acquire "knowledge of the population of the new colony, knowledge that will be useful both from a scientific and from a practical standpoint."[65] The penal colonies in Southern Italy, including the empire's extraterritorial outposts in Libya, were viewed by criminal anthropologists as supplying invaluable data and source material that could be used to validate their theories of congenital criminality, a racist gaze that was also fueled by "scientific" discourse on human "races" based on the theses of the Positivist School of which Cesare Lombroso was an instrumental part. The criminal anthropologist was a frequent visitor of Italian prisons and domicilio coatto where he trialed his method of preventive policing that considered those most deviant from the norm of the white European as prone to criminality, a legacy that strongly echoes through Southern EU hotspots as they frequently serve not only as a first entry point for migrants and their (biometric) data doubles[66] but as strategic sites for EU border security and counterterrorism by vetting migrants as potential security threats.[67]

## FINGERPRINTS AND BERTILLONAGE: THE TRUTH APPARATUS AT THE BORDER

In a court hearing on the use of physical force in biometric data collection, Frontex Coordinating Officer Nicolau presents fingerprints as the only medium that allows making "the presumption of the nationality of a migrant as accurate as possible" and, therefore, establish migrants' identity at the border:

> Fingerprints are the only tool the police have to cross-check someone's iden-
> tity and verify whether there is information about the person in Europe or
> even a Third Country. . . . All other sources of identification are questionable.
> Therefore, all statements released by the person who arrived cannot be reliably
> verified, not even by us.[68]

Nicolau's proclaimed necessity to identify migrants with fingerprints is rooted in the EU's Dublin Regulation, which states that the first country where an asylum applicant arrives is ultimately responsible for her application, thus excluding one country passing refugees on to another, as well as the simultaneous submission of applications in several EU member states. EU border authorities take the applicants' fingerprints whenever a person asks for asylum in a member state and subsequently transmit them to EURODAC, the EU's fingerprinting database. Since its implementation in 2003, EURODAC has been used for asylum purposes only, filing fingerprints to determine whether a person has already applied for asylum in another country.[69] The system presents the largest multijurisdictional AFIS (Automated Fingerprint Identification System) globally. It operates based on the Henry Classification system invented in British India that would later be exported to the British metropole and across the world.[70] Created by Edward Henry, Hem Chandra Bose, and Azizul Haque, this method for classifying fingerprints served as the basis for many modern-day AFIS until the 1990s and was only replaced by ridge flow classification approaches in recent years. The filing system assigned a numerical value based on the number of whorls, loops, and arches on a fingerprint, a mathematical foundation that, according to its inventors, gave the system "increased credibility."[71] It promised that the "raw data of Indian life would be mastered if they could simply be assigned an appropriate location in that grid."[72]

Fingerprints were in use before biometrics were formalized in the nineteenth century and present identificatory markers predating the scientific history of biometrics; hence they are only retrospectively constructed as a sort of "ur-biometrics."[73] Only after fingerprinting established itself as the means by which "others—colonial populations, immigrants, people of color, and women could be drawn into the web of state-sponsored identification" did the system become a technique targeting everyone in the metropole, regardless of gender, race, and class.[74]

The name associated with fingerprinting in India is British colonial official William James Herschel, chief administrator of the Hooghly district of Bengal.[75] Herschel was in close conversation with Francis Galton, who was the first to place the study of fingerprints on a scientific basis and so lay the groundwork for their use in criminal cases. Galton considered the fingerprint to be of continual good service in our tropical settlement, where the individual members of the swarms of dark and yellow-skinned races are mostly unable to sign their names and are otherwise hardly distinguishable by Europeans. And, whether they can write or not are grossly addicted to impersonation and other varieties of fraudulent practice.[76]

While the habitual identification of residents may have been unthinkable in Europe, the British Raj considered the Indian population to be "another matter" where "unquestioned authority went hand in hand with pervasive fears of being deceived by the populace."[77] Fingerprints were seen as reliable images that could supersede the perceived "falsity of Indian tongues."[78] They were officially introduced to suppress anticolonial resistance when Indian conscripts rose against colonial rule in 1857. The technology was born out of a crisis moment in colonial governance and what was seen as a response "to the problem of administering a vast empire with a small corps of civil servants outnumbered by hostile natives."[79] According to British officials, they could not "tell one Indian from another"[80] and sought to enforce law and order upon an unruly population that was perceived, in racist terms, as an undistinguishable colonized mass.

Much later than in British India, fingerprinting was also used in the German colony of Southwest Africa, where colonial administrators were greatly influenced by technologies from neighboring colonies, namely British South Africa and Portuguese East Africa. Fingerprinting was considered to replace the "native crosses" used to sign documents and treaties that caused dissatisfaction among colonial officials and promised to symbolically enforce the implicitness of colonial modernization. In 1912, the government issued a statement stipulating that all official identity cards, passports, and other paper documents "must always bear the owner's right thumbprint for identification purposes."[81] For German colonial officials, biometrics promised to "guarantee the definite identification of a person" because "the pass tag, which can be easily swapped, does not do this."[82] Contrary to the British colony, however, German Southwest Africa never established a proper biometric apparatus to govern colonial subjects.

Like biometrics in the colonies introduced to counter the assumed "litigiousness, wiliness, and inveracity"[83] of the colonized, the capturing of biometrics at the European border imbues the fingerprinting technology with the cachet of scientificity, objectivity, and credibility that is launched against the speaking subjects. In Frontex officer Nicolau's narrative, fingerprints are the only means to determine a migrant's nationality because "all other sources of identification are questionable, all statements released . . . cannot be reliably verified."[84] Migrants' text and biography-based testimonies recede into the background while fingerprints emerge as the only valid medium to reveal someone's identity. Biometrics emerge as truth apparatuses instituting a "regime of truth" that Foucault[85] understood as the types of discourses a society "accepts and makes function as true," rooted in the "techniques and procedures accorded value in the acquisition of truth." These technologies are deployed to counter the assumed false testimonies of those apprehended at the border by at once delegitimizing and locating truth within the metrics of the refugee body.

In the many cases where an asylum applicant refuses to give fingerprints, some EU member states "complete the identification through the taking of a picture and an individual description without transmission of fingerprints."[86] Combining a photograph with the description of a person's physical traits has its uncanny history in the spoken portrait or *portrait parlé* that formed part of the Bertillon System of Identification, a critical forerunner of contemporary biometrics. The method coemerged with photography and criminology in the late nineteenth century where it was seen to enable the professionalization of police work and criminal investigations. Its inventor, Alphonse Bertillon, sought to standardize the police gaze by transmuting bodily data onto a surface (the fiche), which, in turn, was then assessed as part of the more comprehensive statistical apparatus of the filing cabinet.[87]

Bertillonage was born at the intersection of photography and statistics to provide a scientific approach for identifying criminals by grounding photographic evidence in statistical methods. Contemporaries regarded photography as providing "evidence of a novel kind" as it was only the photograph that enabled a new kind of truth that was pitted "against the protean oral texts of those accused with crimes" and presented a mute testimony taking down "the alibis, excuses and multiple biographies of those accused."[88] By the 1840s, this new juridical photographic realism was widely recognized and bolstered by efforts to regulate the presence of the growing urban subproletariat. Replacing oral and textual testimonies with the visual truth apparatus of photography, the discourse on early photography introduced an episteme that will again emerge in the technological truth apparatuses of the European border regime: the notion that biometric apparatuses are more truthful than the testimonies and self-narrated biographies of those persons considered suspect.

The nineteenth-century Bertillon card is an early paradigmatic example of an organizational model between data and images of which a variation is still in use today in the form of driver's licenses, passports, mugshots, and criminal records. In Bertillonage, the relationship between images and data was characterized by a "supplemental mode" as these distinct modes relate to each other in additive ways allowing the deficiencies in the descriptive capacity of images to be "supplemented by those of data and vice versa."[89] The method functioned as a bipartite system. It positioned an individual microscopic record within a macroscopic aggregate by combining photographic portraiture, anthropometric description, and standardized written notes on a single fiche or card and, subsequently, organized these cards in a statistically based filing system. Like today's biometric technologies that are based on the template of white masculinity, Bertillonage was unable to accurately record women or children, as it was designed for men who had short hair and reached full physical maturity.[90]

First put into practice at the Parisian Police Prefecture amid Baron Haussmann's destruction of working-class Paris,[91] an early moment of gentrification[92] that was bolstered by efforts to regulate the "dangerous classes," Bertillonage spread rapidly from the metropole to French and other colonial territories where it was adopted as a "progressive" tool by numerous actors, including police institutions and specialists of criminal anthropology.[93] Also, in German Southwest Africa, the government dictated in 1912 that the record to be produced for apprehended criminals should consist of fingerprints and a standardized anthropometric description combined with a mugshot and a *portrait parlé*.[94] Not being able to permanently attach data onto bodies via pass tags or coerced tattoos, colonizers sought to generate biometric bodies of data by locating the truth in the metrics of the body itself. A commentator from GSWA notes: "It turns out that the control of metal tags is entirely insufficient. The idea of photographing the many thousands of colored workers is unfeasible due to an almost impossible extra burden on police work and because the Blacks are such good gurners and actors that one could never recognize the same man."[95] Anticipating a lack of resources and anticolonial resistance (packed in the racist stereotype of the comical Black person pulling faces), a large-scale photographic archive, while to a minimal extent achieved for colonial policing purposes,[96] was quickly dismissed in the German colony.

"The machine readable bodies," Irma van der Ploeg writes, "are believed to be more truthful than the speaking persons themselves, who, in the process of being bypassed, are defined as 'suspect.'"[97] This claim becomes particularly salient in the European border regime, where the testimonies of Europe's others are weighed against biometric apparatuses. Browne termed this dynamic "digital epidermalization"; the disembodied gaze of certain surveillance technologies such as identity cards and e-passport verification machines is employed to do the work of alienating a subject by producing a truth about the body and one's identity *despite* the subject's claims.[98] Galton's proclaimed accusation of the colonized practicing "impersonation and other varieties of fraudulent practice" resurfaces again at the border, where, like the juridical photographic realism of the nineteenth century that posited the photograph against the oral texts of those accused with crimes, the postvisual fingerprint—the fingerprint's visualized metrics—are seen as superseding refugee narratives, thus taking down the testimonies and multiple biographies of those apprehended at the border.

## IMPERIAL FACIALITY FROM THE FILING CABINET TO THE DATABASE

When Anas Modamani took a selfie with German chancellor Angela Merkel in 2015, it came to symbolize Germany's often-proclaimed *Willkommenskultur*, the notion of a permissive refugee admission policy that led hundreds of thousands of migrants into the country. Modamani arrived in Germany in July 2015 after leaving his friends and family behind in Darayya, a suburb of Damascus. His journey took him across the Aegean Sea from Turkey to Greece, and along the Balkans, he moved from one refugee camp to the next. Only a few days after his arrival in the German capital, the chancellor visited his refugee center outside of Berlin, and it was in that moment when he took the selfie that would instantly go viral and develop a life of its own. In the weeks following his snapshot, the media embraced Modamani as a model refugee and considered him to give a face to the many people seeking protection in Germany. He was invited to German talk shows where he was praised for his commitment to learning German and his friendly relationship with the host family. While his "Merkel selfie" continued to circulate online, rumors spread that linked him to terrorist attacks. One of the first false posts used his selfie in a montage with a mugshot of one of the terrorists behind the 2016 Brussels bombings. The story claimed that "Merkel took a selfie with a terrorist," a misidentification that spread to Facebook and began to be shared by hundreds of people where Modamani was further associated with the truck attack on a Berlin Christmas market in the same year.[99]

Modamani's selfie surfaces against a slew of other "refugee selfies"[100] produced in the context of the European border crisis that has been dubbed the first event of large-scale displacement in an age of ubiquitous smartphone usage. These visual products must be situated as part of refugees' "digital passage" to Europe that scholars have described as profoundly ambivalent,[101] and it is in this conflicted terrain where the refugee selfie emerges: between the vulnerability to (biometric) surveillance and the opportunity to narrate and represent the self. While EU border biometrics produce "forced portraits"[102] such as mugshots and photographs taken during asylum assessment procedures, migrants have long appropriated biometric technologies to narrate their stories despite and against the biometric apparatuses' claims. Visual and digital self-representation presents a crucial tool in a setting where biometric and other surveillance technologies take on the role of representing and speaking for the body, telling its story while bypassing and discrediting the narratives and testimonies of those subjected under the surveillant gaze. And it is particularly the selfie, defined as "a photograph that one has taken of oneself, typically one taken with a smartphone or webcam and uploaded to a social media website,"[103] that sits at the intersection of voluntary self-representation and biometric surveillance for its emergence "cannot be separated from the rise of biometric governance, and in particular the use of facial recognition in surveillance and policing of individuals and communities, in border control or military operations."[104] The selfie "appears in a time when citizenship is to a great extent managed through biometric recognition and the datafication of personal information,"[105] a context characterized by faces' machine readability, which is used to determine eligibility for citizenship and asylum. If today the selfie surfaces in its entanglement with biometric surveillance, it were also technologies of surveillance that brought forward its technological forerunner, the nineteenth-century bourgeois portrait.[106] The enormous prestige and popularity of Physiognomy in the 1840s and 1850s was not only crucial for the popularity of the portrait, but the science also provided the epistemic background for the mugshot to emerge, thus neatly entangling the voluntary self-representation of the portrait with the forced capture of the face in the mugshot that sought to measure and archive facial metrics.[107]

The rise of the selfie and the fixation on the face reside in what Zach Blas[108] termed "global face culture," a culture driven by "impulses to know, capture, calculate, categorize, and standardize human faces." In the philosophy of Gilles Deleuze and Félix Guattari,[109] "faciality" establishes the conditions of subjects to have and assume a face by subjecting the entire body under the regime of the face. According to them, the totalitarian experiences of the twentieth century have taught us about the power and dominance of one type of image over others: the image of the face. Facialization introduces a regime of signs necessary to the politics underpinning Western Christianity. It not only proliferated a star system gravitating around famous faces but a political logic that is unthinkable without the hegemony of the face. The intersection of fascism and face ranges from the iconic totalitarianism of Hitler, Mussolini, Stalin, and Saddam Hussein to Trump's orange face. The "faciality machine," Deleuze and Guattari claim, "performs the facialization of the entire body and all its surroundings and objects' by establishing the condition of subjects to have and assume a face." The birth of faciality began with Christianization when Europeans spread the Christ-face across Europe and the globe: "If the face is in fact Christ, in other words, your average ordinary white man, then the first deviances, the first divergence-types, are racial: yellow man, black man. . . . They must be Christianized, in other words, facialized."[110]

From Blumenbach's perfect Caucasian to Leonardo Davinci's vision of ideal corporeal symmetry, the white man face serves as the template from which all others are derived and racialized. Racism, then, "operates by the determination of degrees of deviance in relation to the white-man face."[111] Insofar as faciality establishes an "imperialism of the face" by hierarchizing faces according to a white and androcentric template, it also introduces a binary grid organized around a zero and one logic, determining whether someone is compliant with the template.[112]

Although biometrics claim to offer neutral means to capture and authenticate bodies, scholars[113] have shown that biometric technologies are built on the template of the white Man, as they have difficulties detecting the faces of people of color and are more prone to produce a failure to enroll (FTE) regarding women of Pacific Rim/Asian descent.[114] Biometrics further introduce the scientific means to establish and justify typologies (the bona fide traveler, the bogus refugee, the criminal, the terrorist), not unlike the racialized profile catalog created in scientific racism. Biometric technologies are "infrastructurally calibrated to whiteness"—that is, "whiteness is configured as the universal gauge that determines the technical settings and parameters for the visual imaging and capture of a subject."[115] Such as biometrics were introduced when British officials were not able to "tell one Indian from another,"[116] Modamani's misrecognized facial features are part of a racism underpinning technological infrastructures that has significantly increased under digital conditions: all derivatives from the white Man template are thought to look the same and are, thus, interchangeable.

In Blumenbach and, even more so, in Lavater's Physiognomy, we see early examples of how the face was used as a truth apparatus. Its singling out and capturing were believed to reveal someone's real identity in the form of race, criminal character, moral flaws, and virtues. Contemporary facial recognition software used in biometric identification and mass surveillance continues to draw from scientific methods that rested on the notion that an isolated representation of the face can give away a person's truth. The attempt to "bind identity to the body"[117] via the singular representation of the face fractures the body into dehumanized facial traits and simultaneously disavows the fact that faces change over time and context. Similar to the measuring instruments built in the disciplines of racial science, today's facial algorithms treat the face as a truth-telling and static repository. Recent examples for this episteme are the building of algorithmic software that attempts to detect a person's sexuality,[118] personality, and criminal status,[119] including whether someone is a terrorist,[120] by using a single facial portrait.

From the anthropometric portrait and the mugshot to today's biometric facial images stored in EURODAC, the privileging of the face strips the body of its three-dimensionality by reducing lived experience and the body's abundant visceral life into a single facial surface. Like fingerprinting, facial recognition technology is inherently defined by its postvisual mode. It stands as symptomatic of a paradigm whereby the truth of computation precedes over the truth of photographic and human recognition. Steve F. Anderson[121] termed this the "translational mode," a mode in which visual phenomena become readily transformed into computable data as they generate a technical basis that translates "facial contours into quantifiable data points." For Kelly Gates,[122] the dual aim of facial recognition technologies is to "automate the mediated process of connecting faces to identities and to enable the distribution of those identities across computer networks" to enhance the searchability of individuals in vast populations. Moreover, algorithmic environments dissect the face in facial features. Alexander Galloway maintains that "there is no 'faciality' with the computer," meaning that neither objects, faces, nor bodies are human to computers, inevitably breaking with the arts that fixated upon the embodied human form (such as painting, photography, and cinema).[123] Facial biometrics and recognition technologies treat the face as a static and standardized repository for identity over time and place. Facebook's auto-face-tagging and the iPhone's *RecognizeMe* application, which uses face scanning to unlock phones, eclipse a romanticized notion of qualitative facial attributes in favor of the face as a quantitative code and template that can be standardized and measured.

The Christ-face is encoded into technology as androcentric whiteness and as a broader template of representation, often in combination with suffering. In response to the November 2015 Paris attacks, some Balkan governments blocked refugees who could not prove citizenship from Syria, Afghanistan, or Iraq. The measures were enacted only four days after the attack and rejected all incoming people, except those from white-listed countries, as "economic migrants." In protest of these decisions, a group of Iranian and Kurdish migrants stranded at the Greek–Macedonian border in Idomeni sewed their lips together and went on a hunger strike. A press photograph by Yannis Behrakis captures the Idomeni protest like the *Cimabue crucifix*: the Passion (from the Latin verb *patior*, to suffer, bear, and endure) of Christ emerges here to align the suffering of the other into a standardized and familiar template of pain. Evoking Christ as the zero template from which all other faces emerge as derivatives might provoke *com-passion* from a Western audience: the suffering-with the other who is often considered as not capable of feeling pain. It might further realign the suffering face into the teleological and necessary suffering of the Passion and thereby cast the violence inflicted on refugee bodies as contingent upon their behavior, not as systemic and gratuitous. The imperial regime of faciality emerges in a twofold way here. It first provides the deviant template of the terrorist against which the other is marked as potentially dangerous, and second, it centers the spectacle of suffering onto the mutilated body and not the systemic violence targeting it. The group of refugees protested precisely against that. They defied the system that profiled them as not deserving protection, an action that was borne out of the racist panic conflating refugees with terrorists. By inflicting violence on themselves, they made visible the violence inherent in these classifications and demonstrated the necropolitical effects that states of emergencies have in the wake of terrorist attacks. By sewing their lips together, they protested against a regime and its biometric backbone that speaks for and silences them: who are you and what have you done.

While the selfie also presents a disciplinary tool that obliges us to shape ourselves in ways permitted by our visual culture,[124] its main characteristic is, as media scholars have pointed out, its intimate entanglement with our digital networks. The "instantaneous distribution" via social networks differs the selfie from its earlier photographic precursors.[125] The selfie is a "progeny of digital networks," and its distinctiveness derives from nonrepresentational changes: innovations in distribution, storage, and metadata—all phenomena not directly concerned with the production or aesthetic design of images.[126] Jill Walker Rettberg even argues that machines are an important—if not the primary—audience of our selfie practices[127] as selfies organize our close alignment to machine readability and treat our faces not as visual entities but as data. Through selfies, we get used to having our faces read by machines; they casualize biometric surveillance and get neatly entangled with our everyday lives.

If the selfie is entangled with the metrics of the social media systems that facilitate its circulation, this is to some extent mirrored in the technologies of photographic capture that have coemerged with statistical filing systems and, by means of this postvisual entanglement, anticipate the logic of storage and information handling of present digital databases. Photography depended, since its very inception, on the metrics of the filing cabinet with the archive serving as its dominant institutional basis:

> In short, we need to describe the emergence of a truth-apparatus that cannot be adequately reduced to the optical model provided by the camera. The camera is integrated into a larger ensemble: a bureaucratic-clerical-statistical system of "intelligence". This system can be described as a sophisticated form of the archive. The central artifact of this system is not the camera but the filing cabinet.[128]

The postvisual genealogy from the mugshot/archive to the selfie/database makes the confusion of faces in Modamani's case not incidental but encoded into the selfie as a progeny of biometric apparatuses invented to measure and capture human features such as facial traits. The photographic archive was organized according to an overriding logic of surveillance invested in constructing middle-class norms against criminal deviance. Practices of seeing instituted by photography were linked to the racist science of eugenics as practiced by Galton, who connected racial differences to criminality.[129] Consequently, "photography came to establish and delimit the terrain of the other, to define with the generalized look—the typology—and the contingent instance of deviance and social pathology."[130] The refugee selfie is thus always already a mugshot, caught in the template of the refugee-as-terrorist that criminalizes refugees' portraits because of the seemingly criminal act of having crossed a border.

As months passed and more posts started appearing, Modamani launched a self-designed campaign to counter the misinformation by writing directly to the people who shared the fake news. He eventually began legal proceedings against Facebook, claiming it had failed to take sufficient action against the defamatory posts he flagged. His charges present the first instance formal action was taken against Facebook in Germany concerning fake news. In January 2017, the German court ruled against him and decided that Facebook does not have to seek and delete defamatory posts linked to him. In Modamani's powerful stance against the company, he not only defied the racialized template of the terrorist but went against the faciality machine that (de)authorizes faces according to citizenship status and race. His struggle makes even more visible that under conditions of digitality, Facebook's facial archive becomes a dangerous locus for expropriating identity in the service of imperial faciality. In this context, to reclaim face against its attributed template becomes unruly as it rejects the way faces are governed by systems that still bear the imprint of scientific racism.

## NOTES

1. The Smart Border Package includes the Entry/Exit System, which electronically records the time and place of third-country nationals entering and leaving the EU and issues an alert to national authorities when there is no exit record by the expiry time. The same package entails the Registered Traveller Programme (RTP), which allows business travelers from third countries to use simplified border checks by subjecting them to prescreening and vetting. The RTP, as Didier Bigo remarked, effectively institutionalizes a two-tier border control system based on indicators such as wealth, nationality, employer, and travel history. Bigo et al., "Justice and Home Affairs Databases and a Smart Borders System at EU External Borders," 3.

2. Mathiesen, *On Globalisation of Control*, 2.

3. M'charek, "Dead-Bodies-at-the-Border," 223.

4. Foucault, *Society Must Be Defended*, 254.

5. Bancel, David, and Thomas, *The Invention of Race*, 1.

6. The process of establishing racial differences according to visual signifiers was profoundly ambiguous. Stoler describes how racial discourse often slips between somatic and visual difference. The ambiguity of these sets of relationships (somatic/

inner self, phenotype/genotype, skin color/psychological traits) are not obstacles to racial thinking but rather enable its proliferation. "The force of racisms," Stoler writes, "is not found in the alleged fixity of visual knowledge . . . but on the malleability of the criteria of the psychological dispositions and moral sensibilities that the visual could neither definitely secure nor explain." Stoler, *Duress*, 198–200. While seeing racial difference in external signifiers is itself evidently tied to racial formations, the linking of visible traces of the body to invisible characteristics is marked by a deep uncertainty that eventually challenges the racio–visual epistemology the practice is based on: the modern conception of racial identity maintains an uneasy relation to the visual; the visible marks of the racialized body are only signs of a deeper, interior difference, and yet those visible marks are the only differences that can be observed. The body is the sign of a difference that exceeds the body. The modern concept of race is therefore predicated on an epistemology of visibility, but the visible becomes an insufficient guarantee of knowledge. As a result, the possibility of a gap opens up between what the body says and what the body means. Kawash, *Dislocating the Color Line*, 130.

7. Flint, *The Victorians and the Visual Imagination*, 14–15.

8. Bernal, *Black Athena*, 219.

9. Sekula, "The Body and the Archive," 11.

10. Schiebinger, *Nature's Body*, 149–50. Besides, Camper was famous for his public anatomical dissections, which dreadfully exemplify how early biometrics at once subjected non-white bodies to a lower position on the human hierarchy and depended on their flesh for scientific inquiry and Western medicine. In these public postmortems, the non-white body is penetrated and literally turned inside out, "an analogue of the colonial voyage of discovery." Pugliese, *Biometrics*, 34.

11. Quoted from Stafford, *Body Criticism*, 84 and 95.

12. Gray, *About Face*, 327.

13. Haggerty and Ericson, "The Surveillant Assemblage," 606 and 613.

14. This principle is to some extent mirrored in accounts that underscore biometrics as a technological project, shorn of the messy realities of gendered and raced bodies and the flesh that is conceived as holding data. Charles Shoniregun and Stephen Crosier, for example, claim a distinction between what they term "regressive" and "progressive biometrics." While progressive biometrics refer to the widely known application of biometrics for identification and security purposes, regressive biometrics, in contrast, consist of "barbaric acts" such as cutting "the criminal's finger(s), toe(s), leg(s), ear(s) and removing their eye(s)." The authors locate the use of biometrics as punishment in the ancient Roman Empire and claim that today "some countries still use regressive biometrics" to punish criminals. While they do not specify which countries "still" use regressive biometrics, they nevertheless indicate to a prominent discourse that conflates the historical past with the non-Western outside. With this, they firmly distinguish a modern use of biometrics as located on a progressive, read technological trajectory, and its barbaric equivalent, the corporeal punishing of criminals often assumed to be exterior to our current time and place. Shoniregun and Crosier, *Securing Biometrics Applications*, 127.

15. Magnet, *When Biometrics Fail*, 2.

16. Federici, *Caliban and the Witch.*

17. Ibid., 141. Still in 1651, this paradigm had to be consolidated as Thomas Hobbes wrote that "[n]o man therefore can conceive anything, but he must conceive it in some place . . . not that anything is all in this place and all in another place at the same time; nor that two or more things can be in one and the same place at once." Hobbes, *Leviathan*, 14.

18. Taussig, *Mimesis and Alterity*, 221–22.

19. M'charek, "Dead-Bodies-at-the-Border," 233.

20. The practice of fingerprinting must be located in a general obsession with the hand in the nineteenth century. Aviva Briefel notes yet another numinous moment that cemented the faith in fingerprinting. While various body parts were scrutinized in racial sciences and used as evidence to establish racial classifications, facial features such as lips, and angles, it was particularly "the hand [that] provided resistance to the post-Enlightenment scientific faith in the body's ability to expose racial particularities." Beginning with the rise of chirognomy, palmistry, and fingerprinting, the hand was perceived as an appendage capable of revealing individual identity in its shape, size, and surface characteristics. Although none of the features analyzed in racist disciplines can be used to distinguish people according to their race, pace Briefel, it was particularly the hand that had to be racially coded as it did not offer signs that could be readily inscribed into preexisting codes of racial difference. Briefel, *The Racial Hand in the Victorian Imagination*, 21.

21. Scherer, "'No Fingerprints!' Chant Migrants in Italy as EU Cracks Down."

22. Moving Europe, "Can't Stop a Movement!"

23. European Commission, "Progress Report on the Implementation of the Hotspots in Italy." The European Union also endorsed a "proportionate degree of coercion" in the case of minors; see European Union, "Asylum."

24. Italian Ministry of Interior, "Circular n. 27978."

25. Commissione Centri Accoglienza Immigrati, "Commissione parlamentare di inchiesta sul sistema di accoglienza e di identificazione nonché sulle condizioni di trattamiento dei migranti nei centri di accoglienza, nei centri die accoglienza per richiedenti asilo e nei centri di identificaazione ed espulsione," 5.

26. Amnesty International, "Hotspot Italy." The report states that border guards make use of coercive measures, including prolonged detention, severe beatings, electrical shocks, sexual humiliation, and causing severe pain to the genitals. The victims interviewed in the report were mostly from Sudan, and included women and unaccompanied minors.

27. Ishaq, whose name has been altered in the report, was interviewed in Ventimiglia on July 9, 2016. Ibid., 52.

28. Scarry, *The Body in Pain.*

29. M'charek, "Dead-Bodies-at-the-Border," 234.

30. Feldman, "On the Actuarial Gaze"; Mirzoeff, "Invisible Empire"; Razack, "How Is White Supremacy Embodied?"; Puar, "Abu Ghraib."

31. Feldman, "On the Actuarial Gaze," 218. The presence of the female police officer in Ishaq's testimony further recalls the much debated participation of Lynndie England in the scandal. In the Abu Ghraib scandal, female soldiers participating in

torture and sexual violence became a prominent focus of scholarly and media debate, and it was particularly England, a soldier who became infamous for posing thumbs-up behind a pile of naked detainees as well as holding a leash attached to a naked Iraqi prisoner, who received much media attention.

32. Ibid., 219–20.

33. Taussig, *Shamanism, Colonialism, and the Wild Man*, 72.

34. Pugliese, *State Violence and the Execution of Law*, 1.

35. Parker and Vaughan-Williams, "Lines in the Sand?"

36. Van der Ploeg, "Genetics, Biometrics and the Informatization of the Body," 48.

37. Balsamo, *Technologies of the Gendered Body*, 6.

38. Angenendt, Kipp, and Meier, "Mixed Migration."

39. Funded in 1926 in Chicago, McKinsey was among the top management consulting firms who replaced Taylorist companies in the United States during the 1930s. The consultancy experienced its breakthrough when U.S. president Roosevelt promoted social reforms with the New Deal and helped to defend corporations against perennial welfare claims from workers and trade unions. McKenna, "The American Challenge."

40. Rügemer, *The Capitalists of the 21st Century*.

41. The hiring of McKinsey is part of a larger "consultant scandal" (*Berateraffäre*) alleging nepotism and the mishandling of public funds against German defense minister Ursula von der Leyen. Delcker, "The Scandal Hanging over Ursula von Der Leyen"; Stanley-Becker, "How McKinsey Quietly Shaped Europe's Response to the Refugee Crisis."

42. In late 2016 and early 2017, the company worked to reduce the backlog of asylum claims in Greece. First, with the European Commission, and then through a project funded by the European Asylum Support Office. McKinsey brought the same economic rationality to the U.S. border regime, where the company worked with ICE, the U.S. Department of Homeland Security, Immigrations and Customs Enforcement, and proposed measures to accelerate the deportation process along with cuts in spending on food and medical care. MacDougall, "How McKinsey Helped the Trump Administration Carry Out Its Immigration Policies."

43. McKinsey and IOM, "More than Numbers—How Migration Data Can Deliver Real-Life Benefits for Migrants and Governments," 18. The firm's proposals have resulted in the legal introduction of the subsidiary or limited protection status (*subsidiärer Schutz*), a status that recognizes an asylum seeker may suffer serious harm in her country of origin but does not qualify as a refugee under the German Asylum Act or the Geneva Refugee Convention. McKinsey's drive to decrease the number of incoming people is further mirrored in the restriction of family reunification that those people granted subsidiary protection encounter. A new law of March 16, 2018, abolished the right to reunite with family members for two years and subsequently replaced it with a "humanitarian clause," which places family reunification at the discretion of the authorities by introducing the quota of one thousand German visas granted each month. Its measures conducted in the name of efficiency have, however, triggered hundreds of thousands of appeals that have created a new backlog—not in asylum centers, but in courts.

44. European Commission, "The Hotspot Approach to Managing Exceptional Migration Flows."

45. European Council, "European Council Conclusions, EUCO 22/15, 26 June 2015, Point 4."

46. Bhambra, "The Refugee Crisis and Our Connected Histories of Colonialism and Empire."

47. Tazzioli and Garelli, "The EU Hotspot Approach at Lampedusa."

48. Ibid.

49. Dimitriadi, "Governing Irregular Migration at the Margins of Europe."

50. Elden and Crampton, "Introduction," 176.

51. Tazzioli and Garelli, "The EU Hotspot Approach at Lampedusa."

52. Foucault, Davidson, and Burchell, *The Birth of Biopolitics*, 34–35.

53. Caplan and Torpey, *Documenting Individual Identity*, 51; my emphasis.

54. A similar type of metabody can be discerned in discourses of contemporary genetics, as evinced by the construals of Richard Dawkins and David Hull of the gene as replicator. Mader, "Foucault's 'Metabody.'"

55. Feldman, *Xenophobic Technicities*.

56. Gilmore, *Golden Gulag*, 234.

57. The chosen English terminology to translate this term—African and native—is not so much adequate as the German term merely expresses where someone was born, inside or outside the colony. Strictly applied, an *Eingeborener* could also be a German born in the colony.

58. In a letter to the district office, the imperial governor advocates to subject those "Basterds" to the ordinances, in whom the "colored blood predominates" and who are "not on the same level as Europeans" regarding their "habits and levels of education." Quoted from Lerp, *Imperiale Grenzräume*, 107. Original: "bei denen das farbige Blut offenbar überwiegt und die nach ihren Lebensgewohnheiten und Bildungsgrade nicht auf gleicher Stufe mit Europäern stehen."

59. Rodríguez, "The Coloniality of Migration and the 'Refugee Crisis,'" 20.

60. Aradau, "Political Grammars of Mobility, Security and Subjectivity."

61. Lentin, *Racism and Ethnic Discrimination*, 93.

62. Gramsci, *The Southern Question*.

63. Gibson, *Born to Crime*, 154. While not as widespread as other types of penal colonies in the late eighteenth and early nineteenth century, these police camps established a clear precedent, particularly in the case of Italy, and remained in force until Mussolini seized power in 1922 to serve as an important prototype for *confino di polizia*, the Fascist regime's own system of police-administered exile, implemented in 1926.

64. Later, in 1923, the penal colony in Sghedeida, twelve kilometres from Tripoli, was founded. Two other colonies in Cyrenaica, in Coefia and Berka, were established in 1919 and 1923 respectively. Di Pasquale, "The 'Other' at Home," 217.

65. Gibson, *Born to Crime*, 148.

66. Pollozek and Passoth, "Infrastructuring European Migration and Border Control."

67. Lyman, "Regulating Flow of Refugees Gains Urgency in Greece and Rest of Europe."

68. Commissione Centri Accoglienza Immigrati, "Commissione parlamentare di inchiesta sul sistema di accoglienza e di identificazione nonché sulle condizioni di trattamento dei migranti nei centri di accoglienza, nei centri die accoglienza per richiedenti asilo e nei centri di identificaazione ed espulsione," 4, my translation. Original: "Le impronte digitali sono l'unico strumento che le forze di polizia hanno per fare controlli incrociati sull'identità della persona e verificare se esistono informazioni su di lei in Europa o anche in un Paese terzo. . . . Tutte le altre fonti di identificazione sono discutibili, tutte le dichiarazioni che vengono rilasciate dalla persona che arriva non possono essere verificate con sicurezza neanche da noi."

69. The fingerprint database combines biometric identification technology with computerized data processing and works as a hit/no-hit system. By comparing fingerprints with the templates of fingerprints submitted in other countries, the system produces a hit each time it recognizes a corresponding alert or template, which would mean that someone has applied for asylum before and is likely to be sent back to the country of first registration.

70. Cole, *Suspect Identities*; Sengoopta, *Imprint of the Raj*; Singha, "Settle, Mobilize, Verify."

71. Henry, *Classification and Uses of Finger Prints*, 85–102.

72. Chattopadhyay, "'Goods, Chattels and Sundry Items,'" 263.

73. Pugliese, *Biometrics*, 49. In the United States, the first populations to be fingerprinted were convicts, petty criminals, soldiers, and native peoples. White administrators who imagined Asians, Africans, and Native Americans as a homogeneous and undistinguishable group began to fall back on the infinite uniqueness of fingerprints; the technology thus literally migrated from the colonial periphery to the economic core. Parenti, *The Soft Cage*, 47.

74. Cole, *Suspect Identities*, 166.

75. When Herschel used the fingerprint for identification purposes, he was unaware of any permanent and individual skin patterns. Nevertheless, he conferred some sort of self-referential quality to the handprint. Herschel's unquestioned authority he awarded to the fingerprint as the privileged means of identification was in line with a broader perception of fingerprinting at the time that considered the practice superior to other visual means of identification such as anthropometry and photography but most of all, the written form of the signature.

76. Galton, "Identification by Finger-Tips," 303.

77. Sengoopta, *Imprint of the Raj*, 204.

78. Waits, "The Indexical Trace," 20.

79. Quoted from Cole, *Suspect Identities*, 63.

80. Ibid., 64.

81. Quoted from Zimmerer, *Deutsche Herrschaft über Afrikaner*, 116.

82. Quoted from ibid., 116–17; my translation.

83. Galton, who would become the first to provide a systematic fingerprint classification system that laid the groundwork for their use in criminal cases, promoted this racist narrative: "In India and in many of our Colonies, the absence of satisfactory

means for identifying persons of other races is felt. The natives are mostly unable to sign; their features are not readily distinguishable by Europeans; and in many cases they are characterized by a strange amount of litigiousness, williness, and inveracity." Galton, *Finger Prints*, 149.

84. Commissione Centri Accoglienza Immigrati, "Commissione parlamentare di inchiesta sul sistema di accoglienza e di identificazione nonché sulle condizioni di trattamiento dei migranti nei centri di accoglienza, nei centri die accoglienza per richiedenti asilo e nei centri di identificaazione ed espulsione," 4.

85. Foucault and Rabinow, *The Foucault Reader*, 73.

86. This finding was revealed by the watchdog *Statewatch*, who obtained a confidential EU nonpaper in which the European Commission discussed the "best practices" to ensure that the fingerprints of refugees are taken and recorded in the EURODAC database. The nonpaper is based on the feedback of member states to a survey enquiring about this same issue. When asked whether member states use other techniques (such as multispectral images) in case the person has damaged fingerprints, the survey revealed that the majority of member states did not use different methods, while some countries (Belgium, France, Lithuania, Poland, and Slovakia) used a combination of photograph and individual descriptions. European Commission, "Summary of EMN Ad-Hoc Query No. 588 Eurodac Fingerprinting," 2.

87. Often considered an innovative move to establish photography as a forensic technology, the Bertillon System of Identification was instead a continuation of already existing media techniques within police work. The inventor of the system, Alphonse Bertillon, used the criminal's mug shot along with body measurements to produce a fiche. The method that Bertillon used for this, *signalement*, first measured some of the most characteristic dimensions of the bony structures of the body, then gave a detailed account of shape and movements including perceived mental and moral qualities, and, lastly, recorded what were regarded as the body's peculiarities, such as "deformities" resulting from disease or accident. The photographs, which were placed on a file card, were then extended by a spoken portrait.

88. Quoted from Sekula, "The Body and the Archive," 6.

89. Anderson, *Technologies of Vision*, 23.

90. Fosdick, "Passing of the Bertillon System of Identification," 364.

91. Maguire, "The Birth of Biometric Security."

92. Potyondi, "The Discovery of the Street." Fears over crime conditioned the birth of biometric security in fin-de-siècle Paris. In the 1860s the city was "modernized" with only 40 percent of its buildings remaining untouched by Haussmann, who removed the working class from the center of Paris and left them to live in shantytowns in the outskirts of the city. Retrospectively, the expulsion is analogous to late modern gentrification, such as when Rudy Giuliani cracked down on the homeless in New York at the end of the 1990s.

93. Piazza, "Bertillonage."

94. The parallel use of different methods for police recording was not unusual at that time. But the systematic use of *Bertillonage* in the German colony was only achieved in the coastal towns of Swakopmund and Lüderitzbucht. Rizzo, "Shades of Empire," 9.

95. Ingenieur von Zwergern, "Zur Eingeborenenfrage in Deutsch-Südwestafrika," 789–90; my translation. Original: "Es ergibt sich daraus, daß die Kontrolle durch Blechmarken eine vollständig ungenügende ist. Der Gedanke, die vielen tausend farbigen Arbeiter zu photographieren, ist unausführbar, nicht nur aus Gründen einer geradezu unmöglichen Mehrbelastung der Polizeitätigkeit, sondern auch deshalb, weil die Schwarzen so gute Gesichterschneider und Schauspieler sind, daß man nie denselben Mann wiedererkennen könnte."

96. Another document merging visuality and data were the German colonial *Fahndungsblätter*, search warrants produced between 1908 and 1910. They usually included a mug shot of the criminal along with body descriptions. Compared to police institutions in Berlin, London, Cape Town or Johannesburg, the German version of this colonial forensic practice was less sophisticated. Windhoek insisted that once all police stations were equipped with cameras, photography should play a crucial role in the identification of individuals. It maintained that the successful prosecution of "black criminals, cattle thieves, burglars, and vagrants thanks to photographs" was remarkable and that in some cases, the photographs also enabled the arrest of "white offenders." Rizzo, "Shades of Empire," 11.

97. Van der Ploeg, "Genetics, Biometrics and the Informatization of the Body," 48.

98. Browne, "Digital Epidermalization."

99. Ott, "How a Selfie with Merkel Changed Syrian Refugee's Life."

100. Risam, "Now You See Them."

101. Gillespie, Osseiran, and Cheesman, "Syrian Refugees and the Digital Passage to Europe"; Leurs and Ponzanesi, "Connected Migrants"; Ponzanesi and Leurs, "On Digital Crossings in Europe." On the one hand, online surveillance practices render refugee journeys more dangerous as travelers strive to remain invisible to gatekeepers, and surveillance continues after arrival in Europe, prompting many migrants to "clean" their online profiles. Latonero and Kift, "On Digital Passages and Borders." On the other, smartphones present important lifelines as they facilitate planning, navigation, and "communication rights." Leurs, "Communication Rights from the Margins."

102. Rettberg, *Seeing Ourselves Through Technology*.

103. Oxford Learner's Dictionaries, "Selfie."

104. Kuntsman, *Selfie Citizenship*, 15.

105. Ibid., 12.

106. While the selfie might be easily read as the triumph of individualism of our current times, to represent oneself via the face has a long history making use of various visual technologies, from oil painting to photography. The selfie is, thus, "a fusion of the self-image, the self-portrait of the artist as a hero, and the machine image of modern art that works as a digital performance." Mirzoeff, *How to See the World*, 31.

107. Sekula, "The Body and the Archive," 12.

108. Blas, "Escaping the Face."

109. Deleuze and Guattari, *Thousand Plateaus*, 187–211.

110. Ibid., 197.

111. Ibid.

112. Ibid., 169.

113. Browne, *Dark Matters*; Magnet, *When Biometrics Fail*; Pugliese, "Biometrics, Infrastructural Whiteness, and the Racialized Zero Degree of Nonrepresentation"; Pugliese, *Biometrics*.

114. Pugliese, "Biometrics, Infrastructural Whiteness, and the Racialized Zero Degree of Nonrepresentation," 112.

115. Ibid., 57.

116. Quoted from Cole, *Suspect Identities*, 64.

117. Gates, "Biometrics and Post-9/11 Technostalgia," 14.

118. Wang and Kosinski, "Deep Neural Networks Are More Accurate than Humans at Detecting Sexual Orientation from Facial Images."

119. Wu and Zhang, "Automated Inference on Criminality Using Face Images."

120. Storm, "Faception Can Allegedly Tell If You're a Terrorist Just by Analyzing Your Face."

121. Anderson, *Technologies of Vision*, 13.

122. Gates, *Our Biometric Future*, 15.

123. Galloway, *The Interface Effect*, 12.

124. Rettberg, *Seeing Ourselves Through Technology*.

125. Tifentale, "The Selfie," 11.

126. Frosh, "The Gestural Image."

127. Rettberg, "Biometric Citizens."

128. Sekula, "The Body and the Archive," 16.

129. Waits, "The Indexical Trace," 35.

130. Sekula, "The Body and the Archive," 7.

## Chapter 5

# Viral Deterrence

## *Sex, Risk, and Contagion ca. 1920 and 2015*

In 2015, Germany's Federal Foreign Office started #rumoursaboutgermany, a multimedia campaign using social and conventional media such as billboards, print, and television to educate, as the office claims, would-be migrants about false information concerning migration toward Europe.[1] As part of the campaign, billboards and posters were placed in high-density areas in the Afghan cities of Kabul, Mazar-i-Sharif, and Herat, asking their readers in the local languages of Dari and Pashto, "Leaving Afghanistan? Are you sure?" and, under the slogan, directing them to the campaign's website. The site presents as an information portal in which the German Federal Foreign Office provides information and "trustworthy facts" to "debunk common rumors that are being spread online by human traffickers."[2] These "rumors" are answered in a simplistic and dichotomous true or false manner. The question "Will you be rescued after two hours in a rubber boat?," for instance, is answered negatively:

> No. This is what smugglers promise, but: Rescue missions may not be where your boat is. Even if they were, your chances of being picked-up in time are extremely small—especially if smugglers leave your rubber boat drifting without a motor. The journey remains very dangerous and continues to cost thousands of lives.[3]

Many of the answers provided by the Federal Office are vague assessments. However, some answers are false from a juridical point of view ("Are you forcibly deported if you come illegally? Yes."). The underlying assumption is that if potential migrants can be made aware of the financial and bodily risks, particularly the dangers of traveling outside legal channels, they choose not to migrate.

European states have been using targeted deterrence in the form of information campaigns since the early 1990s.[4] These campaigns, usually initiated
by states or politicians to address potential migrants and discourage them
from undertaking their journeys, have been criticized for precluding migrants
from the right to claim asylum and not succeeding in preventing migration.
Information campaigns, Ceri Oeppen writes, enable states to control migrants
proactively while maintaining a humanitarian image as they act in the name
of migrants' protection, thus allowing the state to disguise deterrence as a
means of protecting people from potential risks.[5] The discourse of bodies at
risk creates the migrant as "both a life to be protected and a security threat
to be protected against"[6] while constructing smugglers and traffickers as the
real danger to migrants' lives and shifting the responsibility onto migrants
themselves. They represent one strategy of externalizing borders beyond the
geographical territories of the receiving countries and must be placed in the
broader dynamic of the politics of preemptive securitization as they aim to
prevent possible actions in the future tense. Brian Massumi has written about
the ontological structure of preemptive politics:

> An anti-accidental exercise of power, at whatever setting on its operational
> continuum, can only counter the event-driving force of the accident if it catches
> it in the before of incipience. To do this, it must move into that proto-territory.
> It must move as the accident moves, to where it may irrupt, "catching it before
> it actually emerges."[7]

Although Massumi situates the concept in the racialized complexes of
Hurricane Katrina and the War on Terror, he leaves aside the practice's inherent coloniality and racist nature. Information campaigns, however, not only
adhere to the general political imperative of preparedness and preemption that
seek to contain the accident (the terrorist act or the unlawful border crossing)
"before it actually emerges" but inherently depend on the former colony as a
"proto-territory" for migrant deterrence. The "invasive, preemptive, and proactive qualities"[8] of deterrence are innately entangled with the postcolonial
encroachment of the European border apparatus into the African continent,
and it is this setup that allows for the unlawful circulation of deterrence
within media landscapes. It is no surprise that current information campaigns
are historically enchained with colonialism's civilizing mission, specifically
to the use of educational cinema as a civilizing tool implemented to educate
"backward natives" to modern rational subjects.[9]

The paternalistic colonial discourse is further mirrored in the Foreign
Office's campaign in Afghanistan that enlists proper (i.e., state-produced)
knowledge against migrants' informal knowledge. Dismissed by the German
campaign as "rumors," unofficial information channels provide, in fact,

essential lifelines during migrant journeys. Migrants are connected through social media and other information technologies and often get helpful real-time updates during their passage by nonstate actors such as family members and activist networks.[10] In her study of African American rumor-lore, Patricia Turner links the suggestive power of rumors to risk perception and the protection of bodily boundaries[11]—rumors enabled to discuss bodily threats as exemplified by widespread stories about toxic fast-food products targeting Black consumers and conspiracy theories regarding the invention of HIV/AIDS. Allen Feldman generalizes Turner's account to formal mass communication structures and maintains that official state power channels are also characterized by a visual politics that fixates on at-risk social and bodily thresholds and threatened anthropological integrity.[12] If the colonial gesture of information campaigns creates the migrant as "both a life to be protected and a security threat to be protected against"[13] by constructing smugglers and traffickers as the real danger to migrants' lives and shifting the responsibility onto migrants themselves, then the migrant body is rendered as something to be protected on the grounds that it does not infiltrate the social body of the (supra)nation.

Information campaigns can be located in the broader realm of deterrence, a political tool that Global North states have been using since the Cold War to deter migration and prevent refugees from arriving at their territory and accessing their asylum system by reducing so-called "pull factors" or "false incentives." Deterrence, usually defined as "the action of discouraging an action or event through instilling doubt or fear of the consequences,"[14] has accelerated deportations across the globe and effectively created a climate of fear shaping border regimes around the world. A pivotal example in this regard is former Home Secretary Theresa May's "hostile environment policy" that affects numerous immigration acts and policy areas in the UK, ranging from indefinite immigration detention to the controversially high-income threshold for sponsoring a foreign spouse. Scholars importantly understood the hostile environment as an ongoing expression of the colonial system of racial ordering that encourages discrimination by those it deputizes.[15] From nonadmission policies that increasingly limit access to asylum procedures, such as the EU–Turkey deal, to offshore asylum processing and nonarrival measures preventing people from flight or making their routes unsafe by deploying military assets against the logistics of migrant journeys, the European border regime is fundamentally shaped by the deterrence paradigm, a point acknowledged by its critics and policy makers alike.[16] This is emphasized by the fact that since June 2019, the deterrence-based migration policies of the European border regime have been on trial as crimes against humanity at the International Criminal Court in The Hague.[17] Deterrence builds the core argument in the charge against Italy, Germany, and France, the key architects of lethal migration policies that have deliberately sacrificed migrant lives to deter future migratory acts, according to the communication to the criminal court.

As seen in the descriptions above, deterrence is often understood as a host of policies and operational strategies implemented to prevent people from migrating. In this chapter, I will flesh out yet another dimension of deterrence by taking the concept beyond the policy level to define the Cologne 2015–2016 event as a landmark of political deterrence that made use of images and numbers to create a politico-affective landscape in which fear of invasion and contagion thrives. The "night of Cologne" describes the sexual panic unfolding around reported cases of mass sexual assault and rape of women during the New Year festivities at the Cologne cathedral by large groups of men, most of them framed as racialized men of Middle Eastern and North African descent. The initial numbers circulating in the media reported that "2,000 men sexually assaulted 1,200 women"[18] and quoted authorities who linked the sexual assault to the "rapid migration of 2015."[19] CDU Vice-Chancellor Volker Bouffier famously declared that "Cologne changed everything," and Heiko Maas (SPD), the federal minister of justice, denounced the incidents as a *Zivilisationsbruch* (breach of civilization), a term reserved, at least in the German media discourse, for the atrocities of the Shoah.[20]

This chapter locates Cologne in the European border regime's broader media and security environment by approaching this often-repeated turning point in refugee admission through the prism of viral deterrence. I conceptualize viral deterrence as a strategy inherent in policy and media architecture with the primary function to facilitate the mediation and circulation of images of threat, risk, and death by pointing to the porosity and potential invasion/penetration of both (supra)national and individual bodies. According to Allen Feldman, those border figures evoked repetitively, such as the infiltrating terrorist, the drug dealer, the undocumented immigrant, and the foreign sexual abuser, have discursive currency precisely because they are seen as attacking and potentially harming the contours of both national and individual bodies.[21] What Feldman alludes to here is a well-established staple in feminist scholarship that has emphasized, as Mary Douglas did in 1966, the translatability of the body as a bounded system as "its boundaries can represent any boundaries which are threatened or precarious."[22] Central to Douglas's idea about the symbolic nature of purity and pollution is the insight that the human corporeal body is a conceptual microcosm for the body politic, and this is mainly the case in relation to how the flow of phenomena inside and outside of both bodies' openings is conceptualized and controlled. The body metaphor is in charge of policing the boundaries at the threshold of inside and outside, making bodily control an expression of social control. Reading Douglas, Sara Ahmed maintains that the national body is often perceived as soft and permeable, a feminized body prone to be "penetrated" or "invaded" by racialized others.[23] The nation at risk not only bears the potential danger of being penetrated and feminized but also of becoming less white or racially pure. This gendered imagery works to augment the martial power of the state, including border control, framed as masculine power able to protect against this threat.[24] Viral deterrence addresses the fact that those border figures evoked repetitively, such as the foreign sexual abuser during Cologne, have discursive currency precisely because they are seen as attacking and potentially harming both individual and national bodies. These figures work as deterrents to harden borders and securitize the nation. As indicators of "improper circulation," they emerge when border sovereignty is believed to be insufficiently maintained, a moment "symbolized in icons of mobile biosocial pollution."[25]

Feldman termed the visual regime instituted around these conjured bodily transgressions the "actuarial gaze," a tool to understand how the mediation of risk, threat, and emergency—events that commonly elude everyday sensory perception—become socially available in the "prosthetics of media pictures and reports."[26] As much as the actuarial gaze exposes, classifies, and visually edits the events subjected under its gaze, Feldman emphasizes that it not merely curates political events and their perception but shapes the perception of vulnerable groups of people, those classified as risk-bearers, by creating a "moralized and selective scenography of the Other."[27] In the broadest sense, the term *actuarial* relates to actuaries' work of compiling and analyzing statistics to calculate insurance risks and premiums. By using this term, Feldman implies that the mediation of those constructed as risk bearers—the gaze that captures them as posing a risk to the collective body or the ruling classes—simultaneously subjects those so captured to a web of calculations that anticipate, measure, and eventually present solutions to contain the risks. Crucial about Feldman's account is that he understands the contemporary media gaze as intensifying and imperially expanding earlier visual surveillance technologies, most notably the biometric capture apparatuses introduced in the nineteenth century by Francis Galton and Alphonse Bertillon. Inscribed into the actuarial gaze is, thus, an entire history of visualizing, recording, and indeed, calculating that which is perceived as threat: the "dangerous classes," or the subproletariat in the nineteenth century, the terrorist, the "bogus refugee," the refugee-as-terrorist, refugee-as-rapist, and other unlawful trespassers. In actuarial regimes, this mode of calculation is linked to risk perception and prophylaxis. It both introduces the risk and the preemptive politics to tackle it while at the same time representing those targeted by the measures—the risky objects—as not capable of feeling the pain of abjection.

The mode of deterrence disseminated in the Cologne incident had distinct colonial reverberations. To put it in Tina Campt's terms, it was a "resonant echo"[28] from the colonial past. To make sense of the colonial mode of deterrence weaponized during the event, I read Cologne against its (post) colonial precursor: the "Black Shame" campaign of the interbellum period that accused Black colonial troops of raping white German women in the Rhineland. Around 1920, Germans launched a racist media campaign against the non-white soldiers of the French colonial troops, a phenomenon Campt calls "echoes of imagined danger."[29] The "Shame of Cologne" and the "Black Shame" campaign deployed a racialized and sexualized notion of invasion to defame and delegitimize non-white and postcolonial presence in Germany while conflating the body natural and the body politic to cast invasion in viral and sexual terms. Moreover, these campaigns represented invasive others as transgressing an already too permeable border, ranging from the contamination of the purity of blood to undermining Western cultural accomplishments.

## THE "SHAME OF COLOGNE"—A
## SPECTACLE OF POROUS BORDERS

After the long summer of migration in 2015, a phase marked by national and international media reporting about Germany as a bastion of humanitarianism that opened its doors to the many people seeking asylum, Europe turned to a "winter of racism."[30] In the wake of the November 2015 Paris terror attacks, right-wing and conservative forces regained discursive and political territory and swiftly associated refugees with terrorists while demanding restrictive border controls and accelerating deportations. By the end of 2015, several European countries set up increased border control, and the EU suspended the Schengen system of open borders and passport-free travel. In the following year, right-wing nationalist parties across Europe made headway and purported their anti-immigration stances, often with institutional effects. For their xenophobic agenda, the 2015–2016 Cologne event came at the right time. If only months before the terrorist attacks were instrumentalized to produce the figure of the refugee-as-terrorist, the accusations of mass sexual assault during New Year's Eve added yet another stereotype to the vocabulary of racist hatred: the refugee as rapist.

Five years after Cologne, the media reviewed the event in a different light. A report from German news magazine *Der Spiegel* disclosed that from the initial 1,300 police reports filed, only a handful had legal consequences and only three were convicted for sexual offenses. From these initial 1,300 reports, nearly half of those complaints were of sexual violence (the majority reported groping), whereas the rest consisted primarily of petty theft.[31] While every incident of a sexual offense is one too many, the conclusions of the New Year's celebrations demonstrate that Cologne had become a significant media event enabled by a racist truth production that fundamentally reorganized the relationship between Germany and its Others. The swift introduction of the Asylum Package II only one week after the incident substantially broadened the conditions of deportation by declaring Tunisia, Algeria, and Morocco safe countries of origin—former European colonies where many of those accused were seen to originate.[32] Along with the increase of surveillance cameras in public spaces, Cologne further legitimized mass racial profiling in the following year.

The "Shame of Cologne"[33] conjured the specter of a dangerous Muslim patriarchal masculinity targeting German women, Western values, and women's emancipation. The vocabulary of racist hatred unleashed into the public sphere—ranging from the often-conjured "sex mob" and the "pack without inhibitions"[34] to classifying the event as "sexual terror" and a "sexual jihad"[35] against Western civilization—was echoed across the political spectrum, facilitating alliances between far-right, liberal, including feminist and left-wing actors. The comments on Cologne shared a blatant commitment to a racist public discourse that was, at least in the short history of the mediated migration event, a novelty in scale. Cologne was seen as a crime of an "entirely new dimension,"[36] unprecedented in the Western hemisphere, a belief underlined by the repeated use of the term *taharrush* (harassment in Arabic), which portrays group sexual violence as originating from the Middle East and North Africa and, therefore, foreign to German and European culture.[37]

Feminist scholarship was prolific in analyzing Cologne at the crossroads of racism, sexism, and white feminism. Cologne was understood as a crucial "cipher" of these entanglements as it enabled and legitimized anti-Muslim racism via the scandalization of sexism.[38] Furthermore, scholars situated the event as part of a larger historical pattern in which the masculinity of racialized others is perceived as a threat to Occidental values and achievements, spurring an "ethnosexism" that enabled the spilling over of the long history of the "rape-lynching-complex" into the present.[39] The event further allowed the thriving of white nationalist feminism as Cologne was placed at the junction of a "femonationalism"[40] joining forces with a well-worn Orientalism that imagines the white female body as something to protect from the dark male Other.[41]

As the event unfolded in German media, accusations of rape went up to the hundreds. Far-right social media groups, including PEGIDA, an anti-immigration group known in full as Patriotic Europeans Against the Islamization of the West, increasingly began to use the inflammatory term *rapefugee*. The "rapefugee" discourse frequently repeated the claim that refugees are primarily male, often using photographs of migrant men and highlighting the absence of women and children. Indeed, media reports on migration sparsely depict women and children seeking refuge, and if so, they are not represented in masses.[42] Right-wing sympathizers often "aspire to the nation's restoration and repossession and dictate that incomers constitute a security problem which we are obliged to recognize in strongly gendered forms."[43] By shifting their attention to the presumed mass of young migrant men, the sexual panic of Cologne transferred the Orientalist media gaze from focusing on migrating families to young and single migrant men arriving in Europe. Following Miriam Ticktin, the obsession regarding the protection of women from the foreign other must be explained with the fact that sexuality and sexual violence have become the "language and discourse of border control [as] public attention functions as a postcolonial extension that codes race and class in sexual terms."[44] She reminds us that the obsession with mass sexual assault and group sexualities ascribed to the Oriental other harks back to the fantasy of the harem and had a vital resurrection in France in late 2000 when French-Maghrebian teenagers were accused of gang-raping young women of North African origin in the outskirts of French cities. *Les tournantes*, as these mass sexual atrocities conducted by men of former French colonies were called, became a sudden focus in public political debates—after decades of public neglect against issues concerning sexual violence against women.

The challenge of the Cologne campaign was to visually represent and mediate what did not take place to the extent it was narrated. News media frequently illustrated the event using pictures of a massive crowd surrounded by police and immersed in the fumes and sparks of fireworks. Pictures of Cologne were often blurred and low in resolution, transcending the genre of professional journalist photography in favor of evoking digital amateur snapshots that seemed to be taken hastily in the moment. One photograph exemplary of the visual politics depicts a pixelated crowd in front of Cologne central station, leaving a third of the picture manipulated by digital image processing tools. Belonging to what Hito Steyerl terms "poor images" or images that are blurred, amateurish, and full of artifacts and digital manipulations, the image's poor quality "is not a lack, but an additional layer of information, which is not about content but form."[45] Poor images have gained increased currency when it comes to serving as proof of the real. The pixelated snapshot not only suggests proximity to the event but also enters, as a poor image, the genre of visual evidence to produce a criminalization before the fact. Surveillance society widely promotes the "nothing to hide argument," which evokes the ideal subject as transparent and easily identifiable, a subject who does not fear surveillance because she is a good citizen.[46] Embedded in Enlightenment terms, this notion equates visibility and transparency and dismisses all unintelligible as suspicious and potentially criminal. Face pixilation emerges not as a neutral means facilitating privacy and anonymity but as intricately caught in this dynamic, rendering those made unintelligible as having something to hide.

Martina Tazzioli has aptly noted that the lengthened presence and increased visibility of migrants have led to a shift from the language of migration flows to mobs and crowds, partly due to their continued presence and quasi-immobilization in border zones.[47] During Cologne, the "mob"—a term always coded in racist and classist terms—was transposed from the border zone to the metropole and emerged in racial and sexualized terms. The pixels censoring the crowd are primarily dark-colored, ranging from black to brown, hence not merely pointing to the colors of the night and the dark clothing of the crowd, but the racialized notion of a crime that remains in the dark, committed by a mob whose crimes are seen as being covered up by the media. This notion was also reproduced in the "rapefugee" discourse that eventually condensed into a website, inviting its visitors to mark sites of sexual violence purportedly committed by refugees on a so-called "rape map."[48] Given its invitation to participative mapping, the map might eventually serve as the base for vigilante justice, promising to redress crimes seen as covered up by the state and the general public. While over half of the crimes reported on the map were loudly exposed in the media as false (such as the case of the "Rostock rapist"), what stands out in this imaginative geography of rape is the frequent appearance of sexual violence committed against refugee women and minors within detainment facilities and camps. Unbeknownst to the website's initiators, the "rapefugee"-campaign, with its attention to sexual violence, documented the sexual violence of the European border immigration-complex that is, contrary to the sexual violence committed by refugees and migrants, a common and structural phenomenon.[49]

Continuing the conflation of race, citizenship, and religion into an unholy assemblage of the foreign sexual abuser was Slavoj Žižek, who analyzed Cologne as an "obscene version of carnival" that stands in historical line with the Great Cat Massacre of 1730s Paris in which the ritual mass killing of cats during carnival represented the defiance the working class felt toward the bourgeoisie.[50] Equating the historical underdogs with the disenfranchised refugees, Žižek understands the attacks on the master's cats as congruent with the "pussies" assaulted in Cologne and concluded, in proper missionary fashion, that "to enact actual emancipation, [the refugees] have to be educated . . . into their freedom."[51] Here, Žižek feeds into the same sexual-insurgent lexicon put forth by media discourse that evokes a fantasy of invasion from the South. What we might still gain from his historical analogy is less the recurrence of a historical event that has materialized in today's context but the surfacing of Cologne's rejected shadow archive that places the white bourgeois fear of border porosity in Cologne, the German capital of carnival.

Historically, carnival inverted the hierarchical order, or at least performed its persiflage, as people used crossdressing to invert gender and class (such as laypeople in the costumes of clerics and poor people donating to the rich), but it was also the moment when acts of real violence could be committed with impunity, such as the stoning of Jewish people and the killing of domestic animals as in the Great Cat Massacre.[52] Cologne's place in this genealogy enabled not the emergence of sexual violence perpetrated against Western women but, by visually repeating the bodily transgressions enacted during carnival as a historical state of exception, prepared the discursive ground for violent measures to be enacted against refugees and migrants. Looming in the background was not simply the threat of racial mixture and racial parity with fears of non-white men demanding access to white women, a trope, as we will see below, frequently rehearsed in German contexts of postwar defeat, but the "bourgeois hysteria"[53] of porous borders as the ritual inversions and reversals enacted during carnival temporarily repealed the normative order and celebrated not "high" cultural forms, but, as Mikhail Bakhtin[54] noted, the lower strata of the human body by privileging the grotesque and vulgar over the bourgeois and civilized body. Carnival was about inversion, excess, and hybridity and emphasized the body's permeability and viscerality, openings, and orifices, not its closure and finish.[55] In Julia Kristeva's terminology, carnival celebrated the "disgusting" border objects ingested or emitted by the body's openings—a manner fundamentally distinct from the bourgeois body as a restraining shell preventing the circulation of fluids and containing the "inner realm the way a cauldron contains boiling soup."[56] Cologne's staged mass sexual assaults rehearsed this spectacle of border porosity as it laid bare the orifices of the white Volkskörper, casting the white female body as an entry point for pollution and contamination.

The discussion further elucidates why the trope of contagion is so persistent in (visual) border politics. Border staff such as guards, NGO and military personnel, maritime police, and journalists are frequently portrayed wearing mouth masks and protective gloves even long before the emergence of Covid-19. These items speak to the contingency of the visual curating of the border spectacle as not everyone in proximity with refugees wears protective clothing, even when performing the same tasks. Francesca Falk explains this with the fact that disease policy was always crucial for maintaining (border) sovereignty, and it was Hobbes who used medical metaphors in *Leviathan* to equate a harmonious sociopolitical life with health and uproar against the state with illness and death.[57] Falk points us to the famous frontispiece of *Leviathan,* where we find an early visual negotiation of sovereignty and disease management embodied in the two miniature figures wearing beak masks and sanitation costumes, the typical guise of the Plague doctor or epidemiologist at the time.[58] Historically, it was particularly carnivals that presented a constant threat to the governance of epidemics while, at the same time, the virality of mass congregations offered a useful template for governmental aspirations. For Falk, the presence of the Plague doctors in the iconic image of sovereign power undermines the notion of total inclusion into the sovereign state body, as scholarly reception of *Leviathan* often does, but rather points to the constructedness of the body politic and the fact that it needs to be artificially maintained with governmental measures. The visual trope of contagion at the border points to a moment of dangerous virality that renders both the individual and national body vulnerable due to the proximity of the other. The staged exposure to potential contagion visually construes the border as a selective and excluding membrane and points to the intricate entanglement of epidemics, emergencies, and sovereignty. In this analogy, the nation's borders "are like skin; they are soft, weak, porous and easily shaped or even bruised by the proximity of others."[59] The display of a vulnerable body is the decisive moment when the borders of nations are formed. Reading Kristeva's account of abjection in *The Powers of Horror* (1982), Sara Ahmed maintains that "borders need to be threatened in order to be maintained, or even to appear as borders, and part of the process of maintenance-through-transgression is the appearance of border objects."[60] Gloves and face masks present precisely these border objects, staging the parallel threat, transgression, and maintenance of the border while rendering migration as "an attack on the integrity of one's own body."[61] While the emergence of these objects within our visual registers presents the supranational body as porous, they are also an attempt to present border control measures as restoring this porosity, a trope also expressed by the protofascist Freikorps of the Weimar Republic who imagined the ideal fascist body as a "machine component composed entirely of muscle-armor; a whirring, vibrating instrument that contains its inner organs in an impenetrable inner prison."[62]

In Cologne, virality presents a mediological quality facilitating the fast dissemination of information as well as a specific content pointing to the possibility or the fact that borders have been transgressed:

> Virality is most often invoked in contemporary parlance to point to the intensified speed and reach of information transit, especially in relation to the internet. It also refers to indiscriminant exchanges, often linked with notions of bodily contamination, uncontainability, unwelcome transgression of border and boundaries while pointing more positively to the porosity, indeed the conviviality, of what has been treated as opposed.[63]

Viral deterrence emerges as a strategy inherent in policy and media architecture with the primary function to facilitate the mediation and circulation of images of threat, risk, and death by pointing to the porosity and potential invasion/penetration of both (supra)national and individual bodies. Virality is as much about the fast circulation of images within media environments as it is about the message these images convey: the (potential) contagion, pollution, or invasion/penetration of an invasive other. These "invasive others--whether people, plants, pathogens, or ideas—are often described in similar ways, and patrolled and controlled through similar technologies, logics, and policies."[64] It is no surprise, then, that those seeking refuge in Europe are often portrayed as vermin and other forms of nonvital life, low down on the animal phyla and capable of infection and contamination.[65] During Cologne, virality enabled the sexual panic that led to the steadfast accumulation of testimonies of racialized body transgressions. By iterating the figure of the refugee-as-rapist, the moral panic unfolding at the dawn of 2016 mobilized feelings of insecurity, fear of transgression, and other liberal anxieties that rendered the integrity of the national body under attack. These sentiments reterriorialized Europe on the notion of Western civilizational progress and achievements while introducing stricter legal frameworks to deport migrants.

Similarly, the virality of the Black Shame, spurred by then-modern media, proliferated a readily available colonial discourse on sexuality and contagion. The images and data circulated during these campaigns held viral content that got passed around as viral form. The parallel reading of the Rhineland campaign and Cologne suggests that virality—as a mediological concept or form—intensifies when the content is imagined as contagious. Far from being a mere set of policies instilled to discourage future actions, deterrence often holds viral qualities that point to the bodies' openings and viscerality. The figure of the Black rapist evoked during Cologne has a significant history in Germany, a genealogical backdrop generated in the 1920s during the French and Belgian occupation of the Rhineland when the Black colonial soldier was imagined to threaten the white Volkskörper. Before the Rhineland (1919–1930), contact between Germans and Blacks was restricted to encounters in colonial territories or individuals immigrating to Germany, making the Black troops marshaled in the French Rhineland "the first large-scale Black presence in Germany."[66]

## THE "BLACK SHAME" ON THE RHINE

On May 20, 1920, the German Reichstag nearly unanimously denounced the "abusive employment" of Black troops in the occupied Rhineland as a "horrible peril for German women and children."[67] Social Democrats and German nationalists alike condemned the use of "colored troops" as a cultural disgrace that endangered the "purity of blood."[68] Except for the Independent Socialists, all parties of the Reichstag demanded the immediate withdrawal of the Black soldiers from the Rhineland. Only a few months before the denouncement in the Reichstag, the state of war between Germany and the Allied powers was put to an end by the Treaty of Versailles, which required Germany to disarm, pay war reparations, and make ample territorial concessions, including the divesting of its colonies. To enforce the armistice negotiated in 1918, American, Belgian, British, and French troops occupied strategic industrial areas in Western Germany such as Cologne, Koblenz, and Mainz. During the Rhineland occupation, France placed between twenty thousand and forty thousand French colonial troops in the region that it had mustered from its colonial holdings in Algeria, Morocco, Tunisia, Madagascar, Senegal, and Indochina.

Black troops became the focus of attention in 1920 when French forces occupied Darmstadt, Hanau, Homburg, and Frankfurt. Soon after their arrival, allegations of sexual misconduct started to circulate. By the end of the year, mass rallies had been convened in twenty-five German cities, including one with fifty thousand attendees at Hamburg's Sagebiel Hall. This rally was one of the key early events in a racist political campaign that would reach beyond Germany, throughout Europe, and as far as the United States. Known under the racist epithets the "Black Shame," "Black Disgrace," "Black Horror," and "Black Scourge," the campaign used modern media such as newspaper articles, short stories, movies, plays, colportage novels, postcards, medals, posters, and stamps to present the African soldiers of the Allied occupation as racially primitive and sexually depraved. It accused the soldiers of raping German women on a large scale. In reality, however, there were only a few isolated cases of sexual attacks between Black men and German women and many relations between the two groups were mutually elective.[69] The "Black Shame" reached its peak in the early 1920s and ended in 1922 when the Ruhr conflict began to dominate international political discussions in Germany.

Linking rape to the trampling of German national honor and the purity of race, the campaign presented postcolonial and Black male presence in the Rhineland as a crisis threatening Europe—a crisis cast in viral terms for it relied on discourses that portrayed the integrity of the individual and collective body as under attack. By mobilizing a "nationalist-racist myth,"[70] the "Black Shame," as Campt[71] remarks, echoed colonial discourses on the threat of interracial sex and miscegenation.[72] Black soldiers were accused of carrying diseases, and it was cautioned against "infection with foreign race blood and that disease [syphilis]"[73] while also evoking the specter of contamination associated with the negative genetic consequences of miscegenation. According to Fatima El-Tayeb, in Germany at the time, "every relation of German individuals with *Artfremden* (people alien to the stock) was represented as 'infection' of the racial body with 'poor blood.'"[74] The fear that "mulattization" and "syphilization" would result in the decline of both the genes and culture demonstrates that biological and cultural racisms were intimately entangled in discourses on the "Black Shame."[75] Critics further equated the Rhineland occupation with colonization, stating that under the presence of non-white troops, German people had degraded to colonial subjects.[76] This colonial fantasy of reversal uncannily echoes through the contemporary border regime, where narratives of reverse colonization evoke the imperial feeling of being besieged, such as when refugees are deemed as "colonizing Europe" in an act of revenge, a rhetoric Ghassan Hage identified as the distinctly colonial habitus of felt besiegement.[77]

The "Black Shame" provided a platform for white women's demands, and many women's organizations at the time such as the Rheinische Frauenliga (Rhenish Women's League) were at the forefront of organizing against the colonial troops.[78] Social Democrat deputy Elisabeth Röhl from Cologne lamented the landscape of fear that she saw provoked by the presence of the Black soldiers:

By using Black and colored troops, the Belgians and French profoundly disregard the feelings of the Rhineland Germans. This presents both a disgrace and danger as German mothers are held in constant fear for their children. More and more cases are known in which colored troops rape German women and children but only the smallest part of these atrocities is reported. A sense of shame and fear of revenge usually close the mouth of the unfortunate victims. On top of that, it is very difficult to identify the colored perpetrators.[79]

While Röhl is correct to assume that the patriarchal social and legal codex often prevents victims of sexual assault from coming forward, her speech must be placed within the racist moral panic characteristic of the discourse on the "Black Shame" at the time. National and international media played an essential role in popularizing the campaign and not only sought to visualize what remained unseen (or did not happen) but recruited supporters across the political spectrum with sexually charged imagery and rhetoric. The fact that "savages are being used to oversee a cultured people" was seen as breaching the "European laws of civilization"[80] and united conservative, liberal, and left-wing organizations and individuals across Europe by mobilizing the trope of *Demütigung* (German humiliation).

The Black Shame was both a response to a crisis moment and fabricated the narrative of a nation in crisis. The First World War differed from the previous wars due to modern technologies and weapons of mass destruction such as poison gas and powerful explosives. The male soldiers were destroyed, atomized, and reduced to fragments by the weapons of modern warfare,[81] returning home with deformed bodies and suffering from impotence and "male hysteria." Emerging out of the World War I trenches was the trope of the raped white woman that provided, according to Sandra Maß, a vessel for the postwar trauma and the psychological and physical fragmentation of the white male body produced by the decline of traditional heroic warfare.[82] I agree with Maß that the postwar context provided the discursive ground to articulate the fragmentation of white masculinity at the time. Still, I caution against reading the allegory of the white raped woman and the Black rapist as a psychological transferal of war traumata. The mobilization of racist and misogynist discourse does not depend on a psychological a priori but they stand, as discourses, on their own.

The typical iconography of the "Black Horror" used a white and often naked German woman raped by a Black soldier endowed with sexually primitive attributes, as depicted in the satirical coin from 1920 created by Nazi graphic artist Karl Götz. One side of the coin depicts the racist stereotype of a Black soldier, while the French Enlightenment motto refers to the imagined defilement of Western civilizational achievements. On the reverse, a naked blonde woman is shackled to a hyperbolic helmeted penis while the scene of abuse is observed by the icon of oversight, the all-seeing god's eye. The lyre embossed next to the woman, symbolizing music and poetry, refers once again to the desecration of the peaceful civilization of poets and thinkers (*Denker und Dichter*). On this coin, the phallus is, in fact, a gravestone, and buried under it is the German child, symbol of Germany's "reproductive futurism."[83] In this imagined rape scenario, "one is no longer aware of the Negro, but only of a penis. . . . He *is* a penis."[84] The hyperbolized phallus speaks to the fear that the Black other is more potent than his master, a potentiality that needs to be countered with violence: "The primal fantasy of the big Black penis projects the fear of a threat not only to white womanhood, but to civilization itself, as the anxiety of miscegenation, eugenic pollution and racial degeneration is acted out through white male rituals of racial aggression."[85] If the pornographic images of the "Black Shame" used the raped white woman to allegorize "a disarmed, figuratively raped (and thus emasculated) German people,"[86] then, by conjuring the allegory of the disgraced Germania, Germany's defeated Großmachtstellung and loss of colonies was narrated, in the words of a contemporary commentator, as a castration experience and a "decimation, dismemberment and final emasculation."[87]

For scholars of gender and nationalism, the weaponizing of the sexual encounter between the white woman and the Black man hardly presents a surprise. Women have been charged with the task of representing the nation, national honor, and identity[88] and moved, as female allegories, into the formerly sacred center of state power after the end of the absolutist monarchy, where they replaced the image of the male king to be put into the service of the new bourgeois order.[89] With the increase of Black male presence in Europe during and after the First World War, "trans-racial sex between white women and Black men of all classes became an obsession among white males."[90] The racist and misogynist coupling of the Black savage and the white female has long been a core narrative of Western colonial fantasies and was used in the civilizing mission to aid and abet conquest, exploitation, and white supremacy.[91] The fantasy of sexual assault on the white woman is a well-worn trope for imagining the nation's fragility and is often mobilized to redraw national boundaries. Although the physical appearance of the soldiers varied from darker-skinned Madagascans and Senegalese to fairer-skinned Asian troops from French Indochina,[92] the "Black Shame" imagined sexual transgressions in Black and white opposites. This pattern is analogous to Cologne, in which the Otherness of those accused on New Year's Eve is perceived in terms of Blackness.

During the "Black Shame" and Cologne, sexual violence did not occur to the extent it was narrated, a deficiency compensated by using commonplace visual tropes of Oriental and anti-Black imagery. While the testimonies presented during Cologne framed the perpetrators as men from North African and Arab regions, illustrations of the event overwhelmingly juxtaposed imagined sexual transgression in Black and white opposites. If the blurry and low-res images attempted to locate Cologne visuals in the genre of visual evidence, colonial imagery provided a readymade archive to compensate for the invisibility and ambiguity of the event. The magazine and newspaper covers released in the aftershock of the event all presented a similar visual trope: a white woman touched and molested by dark hands.[93] These Black hands on white bodies indicate that the accused men in Cologne were—irrelevant of their skin color—perceived in terms of Blackness. Far from erasing the Orientalism within the Cologne discourse, what this instead reveals is that the other, as mentioned by Fatima El-Tayeb,[94] is always coded as Muslim and Black, making Cologne a pivotal example of how anti-Muslim racism and global anti-Blackness mutually enforce one another.

The images depicting Black and migrant male sexuality are informed by colonial sexuality as such discourses did not remain confined to the colony but moved between the colonial periphery and metropolitan center.[95] Ann Stoler notes that allegations of sexual assault and moral panics often followed periods of tensions and moments of perceived crisis in the colonies, such as after labor strikes. They intensified at the beginning of the twentieth century, when national and anticolonial struggles in the European colonies increased.[96] Also, the Cologne attacks came during the most volatile moments of the European border crisis, the moral panics around racialized sex offenders constructed as a threat to the nation reverberates vigorously in a time of growing precariousness and challenges to enshrined entitlements in the nation.

## CONTAGIOUS FEMININITY

The pornographic imagery peddled during the "Black Shame" presented a channel for male fantasies of female subordination as it were white men's sexual fantasies in which women's bodies were raped, abused, tortured, and sexually humiliated. In 1922, Social Democrat Maria Meyer explicitly denounced the German male fantasies of sexual violence as "phantasmagorias of the torturing to death of German women" by interlinking the misogynist imagery with the unpunished crimes perpetrated by Germans against Black women in the colonies.[97]

Sexual violence against women also presented a crucial discourse among members of the Freikorps movement, German paramilitary units active during "Black Shame." These mercenary groups were composed of veterans who felt lost and humiliated by the war's outcome and fought against the newly formed Weimar Republic between 1918 and 1923. Their operational area was the Eastern border, where they fought against the advancing Red Army and the Baltic nationalists. Within Germany, they took action against uprisings by workers and the radical left and executed Rosa Luxemburg as commissioned by the SPD. Some groups, namely the Freikorps Oberland and the Hanseatische Freikorps, organized armed resistance against the French occupation in the Rhineland and the Ruhr.[98] For many Freikorps members, their participation in counterinsurgency in the colonies was formative for the practices of annihilation they would later conduct in the homeland. Many of them participated vigorously in the annihilating violence in the German colonies in Africa during the 1890s and 1900s and the German imperialist intervention in China during 1900–1901 after the Boxer Rebellion.[99] One such member was Franz Ritter von Epp, an early volunteer to a colonial Schutztruppe, who took part in the genocide of the Herero in German Southwest Africa. Von Epp served as a company commander under Lothar von Trotha and would later, in 1919, form the Freikorps Epp, one of the many paramilitary units to become part of the Nazi elite. In a time of perceived instability and crisis—a subjective structure closely linked to the loss of colonial territories—the men of these protofascist units were invested in militarist culture and the desire for ongoing German imperialism and colonization.

Klaus Theweleit explored the letters, fiction, and propaganda created by the Freikorps and tackled the imaginative world of these "soldier males"—his term for the archetype of fascist manhood.[100] Theweleit uncovered a configuration in which the fear of dissolving boundaries drove militarism, misogyny, anti-Semitism, racism, and a reactive need to affirm the body's boundaries and invulnerability. The Freikorps men were terrifyingly fascinated with female sexuality in general and sexual violence against women in particular.

For the soldiers, femininity was divided into two categories: the white woman was cast as the nurse, the mother, or the sister, distinguished above all else by her sexlessness.[101] This ideal of desexualized white femininity, including its incestuous structure of desire, was contrasted with the "red woman," the category for proletarians and communists, who were depicted as inherently dangerous, sexually insatiable, and castrating whores.[102]

This couplet also formed the narrative backbone of the "Black Shame" as the discourse evoked the parallel existence of German women as both pure and innocent and lacking sexual mores. The Black Shame's political twin was the "White Shame" propaganda that mobilized misogynist tropes of white female innocence and victimhood alongside German women as actively soliciting Black soldiers. The "White Shame"[103] classified women according to their allegiance to race and whiteness into honorable women (*ehrbare Frauen*) and dishonorable women (*ehrlose Frauen*).[104] To control sexuality and reproduction in the occupied Rhineland, white women were instructed to keep their bodies free from alien influences, while those who had mixed relationships were considered a stigma.[105] Similar to the persecution of Black male sexuality in the U.S. south, the discourse was fundamentally racialized insofar as it neither prosecuted cases of the rape of Black women nor rape incidents in which the perpetrator was a white man.

In both the narratives of the Freikorps and the "Black Shame" campaign, white German women figuratively embodied the nation and the white race, and the assumed transgression of their bodily and sexual boundaries corresponded with the imagined penetration and degradation of the national body. And like the "White Shame" campaign of the interbellum period that aimed at closely monitoring women's sexual behavior, Cologne portrayed German women not only as victimized but as responsible for racial–sexual transgressions. The city's mayor, Henriette Reker, held a press conference shortly after New Year's Eve in which she suggested women should always keep men at arm's length to prevent sexual harassment.[106] Her statement caused ridicule and harsh criticism on social media and was rapidly exposed as replicating a perpetrator-excusing, antifeminist discourse. As such, it formed part of the larger patriarchal discourse around Cologne that reaffirmed the bourgeois notion of public space as inherently dangerous for women. However, empirically and in comparison, women's physical integrity and sexual self-determination are more at risk in intimate and domestic spheres, a phenomenon that feminist legal scholarship terms the "fear of crime paradox."[107]

The discursive precursor for the misogynist whore-victim dynamic activated during Cologne and the "Black Shame" was invented and shaped in the colonies. It used the colonial other as a template to contrast, discipline, and shape white bourgeois sexuality and femininity. For the context of European colonialism, Stoler[108] has distinctively shown how the making of racial boundaries turned on the management of sex and how imperial authority and racial distinctions were fundamentally structured in gendered terms, revealing the protean character of sexuality and gender in (post)colonial crisis settings. Sexuality played a crucial role in legitimizing colonial rule as it established a clear line between respectable bourgeois white sexuality and the unrestrained barbaric sexuality of the colonized. While in the colonies, the (self-proclaimed) mission of German women was to serve as a bulwark and barrier against the pollution of the German race via miscegenation, in the postcolonial Rhineland, white female bodies were similarly cast as a "vehicle, conduit, or site of entry point for potential pollution/contamination."[109]

The de facto ban of North Africans seeking asylum instituted one week after Cologne drew nationwide attention and the campaign prepared the ground for racist and anti-immigrant narratives to gain momentum by evoking "a configuration of power whereby the hypervisible rights of white women serve as legitimation for obscuring or excluding the rights of North African refugees."[110] Outside of migration law, the Bundestag reformed the paragraph governing sexual offenses, an overhaul that feminists have long called for but that has been actively blocked by conservative and right-wing politicians. Before the amendment of §177, sexual assault and rape cases required proof that the victim physically resisted the act. Its overhaul institutionalized the feminist demand of "no means no," specifying that "no" is enough to express no consent to the act.[111] The sexual progress, however, was made in parallel to the tightening of migration law as asylum law stipulates that asylum seekers who commit crimes forming part of the catalog established after Cologne, among them sexual offenses and criminal assault, can be deported immediately without due process. The progress in the law governing sexual offenses is reminiscent of the legislation change occurring shortly after the Second World War when German authorities temporarily relaxed the paragraph criminalizing abortion (§218).[112] It was also during that crisis moment, when German defeat was identified with demasculinization, that Black soldiers from Allied personnel were accused of raping white women—a narrative that became central to postwar West German national identity and was readily transformed into one of the founding myths of the West German state.[113] Similar to the "Black Shame," racial stereotypes of sexually predatory Black men tipped the balance in favor of women's applications, and abortions were readily granted to women who provided a sworn written statement of rape.[114] The progress concerning reproductive rights was racially coded as German women were only accused of using abortion in too lenient a way when a potential white father was involved;[115] the implementation of feminist demands was thus enabled by a "hierarchy of state protection" that allowed the "fighting [of] sexism with racism."[116]

As the potential entry point for racial mixture that evoked the threat of racial parity in the background, femininity was also cast as contagious when it was considered traitorous to the white nation. During Cologne, the conjuncture of white feminism and antirefugee sentiment enabled a backlash against antiracist feminist positions.[117] One such position was the collective #ausnahmslos (without exception), a feminist campaign launched in the aftermath of the event that fiercely criticized the racist repercussions of Cologne and demanded the closing of judicial gaps concerning sexual coercion without tightening immigration law. Also, during the "Black Shame," critical voices countered the sexist and racist campaign with what today we would term an intersectional-feminist critique.

A prominent voice in the debate was Luise Zietz, who, along with Clara Zetkin, was the most important representative of the proletarian women's movement and one of the fiercest opponents of German militarism at the time. Zietz addressed the Bundestag in 1920 to denounce the racist hypocrisy underlying the "Black Shame" and the related disavowal for women's issues by pointing out that while the government was quick to denounce incidents of rape and sexual brutalities on the part of the Black soldiers along the Rhine, it had not demonstrated the same kind of outrage when "predominantly white" German soldiers—including many Freikorps—committed similar actions against women in Germany and the colonies.[118] Her entire speech was barracked, and when she criticized German colonial politics as "a single history of atrocities and the oppression of colored people by the Germans" as well as the increasing anti-Semitism in the Weimar Republic, she received a rebuke from the president of parliament and was denounced as a traitor who tried to cover up "the outrageous infamies of the Senegal Negroes."[119] Also, Lilli Jannasch, one of the most ardent opponents of the Rhineland campaign, offered a trenchant critique of the white women's movement and questioned whether German men sincerely valued women's lives by pointing out that German colonizers had abused colonized populations; but back then, when thousands of African women were victimized by white men, the bourgeois women's movement "did not shed a single tear."[120] Like the mainstream response directed at #ausnahmslos, antiracist positions condemning sexual violence in the Weimar Republic were denounced as concealing the truth of sexual crimes and betraying the nation. This also bears repercussions for the struggle against sexual violence as women who condemn all forms of patriarchal and racist violence and do not "place their struggles in the discourse of otherness"[121] by, for example, harnessing Orientalist tropes, have more trouble mobilizing state support in issues concerning sexual violence.

The long durée of colonialism, Stoler writes, can "wrap around contemporary problems . . . and hold tight to the less tangible emotional economies of humiliations, indignities, and resentments."[122] Efforts to securitize the nation along racial and sexual lines had made use of these sexual humiliations, particularly in occupied postwar contexts when white male supremacy was considered to be challenged. If white femininity served as the template to stage pollution and contamination in the postcolonial Rhineland, the contemporary European border regime has, besides the German women attacked during Cologne, mobilized yet another prominent figure of contagious femininity.

In June 2019, the captain of the rescue ship *Sea Watch 3*, Carola Rackete, was arrested for violating an Italian naval blockade that attempted to stop her from bringing the group of migrants she had rescued off the Libyan coast to the Mediterranean island of Lampedusa. Before the incident, Rackete was in contact with the port authorities for over two weeks, asking for permission to dock her ship, which they repeatedly refused. When the conditions on board deteriorated further, she eventually forced her way in past military vessels only to be immediately put in jail after stepping on Italian land. The Agrigento court has since ordered her release from prison and has dropped the charges that Rackete faced at the time: aiding and abetting illegal immigration and attempting to ram a patrol vessel. The incident in the Mediterranean Sea made prominent headlines and was widely discussed by both critics and supporters of Rackete. While it was not the first case to spectacularize the criminalization of migrant solidarity activism,[123] particular about the *Sea Watch 3* incident was that its captain was the prominent center of the media debate, despite attempts to keep her persona in the background.[124]

While Rackete received solidarity for her cause and the virality inherent in social media infrastructure permitted the fast and prominent circulation of the petition #FreeCarola that demanded her acquittal and the suspension of all legal proceedings, she also faced a slew of sexist and misogynist threats and denunciations from predominantly white men. Italy's right-wing interior minister, Matteo Salvini, personally addressed her on social media as the "captain of a pirate ship" and said that he could not wait "to deport this spoiled German communist."[125] Other right-wing spokesmen were fixated on her body and what they perceived as her transgression of ideal femininity: they were obsessed with her armpit hair and outraged when she appeared in court without wearing a bra under her shirt.[126] It was also the men advancing Rackete's smear campaign who condemned her sea rescue as a traitorous act against border sovereignty and the national body. Rackete's saving of lives––her assistance in border transgressions—was conflated with her transgression of a narrow and normative notion of femininity. The belligerent rhetoric around Rackete's perceived transgressive acts were only available in a gendered vocabulary, confirming once again that border discourses maintain a particular place for women and female figures as they are often charged with the task of representing the nation, national honor, and identity.

During the "Black Shame" campaign and Cologne, women were fashioned as the index for the purity of the German *Volk* and European values. Their white bodies-at-risk were mobilized against the threat of postcolonial border transgressions, and their behavior and status (or honor, in the case of the *White Shame*) was measured according to their allegiance to race and whiteness. What emerges in the discursive fringes of these racialized sexuality-complexes is the figure of the dishonorable woman, placing Rackete on the spectrum with the *ehrlose Frauen* of the Rhineland, the communist whores of the Freikorps' fantasies, the female traitor of the nation (as Zietz and other critics of the *Black Shame* were called), and the antiracist feminists of #ausnahmslos who were considered the real threat to Western gender equality. The right-wing men's focus on Rackete's body hair is not coincidental, for it recalls the Freikorps' obsession and fear of all things not hard, firm, dry, and static. In their fantasies, the German mercenary groups of the Weimar period paralleled the flood, mire, and pulp of the Bolshevik revolutionist movement to the swamp and mire of the female body, and specifically the vulva, and brought this in opposition to the hard and clean shaved male fascist body, its desired impermeability a "restraining external shell" and "muscle armor" forming the "conservative utopia of the mechanized body."[127]

## NECROVISIBILITY

Four months before the Cologne event, a shocking image directed the global public's attention toward Europe's maritime borders and tragically made visible what before might have been considered—at least for spectators of the Global North—only the contours of a genuine European border regime. In September 2015, the photograph of Alan Kurdî was broadcasted around the world and caused international outrage as it epitomized the horrific human cost of the global migrant crisis while instantly becoming a pledge for European responsibility. Together with his family, three-year-old Alan fled the Syrian city of Kobanê and boarded a boat from Turkey to Greece to make their way to Europe, from where they would continue to Canada. Alan, his mother, and his brother drowned off the shores of Turkey, leaving his father the sole survivor of this ill-fated journey. Alan's picture was taken when his body washed up on a beach in the Turkish port city of Bodrum and eventually circulated in international media, where it provoked debates about both Europe's humanitarian crisis and the respective role of images in mediating the crisis.[128] Unlike the regimes of representation that cast people on the move as a threatening mass in terms of invasion and contagion, Alan's picture seems to belong to the visual register of empathy that privileges intimate snapshots of individuals or couples, such as a crying child, a mother with her baby, or a rescue worker in action. The picture of the child is particularly emblematic of the individualized visualities of empathy because children, as Erica Burman puts it, "plead, they suffer, and their apparent need calls forth help [echoing a] colonial paternalism where the adult-Northerner offers help and knowledge to the infantilised-South."[129] The image of the drowned child accuses adult failure by placing an unpoliticized and innocent subject as the victim and target of adult politics. For Ticktin, the politico-moral concept of innocence has moved into the center of political life today: innocence promises a space of purity and freedom of contamination as "capturing innocence in the figure of the child reflects this search for purity in the secular world."[130] Innocent figures are seen as free from desire, will, or agency, and innocence is often mobilized in contrast to political subjects claiming their rights up to the point where historical causes of inequality get rendered invisible. Innocence, Ticktin further clarifies, is inextricably tied to sexual innocence, organizing certain bodies around the condition to be pure, unsullied, and chaste. It is also a racial category insofar as certain subjects are deprived of innocence and already regarded as guilty or tainted through their proximity to a specific race or class.

According to Lee Edelman, "every political vision is a vision of futurity," and the political is always already imagined through the image of the "Child."[131] Coming from Anti-Social Queer Theory, for Edelman, politics is always already a heteronormative project as the connection between the political, the social, and the heteronormative is evident in the figure of the Child, whose innocence "we" are supposed to protect by fighting for a "better" future. Acting in the name of the Child results in a shared investment in the future and secures heteronormative identifications and collective beliefs in the present, a psycho-political complex that "endorse[s] as the meaning of politics itself the reproductive futurism that perpetuates as reality a fantasy frame intended to secure the survival of the social in the Imaginary form of the Child."[132] The "Black Shame" and the "White Shame" mobilized innocence as a moral category by which a white nationalist agenda could readily be put into the service of Germany's racist repro-politics. As figuratively emblazoned in Götz's medal, the "Black Shame" buried the white German child under the phallic gravestone, an attempt to visualize that the postcolonial presence of the Black other interferes with Germany's reproductive futurity.

In 2016, a caricature published by the anti-Muslim French satirical magazine *Charlie Hebdo* foreclosed Alan from (sexual) innocence by suggesting that he would have grown up to be a sexual molester of the type blamed during Cologne.[133] In the caricature, two ape-like men with lolling tongues and outstretched arms chase two white women while the question "what would little Aylan [*sic*] have grown up to be?" is answered by "ass groper in Germany."[134] The temporal proximity between Alan's image and Cologne suggests that the image preemptively securitized, indeed immunized, the European social body from his (sexual) maturity, which he was never allowed to reach. If not in psychoanalytical terms, the visual politics put into circulation here performed a castration not only foreclosing the other from his (reproductive) future, but, in a true necropolitical manner, it posited the life, longevity, and futurity of the masses as contingent on the death of the other. This point is underlined by the fact that after the Aegean crisis of March 2020, Germany announced the release of detained refugees from detention camps and their accommodation in German cities, but only in the case of "unaccompanied girls and sick children"[135]—the category of welcomed refugees diametrically opposed to the adult men who were constructed as the vigorous protagonists of Cologne. If, in the name of the Child, "we" are sustaining a reproductive futurism by locating the merits of our political actions in the future, the image of the dead refugee child purports a destructive futurism that proliferates a politics of deterrence through weaponizing necrovisible images by distributing death, social death, and the impossibility of reproduction. By ensuring object lessons of deterrence, the spectacle of violence engulfing the refugee's body becomes an exemplary weapon in warding off other prospective asylum seekers with necrovisibility becoming the only mode of representation commensurate to Mediterranean necropolitics vested in the guise of preemptive securitization.

Alan's image reached iconological status and was appropriated and copied into different contexts. In Frankfurt, artists replicated his image as a vast mural at the banks of the Main River, which was destroyed only a few months later and overwritten with the sentence "borders save lives." At a beach in Gaza, an unknown Palestinian artist built a sand sculpture of Alan's body, commemorating the child's death while at the same time referencing the murder of four Palestinian children who died from Israeli airstrikes in the 2014 Gaza war. In Rabat, Moroccan activists staged a die-in to memorialize his death, wearing a red shirt and blue trousers and imitating the dead child's pose in the sand. The staged die-in is suggestive of another viral moment in history when in the 1980s, ACT-UP contested the structural homophobia that led to the letting-die of thousands of members of the LGBTQ community due to political negligence in addressing HIV/AIDS a fatal and contagious disease. Although Alan's image was brought forward by a depoliticized discourse of innocence that construes the unpolitical subject of the child as the first target of the border crisis, this powerful image could not be contained or neutralized by these depoliticizing forces but established common trajectories between different modalities of racial/colonial and sexual deterrence.

# NOTES

1. Auswärtiges Amt, "Facts, Not False Promises."
2. Ibid.
3. Ibid.
4. Nieuwenhuys and Pécoud, "Human Trafficking, Information Campaigns, and Strategies of Migration Control." One of the most notorious examples of deterrent information campaigns presents a series of advertisements launched on *YouTube* as part of the Australian Operation Sovereign Borders. In one of these clips, commander of operation Angus Campbell warns potential asylum seekers of the dangers of sea crossings and impassively declares to his audience, "There is no way you will *ever* make Australia home." ABF TV, *General Campbell's Message to People Who Travel Illegally by Boat to Australia—English*; see also Lester, *Making Migration Law*, 293–94. The campaign was copied by Dutch right-wing politician Geert Wilders, who declared that there is "no way you will make the Netherlands home." Wilders, *No Way. You Will Not Make the Netherlands Home.*
5. Oeppen, "'Leaving Afghanistan! Are You Sure?' European Efforts to Deter Potential Migrants Through Information Campaigns."
6. Vaughan-Williams, *Europe's Border Crisis*, 3.
7. Massumi, "National Enterprise Emergency Steps Toward an Ecology of Powers," 167.
8. Albahari, "From Right to Permission," 7.
9. Charles Heller analyzed IOM's campaign for the prevention of irregular migration in Cameroon and understood current education campaigns targeting migrants as related to the use of educational cinema in British-colonized Nigeria. Although careful of establishing a link between the two, Heller still points to the connection of the civilizing discourse in both of these campaign tools. Colonizers legitimized violence by referring to a self-proclaimed civilizing mission based on the notion of educating backward natives to modern rational subjects. A similar rhetoric was promoted by the head of mass information activities for IOM who maintained that the organization "would like to have an impact on information levels, then move on to perception, then attitudes, and ultimately try to influence, *for the better*, the behavior of migrants." Quoted from Heller, "Perception Management," 13, original emphasis.
10. Leurs and Ponzanesi, "Connected Migrants."
11. Turner, *I Heard It Through the Grapevine.*
12. Feldman, "On the Actuarial Gaze," 215.
13. Vaughan-Williams, *Europe's Border Crisis*, 3.
14. Oxford Languages, "Deterrence."
15. El-Enany, *Bordering Britain*; Griffiths and Yeo, "The UK's Hostile Environment."
16. Tan and Gammeltoft-Hansen, "The End of the Deterrence Paradigm?" Offshore asylum processing is widely practiced in border regimes around the globe. Already in the 1980s, the United States processed asylum claims in Guantánamo Bay, an approach then emulated by Australia under the Pacific Solution in 2001, which in 2013 became Operation Sovereign Borders and by Europe through the "partnership"

with Libya. Tan and Gammeltoft-Hansen list further deterrence measures such as the criminalization of irregular migration and human smuggling, which they see as having widespread consequences in shaping migration policies and discourses.

17. The lawyer-activists Juan Branco and Omer Shatz filed a communication to the Office of the Prosecutor (ICC), accusing the EU and its member states of crimes against humanity committed with the objective of deterring migration. The charge targets what the lawyers understand to be the key architects of lethal migration policies—Italy, Germany, and France—countries that have, according to them, made use of migrant deaths to deter future migratory acts. Deterrence, defined as "the action of discouraging an action or event through instilling doubt or fear of the consequences" builds the argumentative core of Branco and Shatz's accusation since, according to them, the EU has put in place a set of strategies to deliberately sacrifice the lives of the few to impact the future behavior of the many. The means to this end, they argue, were twofold. First, policies instituting death by drowning as exemplified, for example, in the transition from Operation Mare Nostrum to Triton, have turned the Central Mediterranean into the deadliest migratory route in the world. The situation is further aggravated by the criminalization of NGOs and migrant solidarity activism along with the resultant end to effective search and rescue operations. Second, mass interception and the forcible transfer to Libya prompted by the training and resourcing of the Libyan Coast Guard as executors of mass refoulement has led to devastating consequences for migrants, including unlawful deportation, imprisonment, enslavement, rape, torture, and murder. Shatz and Branco, "Communication to the Office of the Prosecutor of the International Criminal Court, Pursuant to the Article 15 of the Rome Statute." The complaint at the ICC is of particular postcolonial relevance because, since the foundation of the court in 2002, it has exempted Western states and only tried and prosecuted African leaders, prompting the persistent critique of the ICC as a neocolonial institution. Taku, *Conférence de La Défense Du Droit Pénal.*

18. Noack, "Leaked Document Says 2,000 Men Allegedly Assaulted 1,200 German Women on New Year's Eve."

19. Ivits, "Silvesternacht in Köln Am Bahnhof: Männer Umzingeln Frauen."

20. Fried, "Ein Wort Zu Viel."

21. Feldman, "On the Actuarial Gaze," 210.

22. Douglas, *Purity and Danger*, 115.

23. Ahmed, *The Cultural Politics of Emotion*, 2–3.

24. Kim-Puri, "Conceptualizing Gender-Sexuality-State-Nation."

25. Feldman, "On the Actuarial Gaze," 210.

26. Ibid., 206.

27. Ibid., 208.

28. Campt, *Other Germans.*

29. Ibid., 25.

30. Rodríguez, "The Coloniality of Migration and the 'Refugee Crisis,'" 24.

31. Diehl, "Köln."

32. Weber, "The German Refugee 'Crisis' After Cologne."

33. Sat1, "Die Schande von Köln," 1.

34. Bild, "Sex-Mob wütet in Köln."

35. Symons, "Cologne Attacks." Also Alice Schwarzer, the figurehead of German mainstream feminism, linked the "night of horror" to the use of sexual violence as a "traditional weapon of war," inferring that organized radical Islamists weaponized sexuality to infiltrate and destabilize the West. Poschardt, "Kalaschnikows, Spreng-gürtel Und Jetzt Die Sexuelle Gewalt."

36. Deutsche Welle, "Maas."

37. Abdelmonem et al., "The 'Taharrush' Connection."

38. Hark and Villa, *Unterscheiden und herrschen*.

39. Dietze, "Das 'Ereignis Köln.'"

40. Farris, *In the Name of Women's Rights*.

41. Schuster, "A Lesson from 'Cologne' on Intersectionality."

42. Yuval-Davis, *Gender and Nation*, 41.

43. Gilroy, "Agonistic Belonging," 2.

44. Ticktin, "Sexual Violence as the Language of Border Control," 547.

45. Steyerl, *The Wretched of the Screen*, 156.

46. Solove, *Nothing to Hide*.

47. Tazzioli, "The Government of Migrant Mobs."

48. Rapefugees.net, "Vergewaltigungskarte."

49. For a discussion of sexual and gender-based violence in the European border regime, see Freedman, "Sexual and Gender-Based Violence against Refugee Women."

50. Žižek, "The Cologne Attacks Were an Obscene Version of Carnival."

51. Ibid.

52. Lupton, *Risk*, 170; Stallybrass and White, *The Politics and Poetics of Transgression*.

53. Stallybrass and White, *The Politics and Poetics of Transgression*, 171.

54. Bakhtin, *Problems of Dostoevsky's Poetics*.

55. Stallybrass and White, *The Politics and Poetics of Transgression*, 9.

56. Theweleit, *Male Fantasies*, 242.

57. At the same time, it was also *Leviathan* that disrupted some of the common metaphors used to describe and imagine political life. The mid-seventeenth century is often understood as the key point for the entry of life and the biological body into politics. The common usage of body metaphors to describe the political is disrupted when mechanical philosophy transferred the allegory of the body politic to the mechanistic world view, illustrating the state as artificial animal, automaton, and clockwork. Hobbes, *Leviathan*, xxxvii. Importantly, as Roberto Esposito argues, bodily metaphors did not give way to the popular image of body mechanics but were instead continued and intensified via the paradigm of immunity. The machine lexicon introduced in *Leviathan* did not oppose but reinforce the allegory between state and body despite the thorough rationalization of the body's faculties by understanding it as a machine. "The machine metaphor," Esposito writes, "is meant to strengthen the precarious connection between life and body, like a sort of metal skeleton designed to keep the body alive beyond its natural capacity."

58. Falk, "Invasion, Infection, Invisibility," 89.

59. Ahmed, *The Cultural Politics of Emotion*, 2.

60. Ibid., 87.

61. Falk, "Invasion, Infection, Invisibility," 101.

62. Theweleit, *Male Fantasies Vol. 2*, 382.

63. Puar, "Homonationalism as Assemblage," 42.

64. Ticktin, "Invasive Others," xxii.

65. O'Brien, "Indigestible Food, Conquering Hordes, and Waste Materials"; Anderson, "The Politics of Pests."

66. Campt, *Other Germans*, 35.

67. Quoted from Fehrenbach, *Race after Hitler*, 53.

68. Quoted from Mamozai, *Schwarze Frau, weisse Herrin*, 289; my translation.

69. Wigger, *The "Black Horror on the Rhine,"* 1f.

70. Lebzelter, "Die 'Schwarze Schmach.'"

71. Campt, *Other Germans*.

72. The discourse was alive and well as it fed back into the popular notion that racial mixture serves as proof for the ultimate difference of the races. The predominant view of early twentieth century geneticists was that racial mixture leads to the "pauperization" of the genetic traits of the superior white race, a discourse mirrored in German debates on mixed marriages held only six years before the Rhineland campaign. Governor Friedrich von Lindequist issued the first such measure banning interracial marriages in German Southwest Africa. Following his order, similar bans were published in other German colonies, although they could never effectively be enforced. The bans were unique among European colonial regimes and marked the first attempt to include racial definitions into German citizenship law. Wildenthal, "Race, Gender, and Citizenship in the German Colonial Empire." Although the debate centered on marriages, biracial children did, to a great extent, result out of wedlock. Therefore, at stake in discussions on the legality of mixed marriages was to hinder the claims of Afro-German children to citizenship and the status of Blacks as German citizens. Campt, *Other Germans*, 47.

73. Quoted from Wigger, *The "Black Horror on the Rhine,"* 218.

74. El-Tayeb, *Schwarze Deutsche*, 119.

75. Echoing broader concerns of eugenics and racial hygiene, the "Black Shame" further prepared the ideological ground for the sterilization of the "Rhineland Bastards," a derogatory term used for children born to German mothers and fathers of the French African colonies. German professor Eugen Fischer took his colonial experiments to the metropole to follow up on his "Bastard Studies," which he conducted in 1908 in German Southwest Africa. Fischer believed that Afro-German children should be sterilized to protect the racial purity of the German *Volk*. He aimed to prove the inheritance of "race characteristics" and establish and consolidate race in biology. After 1933, Afro-Germans who were classified as "Rhineland Bastards" were persecuted under Nazi policies, and in 1939, the Kaiser Wilhelm Institute for Anthropology, Human Heredity and Eugenics (KWI-A), spearheaded at the time by Fischer, conducted the forced sterilization of hundreds of children and young people in Germany.

76. Poley, *Decolonization in Germany: Weimar Narratives of Colonial Loss and Foreign Occupation*.

77. Hage, "État de Siège."

78. Maß, "Von der 'schwarzen Schmach' zur 'deutschen Heimat'. Die Rheinische Frauenliga im Kampf gegen die Rheinlandbesetzung, 1920–1929."

79. Quoted from Mamozai, *Schwarze Frau, weisse Herrin*, 289; my translation. Original: "Die Belgier und Franzosen nehmen absolut keine Absicht auf die Gefühle der Deutschen im Rheinlande, wenn sie dort schwarze und farbige Truppen verwenden. Das ist eine Schmach und zugleich eine Gefahr. Deutsche Mütter werden dauernd in Angst um ihre Kinder gehalten. immer mehr Fälle werden bekannt, in denen farbige Truppen deutsche Frauen und Kinder schänden. Nur der kleinste Teil der Scheußlichkeiten wird gemeldet. Schamgefühl und Furcht vor Rache schließen den unglücklichen Opfern meist den Mund. Auch das Wiedererkennen der farbigen Übeltäter ist sehr schwer."

80. Quoted from Pommerin, "Zur Praxis Nationalsozialistischer Rassenpolitik," 158; my translation.

81. Tate, *Modernism, History and the First World War*, 76.

82. Maß, "Das Trauma des weißen Mannes."

83. Edelman, *No Future*. Götz produced two different versions of the coin: one with an explicit representation of a penis wearing a helmet and a more abstract depiction of a phallic gravestone, which underlines the fact that the helmeted gravestone is, indeed, a phallus.

84. Fanon, *Black Skin, White Masks*, 170.

85. Mercer, *Welcome to the Jungle*, 185.

86. Wigger, "'Black Shame,'" 38.

87. Kreutzer, *Die schwarze Schmach, der Roman des geschändeten Deutschlands*, 191f.; my translation.

88. McClintock, *Imperial Leather*; Yuval-Davis, *Gender and Nation*.

89. Brandt, *Germania und ihre Söhne*.

90. Bush, "'Britain's Conscience on Africa,'" 215.

91. Davis, *Women, Race & Class*.

92. According to Gilman, there were even few Black soldiers among the troops, revealing the Blackness attributed to the French groups as a relative assessment. Gilman, *On Blackness Without Blacks*, xiii.

93. Abdelmonem et al., "The 'Taharrush' Connection"; Dietze, "Das 'Ereignis Köln'"; Hark and Villa, *Unterscheiden und herrschen*; Weber, "The German Refugee 'Crisis' After Cologne."

94. El-Tayeb, *Schwarze Deutsche*.

95. Cooper and Stoler, *Tensions of Empire*.

96. Stoler, "Making Empire Respectable."

97. Meyer, "Die Schwarze Schmach."

98. The Freikorp's struggle was state-backed by Berlin with financial support. Vialatte and Pourrat, *Correspondance Alexandre Vialatte–Henri Pourrat*, 264.

99. The postcolonial aspect remained manifestly absent in Theweleit's work on the Freikorps. Amidon and Krier, "On Rereading Klaus Theweleit's Male Fantasies."

100. Theweleit, *Male Fantasies*.

101. Ibid., 100.

102. Ibid., 113.

103. The "White Shame" propaganda was prominently led by the American actress, journalist, and far right-wing populist Ray Beveridge, who ran several protest meetings against the Black occupation, publicly demanded the lynching of the Black soldiers, and produced the slandering pamphlet *The Black Horror—the White Shame (Die Schwarze Schmach—die weisse Schande)*.

104. Wigger, "'Black Shame'"; Wigger, *The "Black Horror on the Rhine."*

105. The campaign further had classist dimensions as women from working-class backgrounds were considered more likely to engage with the racialized other. The *White Shame* campaign specifically addressed German workers, asking them to demonstrate national rather than class solidarity by fabricating the image of Black troops attacking German working-class women. Wigger, "The Interconnections of Discrimination."

106. Scheer, "Übergriffe in Köln."

107. Spalek, *Communities, Identities and Crime*.

108. Stoler, *Carnal Knowledge and Imperial Power*.

109. Campt, *Other Germans*, 41.

110. Weber, "The German Refugee 'Crisis' After Cologne," 82.

111. Hark and Villa importantly note that before the law's alteration, the majority of the attacks reported during Cologne would not have constituted a criminal offense and could, therefore, not have been legally prosecuted. Hark and Villa, *Unterscheiden und herrschen*, 45.

112. Notably, §218 is still in use today and mandates that abortion is illegal but exempt from punishment. The abolishment of the paragraph presents a core demand of feminists and pro-choice activists in Germany who fight for the decriminalization of abortion.

113. Into the 1950s, the discourse of German women's brutal rape by the victorious enemy played a dominant role in the postwar society, accusing mainly Soviet and, to a lesser extent, French Moroccan troops and African American GIs. These allegations were racially coded as sexual offenses committed by white Allied soldiers and white German men were not recounted similarly. In the late spring of 1945, the Bavarian Landesregierung issued a secret memo, which was later burned, encouraging abortion in the case of "colored troops." Quoted from Fehrenbach, *Race after Hitler, 57*.

114. Ibid., 112.

115. In cases of alleged rape by non-white Allied personnel, abortion was seen as a tool to alleviate the psychological and emotional suffering the carriage of a *Mischlingskind* would bring for white German women. Fehrenbach, *Race after Hitler*, 57 and 113.

116. Razack, "Domestic Violence as Gender Persecution."

117. Boulila and Carri, "On Cologne."

118. Addressing the Bundestag, Zietz noted: "I want to further point out that the petitioners, who are now justifiably turning against the beastly acts of brutality in the occupied territory, found no words of protest when in Germany our own mercenaries perpetrated such beastly acts of brutality against German women . . . At a time reports were substantiated that in China, Germans set up bordellos, to which Chinese women were brought and abused by German soldiers. Fearful of being taken to these

bordellos or being raped by the soldiers, the Chinese women jumped into the well, preferring to drown in the water than to be subjected to the brutalities of the German soldiers." Quoted from Opitz et al., *Showing Our Colors*, 45. Other opponents were the Rhenish separatists, who condemned the anti-French approach of the campaign, and the U.S.-based *National Association for the Advancement of Colored People* (NAACP), who refused to sign a petition demanding the withdrawal of Black troops in the Rhineland, stating that "[t]he infamous acts of black French troops are not more numerous or worse in their kind than those of the white occupying forces." Quoted from Mamozai, *Herrenmenschen*, 290; my translation. The Rhenish separatists satirically asked what was worse for the Rhinelanders, "the humiliated [N-word], who is also a human being, or the deceitful Schnapspreuße, who has penetrated the region from beyond the Rhine?" Quoted from Traore, *Schwarze Truppen im Ersten Weltkrieg*, 40. My translation, original: "der gedemüdigte [N-word], der doch auch ein Mensch ist, oder der hinterlistige, von jenseits des Rheines eingedrungene Schnapspreusse?"

119. Deutsche Nationalversammlung, "177. Sitzung (20.5.1920)," 5695; my translation. Original: "eine einzige Geschichte der Greuel und der Unterdrückung der Farbigen durch die Deutschen."

120. Quoted from Sharp and Stibbe, *Aftermaths of War*, 105. Jannasch acted as a secretary of the most radical bourgeois pacifist organization in Germany, the *Bund Neues Vaterland,* and offered her critique in the 1921 pamphlet *Schwarze Schmach und schwarz-weiss-rote Schande (Black dishonor and Black-White-Red disgrace)* and in a German magazine article in November 1920.

121. Ticktin, "Sexual Violence as the Language of Border Control," 883.

122. Stoler, *Duress*, 3–4.

123. In summer 2004, a ship of the humanitarian aid organization *Cap Anamur* rescued thirty-seven refugees from distress at sea close to the Italian island of Lampedusa. Their rubber dinghy was unable to maneuver between Libya, Italy, and Malta due to engine damage. For three weeks, Italian and Greek authorities refused to let the ship dock their ports and sent a fleet of naval, customs, police, and coastguard vessels to block the ship in the open sea. Only when the conditions for the people on board were regarded as untenable was the ship allowed to head for the port of Empedocle in Sicily. On the Italian shore, refugees were immediately deported without legal process and the captain and other employees of the ship were accused of aiding and abetting illegal immigration and smuggling. The Sicilian court eventually acquitted Captain Elias Bierdel and his two codefendants in Agrigento, and Bierdel was awarded the Georg Elser Prize for Civil Courage.

124. Modrow, "Eine Heldin wider Willen."

125. Spiegel Online, "Streit Um Sea-Watch-Kapitänin."

126. Thorwarth, "Der Hass der weißen Männer."

127. Theweleit, *Male Fantasies*, 242.

128. Some media outlets argued in favor of publishing Alan's picture, emphasizing the image's potential for eliciting compassion as well as global visibility of the border crisis, which resulted in an increased amount of donations to charities for migrants and refugees. In Britain, for example, Alan's picture was published by all major

newspapers, tabloids and broadsheets alike, while in Germany, many papers refrained from reproducing the image of the dead child out of respect for Alan, as they argued.

129. Burman, "Innocents Abroad," 241.

130. Ticktin, "A World without Innocence," 579.

131. Edelman, *No Future*, 12.

132. Ibid., 14.

133. Meade, "Charlie Hebdo Cartoon Depicting Drowned Child Alan Kurdi Sparks Racism Debate."

134. The cartoon was published a week after the anniversary of the attacks on *Charlie Hebdo* when a gasoline bomb destroyed the magazine's offices after it published a caricature of the Prophet Mohammed. The cartoon sparked an immediate reaction on social media with many labeling it offensive and racist and questioning whether the wave of solidarity performed in the aftermath of the attack would question people's allegiance to #JeSuisCharlie.

135. Melzer, "Flüchtlingskrise in Griechenland."

## Chapter 6

# A Thousand Crises

## *Notes on the State of Exception*

When, in 2007, the global financial market crashed as a result of the collapse of the U.S. housing market, the recession of Eurozone economies swiftly followed suit. The European sovereign debt crisis began in 2008 with the collapse of Iceland's banking system and, starting in Greece, soon spread to the peripheral EU member states of Ireland, Portugal, and Cyprus. By the end of 2009, these member states were unable to refinance their government debt or bail out indebted banks without the assistance of other Eurozone countries and international finance conglomerates such as the European Central Bank. As part of the loan agreements for receiving bailout funds, these countries, and most prominently Greece, were required to enact austerity measures to reduce the public sector. With the sovereign bond yields rising, Germany was one of the main beneficiaries of the Eurozone crisis. Its export performance and limited wage increases have given German exporters the competitive advantage to dominate trade and capital flows within the Eurozone.[1] While during that time, crisis-talk dominated public discourse, the global economic recession should not have come as a surprise. For years, growing public and private indebtedness was facilitated and manipulated through financial markets and made vulnerable to speculation. In the wake of the 2007–2008 financial crisis, the speculative logic of these markets through which debt had come to be financed increased public debt exponentially to the inordinate benefit of banks and the detriment of social welfare. What has been described as the worst economic downturn since the Great Depression was, in fact, far from unprecedented. According to David Harvey,[2] there have been hundreds of financial crises worldwide since the last big crisis of capitalism in the 1970s and early 1980s. These crises are usually triggered by property and urban development markets, a process forming part of what Harvey termed "accumulation by dispossession."[3] The trigger of the European sovereign debt crisis, the collapse of the U.S. housing market known as the U.S. subprime mortgage crisis,[4] was itself a repercussion of speculative racial capitalism in the form of government housing policies,[5] situating the collapse within the racial and colonial logic of global capitalism.[6]

These crises, however, did not signal the end of capitalism but a reorganization of capital to meet new circumstances. Crises are essential to the reproduction of capitalism, and it is in the course of crises when the instabilities of capitalism are confronted and reshaped to create a new version of what capitalism is about.[7] This denotes a general feature of crisis capitalism or "disaster capitalism," a neoliberalism that has been facilitated by the opportunistic use of crises to enable the imposition of its economic policies.[8] The neoliberal restructuring project that arose in response to the global economic downturn of the 1970s and that became associated with the Reagan and Thatcher administrations in the 1980s marked the consolidation of an increasingly repressive governmental regime that sought to secure rising rates of corporate profitability by imposing market discipline on those at the bottom of the social order. Not coincidentally, it was within this same context that Stuart Hall and his collaborators observed an increase of moral panics over race, crime, national security, and the emergence of the exceptional state:

> It is important to note that [the exceptional state] does not entail a suspension of the normal exercise of state power—it is not a move to what is sometimes called a fully exceptional form of the state. It is better understood as—to put it paradoxically—an "exceptional moment" in the "normal" form of the late capitalist state. What makes it "exceptional" is the increased reliance on coercive mechanisms and apparatuses already available within the normal repertoire of state power, and the powerful orchestration, in support of this tilt of the balance toward the coercive pole, of an authoritarian consensus. In such moments the "relative autonomy" of the state is no longer enough to secure these measures necessary for social cohesion or for the broader economic tasks which a failing and weakened capital requires. The forms of state intervention thus become more overt and more direct. Consequently such moments are also marked by a process of "unmasking". The masks of liberal consent and popular consensus slip to reveal the reserves of coercion and force on which the cohesion of the state and its legal authority finally depends; but there is also a stripping away of the masks of neutrality and independence which typically are suspended over the various branches and apparatuses of the State—the Law, for example. This tends further to polarize the "crisis of hegemony", since the state is progressively drawn, now in its own name, down into the arena of struggle and *direction*, and exhibits more plainly than it does in its routine manifestations what it is and what it must do to provide the "cement" which holds a ruptured social formation together.[9]

The introduction of coercive practices at the time—policing, punishment, and confinement—were key social policy instruments and legitimating frameworks for securing ever-narrowing bases of popular consent. These practices, Hall et al. make clear, are not exceptional themselves—they are already available within the normal repertoire of state power. The exceptionality lies in the unmasking of state power that is revealed to depend on these coercive measures but that already form the core of state power. The racialized law-and-order project introduced during the period presents an opening wedge in the broader reorientation of the very forms and dispositions of governance. Crises are essential for the reproduction of capitalism, and they often introduce more ruthless practices of capital accumulation; more than this, they reterritorialize state power and popular consent with racist policies as part of the standard modus operandi.

The repercussions of the financial crisis are best understood as the "unsettling, destructive, and violent features of the normal functioning of capitalism, rather than some unforeseen and unfathomable anomaly."[10] Similarly, informal migration toward Europe, including the lethal outcome of migrant journeys, does not present an exceptional event but the predictable effect of neocolonial governance and warfare in Africa and the Middle East and a migration regime foreclosing mobility to the great majority of people. Crisis talk and crisis-mongering have put forth the idea that the transformations we are witnessing today disrupt a state of stability and unfold as a singular event. They tend to conceal "the violence and permanent exception that are the norm under global capitalism and our global geo-politics"[11] by singling out moments of presumed emergency and crisis from an already crisis-driven status quo. The narrative of the exceptional tends to conceal the conditions that have led to the emergency in the first place. "The state of exception is not simply the sovereign declaration," Didier Fassin and Mariella Pandolfi write, "it is also the notion of emergency itself, not only because it is the counterpart to the very idea of order but also because it carries a demand for action."[12] Emergency is not merely a trope that is evoked but a way of grasping problematic events and representing them in their apparent unpredictability, abnormality, and brevity. Greg Calhoun further notes that "the managerial response to an emergency focuses on restoring the existing order, not on changing it."[13] Maurizio Albahari, however, asks whether such an order is truly preexisting: "Emergencies . . . serve as a political technique that bypasses and makes exceptional what would need to be thoroughly, more deliberatively addressed via democratic methods. Emergencies methodically procrastinate to a never attainable future the analysis of the conditions that enable them."[14]

After 2008 and the ensuing decade of austerity measures that fundamentally expanded neoliberal policies, we see the countries that formed the epicenter of the European debt crisis take center stage once again. The countries located at the threshold to Africa and the Balkans—the southern European member states with Greece as erosion center—have endured most of the protracted ramifications of the global economic crisis. These same countries also form the dreadful backdrop of the European border spectacle by having been transformed into a veritable crisis and buffer zone sealing off dominant northern EU member states from migrants coming from Europe's peripheries. The collapse of the Greek government and banking system at the height of the debt crisis in 2015 coincided with one of the most volatile moments of the European border regime when an increased number of migrants entered via Turkey to the Greek islands of Kos, Chios, Lesvos, and Samos.

The interdependency between the two crises—the Great Recession and the migrant crisis—has been stated both discursively and in terms of policy responses adopted by the European Commission. As part of a "vulnerability assessment," the EU introduced a "border stress test . . . in parallel to the stress tests in the Banking Union" to ensure that "the European Border and Coast Guard have the capacity and means to be ready to face challenges at the external borders."[15] The test is part of a broader narrative accusing southern member states, and particularly Greece, of failing to properly guard its borders while attesting fiscal irresponsibility as the leading cause for its precarious status in the sovereign debt crisis. Although the debt crisis is a product of speculative capitalism and the uneven geography of the EU and aggravated this unevenness even further, Greece faced accusations and the warning to suspend its inclusion in the Schengen zone "unless it overhauls its response to the migration crisis."[16] The de facto degradation of Greece into an economically colonized member state, whose every parliamentary act depends on sanction from Brussels (if not the IMF), has led Nikos Kotzias to suggest that the "economic racism" of the "German occupation" has transformed Greece into a veritable "debt colony."[17] Étienne Balibar has claimed that the increasing core-periphery dynamics in Europe have led to the point where "one part of Europe is transforming another part into an internal post-colony" through a process of "zoning" in which "the inequalities of globalization reproduce themselves in the heart of these countries and regions."[18] While these comparisons have their limitations, indeed, it is crucial to note that Southern European or Mediterranean capitalism is to some extent the boomerang effect of European colonization: like Europe's peripheral member states in the south, the EU makes the economic and political participation of former African colonies in the European and international community dependent on their ability to halt migration toward Europe.

The current crisis manifests itself in the plural as we see the simultaneous proclamation of multiple crises: a migrant crisis, refugee crisis, humanitarian crisis, border crisis, a crisis of European values and its political and juridical apparatuses, a crisis of Europe as an idea, and a crisis of Europe itself. The shorthand border crisis, for example, refers to both the failure of bordering practices (the lack and incapability of border sovereignty in warding off migration), as well as the becoming-fragile of postcolonial borders during moments of increased migration across the globe, of which the Arab Spring remains one crucial point of origin. When, in 2011, people's uprisings and antigovernment protests shattered oppressive regimes in the region, this led to the collapse of Europe-held walls and threatened the many pacts the EU had with dictators and other emigration gatekeepers.[19] The collapse of the Gaddafi regime enabled migration from across Africa through Libya until it was impeded by the Italy–Libya partnership that sought to increase the discretion of Libyan bordering practices with EU-supported coast guards and militias. So, together with the "crisis in the Middle East" that is often considered both a cause and a byproduct of the European migrant crisis, a set of multiple crises emerges that inflects and coexists with the migrant crisis.

The contemporary understanding of crisis is synonymous with disaster and emergency, yet the etymological history reveals multiple meanings of the term. The Greek term *krisis* meant "judgment, result of a trial, or selection" and originated from the Proto-Indo-European root *krei*, which meant to sieve and separate grain, and, in more abstract terms, to distinguish and discriminate.[20] The etymological root reveals the intricate entanglement of the reorganization of a body politic with the biopolitical techniques of sorting, distinguishing, and discriminating. The process of sieving includes the use of a filter that separates the valuable from that which can be discarded according to a zero/one logic. This process recalls the account of borders presented by Mezzadra and Neilson, who understand borders as not merely obstructing and blocking migratory flows but as filters that include some subjects by way of "differential inclusion."[21] Borders are defined by their high degree of permeability, for they include some subjects and, by means of inclusion, create racial differences that are eventually put into the service of surplus production by extracting value created in illegalized labor markets. Differential inclusion is organized such that illegality remains a steady and beneficial component of the labor market and reinforces the crucial position of the border for the circulation and accumulation of capital. While it would be false to identify capital accumulation as the sole endgame of the border apparatus,[22] what the structural proximity of the filtering mechanism of both the border and the crisis reveals are the defining features of selection and stratification in the production of racial differences that are each amplified in the spatio-temporal moments of border and crisis. If the history of the term "crisis" denotes the crisis as a selection machine—the crisis as border—one that brings the border as a permeable membrane into play to define the trajectory of change by selecting and stratifying, we need equally to assess the structural moment of the border-as-crisis and demonstrate how the process of bordering is always already crisis-driven, particularly in democratic contexts, as it implies the sovereign technologies of distinguishing and discriminating.


## THE COLONIALITY OF EXCEPTION

In contemporary accounts of (forced) migration, border regimes and other imperial infrastructures such as camps, prisons, and black sites, Giorgio Agamben's concepts of bare life and the state of exception, along with Foucault's biopolitics, remain the dominant frameworks for conceptualizing the violence inherent in these spaces.[23] Many scholars, however, challenged the universality and transposability of the concepts Agamben developed in his famous trilogy *Homo Sacer, State of Exception,* and *Remnants of Auschwitz,* and pointed to his occlusion of racism and coloniality.[24] Agamben's identification of Auschwitz as the exemplary site for the state of exception ignores the historical antecedents of the Nazi camp, namely, the Indian reservation camps in the settler societies as well as the residential schools that sought to "Kill the Indian, Save the Child";[25] the slave plantation and the Bantustans,[26] and the native quarters and medinas in European colonies.[27] When Agamben mentions some of these antecedents, such as the Algerian war, or the incarceration of Japanese American citizens, he does so in passing, noting the latter's "solely racial motivation"[28] but eschewing its political, juridical, and economic contribution for the maintaining of the permanent and normative order of the state of exception.[29]

Agamben traces the state of exception back to the historical emergence of the state of siege in the French Revolution when revolutionaries introduced the option of suspending the constitution in the face of great danger. According to him, the state of exception is a French invention that has morphed from strictly being a wartime measure (*état de siège*) to become an "extraordinary police measure to cope with internal sedition and disorder."[30] He tacitly leaves aside the (post)colonial framework that enabled the invocation of a state of emergency in France since the law was first forged in the context of the Algerian War. Unlike other French territorial possessions, Algeria was considered part of France rather than a colony, and Algerians had French citizenship beginning in 1947. When Algerians organized resistance in October 1954, France treated the struggle for independence as a civil war and answered with oppressive measures, adopting a law that allowed the French government to decree a state of emergency without declaring a state of siege. Since the law was created in the Algerian War in 1955, France has decreed a state of emergency six times. Half of those declarations occurred during the war of independence,[31] while the recent three were all closely related to France's colonial past. In 1984, pro-independence uprisings in New Caledonia—a French colonial holding in the South Pacific that remains under France's jurisdiction since the referendum for independence was rejected in 2018, 2020, and 2021—provoked the summoning of the law. Decades later, back at the fringes of France's metropoles, second-and third-generation immigrants from former French colonies burned cars and public buildings in the Arab suburbs of Paris, Lyon, and Lille. The 2005 French riots were a painful reminder that the French project of *égalité*, itself a byproduct of France's colonial past that made its way from Saint-Domingue to the metropolitan center, had failed to address the social inequalities produced by its colonial legacy. Although the riots only erupted for three weeks, the state of emergency lasted for three months and sought to smoothen the colonial fractures that France's past brought to the peripheries of its capital. A decade later, President François Hollande invoked the state of emergency immediately following the 2015 Paris terror attacks. Under the law, almost 3,600 raids were conducted that disproportionately targeted French Muslims, especially those of North African descent, serving as a painful reminder that "exceptionalism does not just play upon public panics, but also institutionalizes fear of the enemy as the constitutive principle for society."[32] Although the perpetrators of the attack had either French or Belgium citizenship, the event was instrumentalized to rally fear against migrants and refugees and suspended free movement of people within the Schengen zone, summoning the state of emergency as part of a national anxiety that regarded the contours of the former empire as under siege. For two years, the nation remained in a state of self-proclaimed crisis and only abandoned the status after being replaced by an extensive counterterrorism law that gave authorities more discretion in fighting violent extremism.

When Agamben notes that the state of exception becomes the norm, or "the dominant paradigm of government in contemporary politics,"[33] the (post)colonial history of the French state of emergency fundamentally reassesses this claim by situating the exception in a racial/colonial framework that, each time, has brought it into existence. Recalling Hall's reflections on racialized policing that reveal the already normative status of coercion and repression for racialized others, Agamben's account cannot explain why not all bodies are targeted by exceptional measures and captured by sovereign power in the form of bare life.[34] "Once race enters the analytic frame," Sunera Thobani[35] writes,

> it becomes evident that the "state of exception" has been no such thing in the colony, the inextricable Otherside of the "West" and governed by particular forms of deadly and genocidal violence. Indeed, in the colony that was

co-constitutive of the West, the "state of exception" was normalized, rendered banal in the ordinary workings of power.

"One of the paradoxes of the state of exception," writes Agamben,[36] "lies in the fact that in the state of exception it is impossible to distinguish transgression of law from the execution of law." The liberal democratic state at once legislates and executes the law and places subjects beyond the reach of the law. This aporia effectively creates zones of exception that we can trace into multiple geopolitical contexts: U.S. prisons that forego the Thirteenth Amendment, the black sites of the U.S. War on Terror that suspend the Geneva Convention, the camps of the Australian border regime on Manus Island and Nauru, and the unlawful detainment of refugees in Libya and the camp archipelagos of the Mediterranean Sea. In the European context, the adoption of the EU–Turkey deal (2016–2019) was a product of the aporetic contradiction between the execution and the transgression of law that left thousands of people stranded and incarcerated on Greek islands outside of any legal framework. The deal stipulated that all migrants arriving on the Greek islands facing the Turkish coast are returned to Turkey. For every returned Syrian refugee, one asylum applicant residing in Turkey would be relocated to EU territory. The purpose of the deal was to reduce the number of migrants arriving via Turkey and provide a legal framework that could immediately react to the migratory influx of 2015. The agreement was enabled by a crisis narrative demanding swift solutions during exceptional times and providing the legal basis to administer unexpected mass migration. Contrary to the EU's argument that there was no prior legislation in place, Zeynep Kıvılcım[37] reminds us of *The Temporary Protection Directive* of 2001, a piece of legislation elaborated following Europe's refugee crisis at the end of the 1990s and explicitly designed to deal with exceptional migration. Since the directive was created and adopted to respond to migration from former Yugoslavia, the EU never activated it again but, instead, bypassed the existing legislation to forge new deals with Turkey and its former colonies. According to Kıvılcım,[38] the EU–Turkey deal is in clear breach of the EU's and Turkey's obligations under international refugee law and international human rights law and thus "constitutes an important precedent of an international outlaw refugee regime."

"The danger of fetishizing the concept of exceptionalism in the context of law," Joseph Pugliese[39] writes, "is that it functions to erase the serial practices of violence actually constitutive of the internal operations of the state and their very normalization precisely through law." By outlawing migration law, the EU reiterates its monopoly of violence and uses law to present an official front of due process. The EU outlaw regime not merely dodges its legal codex but, by adopting deals with third countries, precludes refugees from the right to claim asylum. Exceptional and crisis narratives circumnavigate the ethical questions of the racialization of border control due to the perceived need for immediate action. With this, they allow for postcolonial subjects to be governed unquestionably in the name of national and European security. As a consequence, Europe and its political elites can equivocate from their commitment to the values that define its "institutional and civilizational project"[40] as these states are framed as the sole authority capable of remedying such threats. The colonial history of Europe's border and surveillance technologies lays bare the flattening out of the exceptional into coloniality and raciality. It reveals the normative status and permanence of racial governance, along with the moments it is ruptured by postcolonial movements.

The (post)colonial underpinning of the state of exception and the suspension of the law in a proclaimed exceptional migration context demonstrate that it is, in fact, raciality and coloniality that enabled exceptional measures to pass. Denise Ferreira da Silva argues against Agamben's notion of the ban and the stripping off of legal and moral protection that produces bare life and a naked body before total sovereign violence. Contrary to Agamben, she reads the human body as inscribed by the "arsenal of scientific reason" and what she terms "the arsenal of raciality," namely the racial and cultural differences that these scientific signifiers instill.[41] For her, Agamben's defining feature of bare life, the collapsing of the body with total violence, is precisely inscribed in raciality: "For raciality assures that, everywhere and anywhere, across the surface of the planet, that ever-threatening 'other' exists because already named; as such, it is an endless threat because its necessary difference consistently undermines the subject of ethical life's arrogation of self-determination."[42] The analytical moment of raciality allows connecting the many repetitive instances of the deployment of the colonial–racial machinery. At the same time, it provides the necessary condition to understand dispersed events of racial violence as part of activations of this same logic that extends across global contexts. It is in the framework of raciality da Silva claims that the necropolitical violence before Europe's borders does not present an "unprecedented crisis," but rather "business as usual for global capital" in the form of the permanent reproduction of "*the social conditions that produce refugees.*"[43] Raciality and the colonial matrix that sustained merchant capital made its ways to industrial capital from where it proceeded to financial capital—always in the form of raciality, which becomes the a priori of state violence, creating the basis where the torture and killing of these subjects do "not unleash an ethical crisis because these persons' bodies and the territories they inhabit always-already signify violence."[44]

When Greek police used live ammunition against refugees at the Turkish–Greek border in March 2020, the event recalled yet another moment of European border violence: the 2005 killings at the Ceuta and Melilla gates of the EU, when more than ten people were shot dead while attempting to cross the Moroccan border. Although the Moroccan police fired the shots, the EU provided weaponry and infrastructure as part of the externalization of the EU border apparatus into the Maghreb states, Mauritania and Libya. While border violence becomes spectacularly visible in such cases, there is nothing exceptional about it. Since the incident in the Spanish exclaves, the militarization of European borders has not only increased in scale and budget but intensified the rhetoric of migrants as a security problem to be governed by military means. Glenda Garelli and Martina Tazzioli[45] have shown that in the field of migration, military deployments have grown in the past few years, moving from occasional rescue interventions to a warfare approach in the form of military operations specifically enlisted against the logistics of migrant journeys. Border militarization takes place both at the external borders of the EU and in third countries. It includes sending armed forces, providing training and equipment to border guards, erecting security fences and surveillance infrastructure, the increase of autonomous systems such as drones and satellites, and the use of military means by border police and paramilitary forces such as Frontex.

While it might be true, as stated by Didier Bigo,[46] that individual border guards do not intend to combat and kill migrants, the discussion on deterrence in the previous chapter has shown that migrant deaths present a deliberate element of EU necropolitics. The architects of Mediterranean migrant policies are not only fully aware of the fatal effects of their policy framework but use "making die" as a political deterrent for future border transgressions. When leaving aside intentionality and turning to the structural architecture of migrant policies, EU state violence includes the proliferation of lethal extrajudicial violence in the form of pushback operations, outlaw deals with non-European countries, and the often-fatal preclusion of asylum by way of externalizing the border apparatus. While in some of these cases, the policies produce immediate death, EU border violence also fortifies slow death or the imposition of harsh oppressions and physically intolerable conditions of life in the form of detention, legal limbos, and racism in host countries. If these deaths were to be considered collateral (i.e., nonintentional), we would have to acknowledge that state violence organizes and technocratically camouflages extrajudicial murder precisely as collateral damage.[47] The European supra-nation organizes its politics of killing in a manner that makes it increasingly difficult for the (supra)state to be held accountable. Feldman[48] termed this process the "becoming non-state of the state," which, in the European context, means that the EU has liquefied many of its institutional bodies by means of postcolonial extraterritorialization and privatization and is applying, perhaps mimicking, the nonstate tactics of those it seeks to target. Not unlike the counterinsurgent warfare in the Middle East, where signature drone strikes kill people preemptively in the name of national security only to post-humously reveal their innocence, the EU has instituted a cynical relationship with the dead migrant body, for it not only weaponizes migrant deaths for deterrence purposes but uses the dead body as a template to stage its spectacle of European values, such as the eulogy Italy performed in 2013 when it granted citizenship to migrants who had already drowned before reaching its shores.

## FADING COLORS

In April 2016, one month after the EU and Turkey signed a deal that would close the Balkan route and leave thousands of people trapped in Greece, refugees, anarchists, and other migrant solidarity collectives broke the locks on City Plaza, an abandoned former five-star hotel in Athens' Exarchia neighborhood. Warmly, or perhaps comically dubbed the "Best Hotel in Europe" by its inhabitants, the squat quickly grew into the most well-known of over a dozen squats in Athens that provided shelter and basic needs outside the border-industrial complex. After the European sovereign debt crisis and the EU-imposed austerity measures led to widespread poverty, unemployment, and unstable political conditions, a high number of housing and storefronts sat unoccupied, providing the conditions for building infrastructures of solidarity within the center of Greece's shattered crisis capital. Built in the spirit of self-organization, cohabitation, and empowerment from below, the City Plaza is a gesture to reclaim visibility within urban space and defies neoliberal spatial segregation that continually pushes refugees and other undesired urban dwellers into the outskirts of the city. During more than two years, the squat housed over 2,500 refugees from thirteen different countries; its inhabitants and volunteers provided hot meals, language classes, therapy sessions, women's advocacy work, yoga lessons, and childcare. Then, in July 2019, two days after the electoral win of the Greek right-wing party New Democracy, and after consecutive threats of the newly elected minister who made the closure of the squat his priority, the inhabitants of City Plaza were forced to move out.

Among the inhabitants of the Exarchia squat were the Plaza Girls, a collective of young activist women from Afghanistan who describe themselves as "anti-fascist and anti-patriarchy."[49] Its members arrived on the Greek island of Lesvos by boat and were detained in Moria camp, where they went on hunger strike to protest the dire and fatal conditions of the Greek detention center that was named a "concentration camp" by Human Rights Watch.[50] Using a documentarist and poetic approach to articulate their social commentary, in 2018, they produced a satirical video named *Letter to Trump*, in which they fiercely attack Europe's proclaimed hospitality toward refugees. Standing in front of a painted wall with a caricature of the U.S. president and his desired border wall, they address Europe's hypocrisy regarding human rights, which is, they claim, revealed in the "conditions [of] Moria and other camps." While in their poems they openly denounce the racism and racial segregation sustaining the carceral architecture of the European border regime, in their video message to Trump, the Plaza Girls establish a transatlantic link between the United States and the European border regime and take a stance against "fascist policies, in the United States, Europe, [and] anywhere else in the world."[51] By juxtaposing Europe's proclaimed welcome culture and rule of law against Trump's flagrant display of racial hatred, the Plaza Girls unapologetically dismantle the optics of the European border regime and its ostentatious upholding of constitutional rights and the modern nomos that undergirds it: the state-sanctioned violence of the refugee camp. In the poem "Moria: Arriving" they share their desperation upon arriving in the camp on the Greek island of Lesvos, contrasting the pristine landscape of the well-known holiday destination with its hosting of one of the most disastrous outposts of the EU border regime:

Lesvos is among the most beautiful islands in Greece. It's covered

with trees and the horizon is water: green and blue. The villa roofs

shine clay-red, hills dotted with olive trees.

From the windows of the bus these colours rush by as we circle

upwards around this hill.

From all this beauty and glitter of the sea, when you enter the camp, all

the colors fade. The reds, and blues and greens of the rainbows

become drained when seeing the conditions and the refugees. Their

faces, the grey walls, everything without colors, around everything

fences. Like zombies.[52]

Moria figures as a colorless space of detention, where colors fade as soon as one approaches the Aegean prison, giving way to everything becoming gray, a mode of lifelessness. The vivid colors evoked in the poem, the green of the trees and the blue horizon, yield to the gray and colorless enclosure of

Moria camp. The fading of colors, they insist, is part of the violent modus operandi of the border regime, wresting life of its colors and gray-washing visual perception.

"Color is not exclusively about vision," Carolyn Kane[53] writes, but "a system of control used to manage and discipline perception and thus reality." In Moria, the becoming lifeless of all things as color alteration pertains to the disciplinary apparatus of the camp that inflicts a zone of exception upon detainees who linger and survive in this imposed reality. If, as the Plaza Girls describe, one aspect of the camp's violence consists in depriving people of the right to see the world in color, we can take their cue and ask how the governing of color, its mediation, synthetization, but also its classifying and hierarchizing is an essential part of racist truth production in border regimes across the globe. The architecture of containment they describe, the fences and gray walls, are indicative of the sovereign politics of letting-die under-girding encampment around Europe. This extralegal production of violence exposes detainees to premature death, "like zombies." The zombie metaphor, the figure pronounced dead but still walking among us, is well placed here, for its myth was born on yet another enclosed space of racial segregation. On the Caribbean slave plantations of Saint-Domingue, the curse reflected Haitians' fear of being imprisoned in their bodies permanently and having to work the Hispaniola plantations for eternity. Taking the sovereign erasure of color beyond the confines of Moria camp, a long history of color as the racist and racial management of differences is revealed, ranging from the racist–misogynist color spectrum presented by the Freikorps, the color-coded pass tag regime in German Southwest Africa to the ethnic and racial profiles used in European hotspots to classify migrants into different groups of people.

Also, in Richard Mosse's video installation *Incoming* (2016–2017), the visuality of the European border regime is rendered in a colorless gray. There, spectators follow refugees on two major routes toward Europe, one starting east of the Mediterranean Sea with imagery from an airstrike on a Syrian village, leading eastwards across the Aegean Sea and through the Balkans, the other route showing the African trail toward Libya and across the Mediterranean Sea, ending with the documentation of the destruction of the "Calais Jungle" before the Channel Tunnel. The installation is screened as a monumental triptych on three large panels and shot on a military thermal imaging camera that depicts the entire footage in a colorless and monochrome gray. Mosse's camera is classified as a weapon under international law; it was developed by multinational defense and security corporations and can detect heat from over 30km. The brochures of the National Gallery of Victoria in Melbourne and Art Basel Unlimited suggest reading the camera and the idiosyncratic visuals it produces as registering the mere biological life of a person, stripping refugees of their individual features by only recognizing the scale of heat difference that indicates the fragile line between life and death. The camera seems to depict the bare life of the incoming people, stripping off any qualities except the biological traces of those subjected under its gaze. This is shockingly caught in the depiction of a hypothermia victim whose body almost disappears from the screen or in the human eyes that appear as black holes devoid of any life.

*Incoming* indeed negotiates the concept of bare life in the context of the European refugee crisis, but in my understanding, what the camera-as-weapon points spectators to is less the *zoē* or the biological substance of those depicted but the process of mediating the European border crisis. As spectators of *Incoming*, we see how missiles see and are thus invited to reflect on our gaze that relies upon the inherent monstrosity, violence, and lethal capacities inherent in the process of mediation. Optical technology creates an aesthetic of detachment, the only mode of perception that can be commensurate to the incursions of technological shock in everyday life. This detachment from human life is hyperbolized in Mosse's heat camera as it points to the structure of alienation and distance that the media infrastructure introduces between spectators and the subjects it portrays. *Incoming* not only perfects and finalizes the blurring of the camera and the weapon but situates refugee journeys on a continuum with warfare that is at the same time (one of) the causes for flight and the instrument to tackle it. Mosse's documentation of an airstrike or the launching of fighter jets on a U.S. aircraft carrier aligns the visual lexicon of warfare with migration and thus reveals the preclusion of migrants from civilian life as they make their journeys through profoundly militarized landscapes. As spectators, we are thus confronted less with the depiction of refugees as mere biological life than with a mediated complex of inhumanization that does not eradicate racial difference in the service of the last biological trace but fosters its weaponization. Under this militarized gaze, what is presented is neither a universal humanitarianism that portrays people as the same despite their colors, nor a bare life exposed, but a reflection of how we deploy media to capture history and narrate the stories that eventually become memory.

## NOTES

1. Young and Semmler, "The European Sovereign Debt Crisis."
2. Harvey, *The Enigma of Capital*.
3. Harvey, *The New Imperialism*.
4. Zestos, *The Global Financial Crisis*.
5. Decades of racist government mortgage policy provoked a cycle of poverty and exclusion for Black and Latinx communities in the United States and established the

"redlining" of neighborhoods deemed uninsurable by the federal government. Lacking inherited property and stocks, and burdened by greater reliance on consumer credit, Black and Latinx communities were less able to weather the sudden decline in home values, which led to the imminent risk of foreclosure and, ultimately, the loss of home for millions. Hernandez, *Race, Market Constraints and the Housing Crisis.*

6. Chakravartty and da Silva, "Accumulation, Dispossession, and Debt."

7. Harvey, *The Enigma of Capital.*

8. Klein, *The Shock Doctrine.*

9. Reiner et al., "Policing the Crisis," 214. Looking at the same historical context, Naomi Klein remarks that it was the postcolonial Falklands War of 1982 that served the Thatcher administration a crucial purpose: the disorder and nationalist excitement resulting from the war allowed the use of tremendous force to crush the striking coal miners and to "launch the first privatization frenzy in a Western democracy." Klein, *The Shock Doctrine*, 12.

10. De Genova, Tazzioli, and Álvarez-Velasco, "Europe/Crisis," 10.

11. Ibid., 10–11.

12. Fassin and Pandolfi, *Contemporary States of Emergency*, 47.

13. Calhoun, "The Idea of Emergency," 55.

14. Albahari, *Crimes of Peace*, 13.

15. Justice and Home Affairs Ministers, "Discussion Paper European Border and Coast Guard."

16. Barker, Robinson, and Hope, "Greece Warned EU Will Reimpose Border Controls."

17. Kotzias, *Ελλάδα Αποικία Χρέοης. Ευρωπαικί Αυτοκρατία Και Γερμανική Προτοκραθεδρία.*

18. Balibar, "Tous Grecs, Tous Européens."

19. Campesi, "Arab Revolts and the Crisis of the European Border Regime"; Campesi, "The Arab Spring and the Crisis of the European Border Regime."

20. American Heritage Dictionary, "Crisis."

21. Mezzadra and Neilson, *Border as Method*, 59.

22. The role of the border as a permeable filter has led many critics of neoliberalism to assume that there is a hidden economic agenda behind Fortress Europe, one that selects and recruits laborers for European capital accumulation. See, for example, Kasimis, Papadopoulos, and Zacopoulou, "Migrants in Rural Greece." Saucier and Woods importantly criticize the prioritizing of the economic rationale and advocate for the priority of anti-Black violence when analyzing the European border regime. Saucier and Woods, "Ex Aqua."

23. The use of Agambenian frameworks to theorize contemporary migration issues is widespread; see, for example, Dines, Montagna, and Ruggiero, "Thinking Lampedusa"; Mabon, "Sovereignty, Bare Life and the Arab Uprisings."

24. Alexander Weheliye has prominently suggested that Agamben has neglected to theorize racialization as the prime mechanism for articulating "a set of sociopolitical processes that discipline humanity into full humans, not-quite-humans, and nonhumans." Agamben envisages a field in which the categories that separate bare life from other forms of life become obsolete; it eradicates divisions among human lives along

the lines of race, religion, nationality, or gender, "because it creates a substance that, albeit in its debasement, transcends traditional social and political markers." Bare life thus aspires to transcend racialization with recourse to pure biological matter and neglects the idea of the modern human as profoundly shaped by race and racism. This allows the concepts "to imagine an indivisible biological substance anterior to racialization." Weheliye, *Habeas Viscus*, 4 and 34. For other critiques see da Silva, "No-Bodies"; Svirsky, *Agamben and Colonialism*; Thobani, "Empire, Bare Life and the Constitution of Whiteness: Sovereignty in the Age of Terror."

25. Monture-Angus and Stiegelbauer, "Thunder in My Soul: A Mohawk Woman Speaks."

26. Patterson, *Slavery and Social Death*.

27. Fanon, *The Wretched of the Earth*; Mbembe, "Necropolitics."

28. Agamben, *State of Exception*, 22.

29. Responding to Foucault's theory of biopolitics, in which human life becomes the target of state power, Agamben argues that there exists a "hidden tie" between sovereign power and biopolitics, forged in the exceptional basis of state sovereignty. After the atrocities of the Shoah, the United Nations General Assembly formulated universal human rights with the stated intention to prevent the recurrence of similar regimes of inhumanity. For Agamben, however, the most inhumane logos of power, the concentration camp, has returned in our current times, enabled by states of exception that suspend the juridical order by proclaiming extraordinary circumstances. Within a state of emergency such as the War on Terror, states of exception extend their governmental reach by diminishing, superseding, and rejecting constitutional rights. Agamben follows Carl Schmitt in defining sovereignty as the power to proclaim the exception. The exception is the fundament of law and "reveals the essence of State authority most clearly." Schmitt quoted from Agamben, *Homo Sacer: Sovereign Power and Bare Life*, 16. Crucially, Agamben stresses that it is during a state of exception where the rule of law is suspended that many countries adopt a doctrine for fighting against terrorism, and it was the same logic that enabled the concentration camps of the Third Reich. In fact, Nazi Germany did not operate in violation of the Weimar Constitution but within the framework of its articles that allowed the government to suspend individual rights in case of necessity. Therefore, "from a juridical perspective, the entire Third Reich can be considered a state of exception that lasted twelve years." Agamben, *State of Exception*, 2.

30. Agamben, *State of Exception*, 5.

31. The declarations provided a legal framework for counterinsurgent measures, including when the law was used to impose a curfew on French Muslims in Paris who defied it on October 17, 1961, as part of a peaceful demonstration. On this day, which later became known as the Paris massacre of 1961, the French police attacked and killed hundreds of pro–National Liberation Front (FLN) Algerians, an act of colonial violence within the French metropole that the government only partially acknowledged decades later. Gallois, *A History of Violence in the Early Algerian Colony*.

32. Aradau and van Munster, "Exceptionalism and the 'War on Terror,'" 689.

33. Agamben, *State of Exception*, 2.

34. It is in the zones of exception where Agamben famously situates bare life, the production of those lives that can be killed with impunity. Based on the distinction between "natural reproductive life" (*zoē*) and a "qualified form of life" (*bios*), bare life emerges from within this distinction. It produces people who have "lost all other qualities and specific relationships—except that they were still human." Arendt, *The Origins of Totalitarianism*, 299. This "life exposed to death" appears in the abandonment of natural life to sovereign violence and can be found in *homo sacer*, a figure of Roman law that has been reduced to bare life for the sovereign has full discretionary power over her natural or biological life. Agamben notes that the abjection of *homo sacer* includes a double movement as the individual is at once barred from political life and at the center of the exercise of biopower, making the figure a primary referent of the sovereign decision. Agamben, *Homo Sacer: Sovereign Power and Bare Life*, 85 and 88.

35. Thobani, "Empire, Bare Life and the Constitution of Whiteness," 6.

36. Agamben, *The Omnibus Homo Sacer*, 50.

37. Kıvılcım, "Migration Crises in Turkey."

38. Ibid., 436.

39. Pugliese, *State Violence and the Execution of Law*, 18.

40. Bhambra, "The Current Crisis of Europe," 7.

41. da Silva, "No-Bodies," 233.

42. Ibid., 235.

43. da Silva, "Fractal Thinking"; original emphasis.

44. da Silva, "No-Bodies," 213.

45. Garelli and Tazzioli, "The Biopolitical Warfare on Migrants."

46. According to Bigo, the "disposition" of border guards is not rooted in the intentionality to kill but in "tutelage"; the political elite and border institutions do not transform migrants into "enemies" to "combat," instead they "see their mission as protecting international order, disciplining chaotic flows of people, avoiding the 'catastrophic consequences of inaction' and of 'free travel between these countries in turmoil and the countries that enjoy peace and development.' Bigo, "The (in)Securitization Practices of the Three Universes of EU Border Control," 212–13.

47. Feldman, *Archives of the Insensible*, 5.

48. Feldman, "The Becoming Non-State of the State."

49. Plaza Girls, "Zine Issue 2."

50. Kokkinidis, "Migrant Camp in Lesvos 'a Concentration Camp' Says Human Rights Watch."

51. Plaza Girls, "Zine Issue 2."

52. Ibid.

53. Kane, *Chromatic Algorithms*, 211.

# Works Cited

Abdelmonem, Angie, Rahma Esther Bavelaar, Elisa N. Wynne-Hughes, and Susana Galán. "The 'Taharrush' Connection: Xenophobia, Islamophobia, and Sexual Violence in Germany and Beyond." *Jadaliyya* 1 (2016).

ABF TV. *General Campbell's Message to People Who Travel Illegally by Boat to Australia*, 2014. https://www.youtube.com/watch?v=BypuBsE_Eq8.

Adey, Peter, Mark Whitehead, and Alison J. Williams. *From Above: War, Violence and Verticality*. London: Hurst, 2013.

Adler, Katya. "Migrant Deaths Renew Pressure on EU." *BBC News*, April 20, 2015, sec. Europe. https://www.bbc.com/news/world-europe-32376082.

Agamben, Giorgio. *Homo Sacer: Sovereign Power and Bare Life*. Palo Alto: Stanford University Press, 1998.

———. *State of Exception*. University of Chicago Press, 2008.

———. *The Omnibus Homo Sacer*. Stanford University Press, 2017.

Ahmed, Sara. *The Cultural Politics of Emotion*. New York and London: Routledge, 2013.

Akkerman, Mark. "Border Wars. The Arms Dealers Profiting from Europe's Refugee Tragedy." Amsterdam: Transnational Institute and Stop Wapenhandel, 2016.

Albahari, Maurizio. *Crimes of Peace: Mediterranean Migrations at the World's Deadliest Border*. Philadelphia: University of Pennsylvania Press, 2015.

———. "From Right to Permission: Asylum, Mediterranean Migrations, and Europe's War on Smuggling." *Journal on Migration and Human Security*, April 25, 2018, 1–10.

American Heritage Dictionary. "Crisis." Accessed March 13, 2020. https://ahdictionary.com/word/search.html?q=crisis.

Amidon, Kevin S., and Dan Krier. "On Rereading Klaus Theweleit's Male Fantasies." *Men and Masculinities* 11, no. 4 (June 2009): 488–96.

Amnesty International. "Hotspot Italy. How EU's Flagship Approach Leads to Violations of Refugee and Migrant Rights." London: Amnesty International, 2016.

Anderson, Bridget. "The Politics of Pests: Immigration and the Invasive Other." *Social Research: An International Quarterly* 84, no. 1 (2017): 7–28.

Anderson, Steve F. *Technologies of Vision: The War Between Data and Images*. Massachusetts: MIT Press, 2017.

Andrijasevic, Rutvica. "Deported: The Right to Asylum at EU's External Border of Italy and Libya." *International Migration* 48, no. 1 (2010): 148–74.

Angenendt, Steffen, David Kipp, and Amrei Meier. "Mixed Migration: Challenges and Options for the Ongoing Project of German and European Asylum and Migration Policy." Gütersloh: Bertelsmann Stiftung, 2017.

Appadurai, Arjun. *Modernity at Large: Cultural Dimensions of Globalization.* Minneapolis: University of Minnesota Press, 1996.

Aradau, Claudia. "Political Grammars of Mobility, Security and Subjectivity." *Mobilities* 11, no. 4 (2016): 564–74.

Aradau, Claudia, and Rens van Munster. "Exceptionalism and the 'War on Terror': Criminology Meets International Relations." *The British Journal of Criminology* 49, no. 5 (September 1, 2009): 686–701.

Araujo, Felipe. "'It's Like Nazi Germany' Fury as Asylum Seekers Forced to Live behind Red Doors." *Express*, January 20, 2016. https://www.express.co.uk/news/uk/636388/nazi-germany-red-doors-outrage.

Arendt, Hannah. *The Origins of Totalitarianism.* Boston: Houghton Mifflin Harcourt, 1973.

———. *The Origins of Totalitarianism.* San Diego: Harcourt Brace Jovanovich, 1979.

Asaro, Peter M. "The Labor of Surveillance and Bureaucratized Killing: New Subjectivities of Military Drone Operators." *Social Semiotics* 23, no. 2 (April 1, 2013): 196–224.

Auswärtiges Amt. "Facts, Not False Promises." *German Federal Foreign Office*, 2017. https://www.auswaertiges-amt.de/en/aussenpolitik/themen/migration/-/608814.

Azéma, Marc. *La Grotte Chauvet-Pont d'Arc.* Paris: Éditions Jean-Paul Gisserot, 2019.

Baker, Aryn. "'It Was as If We Weren't Human': Inside the Modern Slave Trade Trapping African Migrants." *Time.* Accessed August 13, 2021. https://time.com/longform/african-slave-trade/.

Bakhtin, Mikhail. *Problems of Dostoevsky's Poetics.* Minneapolis: University of Minnesota Press, 1984.

Balibar, Étienne. "Tous Grecs, Tous Européens: Intervention d' Étienne Balibar à La Rencontre-Débat Du 31 Mars 2012 Avec Les Signataires de l'appel 'Sauvons Le Peuple Grec de Ses Sauveurs.'" *GrèceHebdo*, April 2, 2012.

Balsamo, Anne Marie. *Technologies of the Gendered Body: Reading Cyborg Women.* Durham: Duke University Press, 1996.

Bancel, Nicolas, Thomas David, and Dominic Thomas. *The Invention of Race: Scientific and Popular Representations.* New York: Routledge, 2014.

Barder, Alexander D. *Empire Within: International Hierarchy and Its Imperial Laboratories of Governance.* Abingdon: Routledge, 2015.

Barker, Alex, Duncan Robinson, and Kevin Hope. "Greece Warned EU Will Reimpose Border Controls." *Financial Times*, December 2, 2015. https://www.ft.com/content/463dc7a0-982b-11e5-9228-87e603d47bdc#axzz3wM7qdqSu.

Baucom, Ian. *Specters of the Atlantic: Finance Capital, Slavery, and the Philosophy of History.* Durham: Duke University Press, 2005.

Behnegar, Nasser. *Leo Strauss, Max Weber, and the Scientific Study of Politics.* University of Chicago Press, 2005.

Bellanova, Rocco, and Denis Duez. "The Making (Sense) of EUROSUR: How to Control the Sea Borders?" In *EU Borders and Shifting Internal Security,* edited by Raphael Bossong and Helena Carrapico, 23–44. Cham: Springer International Publishing, 2016.

Beller, Jonathan. *The Cinematic Mode of Production: Attention Economy and the Society of the Spectacle.* Lebanon: University Press of New England, 2012.

———. *The Message Is Murder: Substrates of Computational Capital.* London: Pluto Press, 2018.

Bentham, Jeremy. *Correspondence of Jeremy Bentham, Volume 3: January 1781 to October 1788.* London: UCL Press, 2017.

———. *Panopticon; Or, the Inspection House (Volume 2).* Dublin and London: T. Payne at the Mews-Gate, 1791.

Bernal, Martin. *Black Athena: The Linguistic Evidence.* New Jersey: Rutgers University Press, 1987.

Best, Stephen. "On Failing to Make the Past Present." *Modern Language Quarterly* 73, no. 3 (January 1, 2012): 453–74.

Bhambra, Gurminder K. "The Current Crisis of Europe: Refugees, Colonialism, and the Limits of Cosmopolitanism." *European Law Journal* 23, no. 5 (2017): 395–405.

———. "The Refugee Crisis and Our Connected Histories of Colonialism and Empire." *Sicherheitspolitik,* 2015. https://www.sicherheitspolitik-blog.de/2015/10 /01/the-refugee-crisis-and-our-connected-histories-of-colonialism-and-empire/.

———. "Whither Europe? Postcolonial versus Neocolonial Cosmopolitanism." *Interventions* 18, no. 2 (March 3, 2016): 187–202.

Bielicki, Jan. "Warum die Medien so spät über Köln berichteten." *Süddeutsche,* January 7, 2016. https://www.sueddeutsche.de/medien/uebergriffe-an-silvester -warum-die-medien-so-spaet-ueber-koeln-berichteten-1.2808386.

Bigo, Didier. "The (in)Securitization Practices of the Three Universes of EU Border Control: Military/Navy–Border Guards/Police–Database Analysts." *Security Dialogue* 45, no. 3 (June 1, 2014): 209–25.

Bigo, Didier, and Elspeth Guild. "Policing at a Distance: Schengen Visa Policies." In *Controlling Frontiers: Free Movement into and within Europe,* edited by Elspeth Guild and Didier Bigo, 233–63. Farnham: Ashgate, 2005.

Bigo, Didier, Sergio Carrera, Ben Hayes, Nicholas Hernanz, and Julien Jeandesboz. "Justice and Home Affairs Databases and a Smart Borders System at EU External Borders: An Evaluation of Current and Forthcoming Proposals." *CEPS Papers in Liberty and Security in Europe* 52 (2012): 1–97.

Bild. "Sex-Mob wütet in Köln: WER SEID IHR?" *Bild,* January 5, 2016. https://www .bild.de/news/inland/sexuelle-belaestigung/wer-sind-die-taeter-aus-dem-sex-mob -44033738.bild.html.

Black, Crofton. "Monitoring Being Pitched to Fight Covid-19 Was Tested on Refugees." *The Bureau of Investigative Journalism.* Accessed May 25, 2021. https: //www.thebureauinvestigates.com/stories/2020-04-28/monitoring-being-pitched-to -fight-covid-19-was-first-tested-on-refugees.

Blas, Zach. "Escaping the Face: Biometric Facial Recognition and the Facial Weaponization Suite." *NMC Media-N*, July 10, 2013. http://median.newmediacaucus .org/caa-conference-edition-2013/escaping-the-face-biometric-facial-recognition -and-the-facial-weaponization-suite/.

Bley, Helmut. *Namibia Under German Rule*. Münster: LIT Verlag, 1996.

Boulila, Stefanie C., and Christiane Carri. "On Cologne: Gender, Migration and Unacknowledged Racisms in Germany." *European Journal of Women's Studies* 24, no. 3 (2017): 286–93.

Brandt, Bettina. *Germania und ihre Söhne: Repräsentationen von Nation, Geschlecht und Politik in der Moderne*. Göttingen: Vandenhoeck & Ruprecht, 2010.

Briefel, Aviva. *The Racial Hand in the Victorian Imagination*. Cambridge University Press, 2015.

Brigida, Valeria. "Migranti: Catania, Gli Sbarchi, Le Persone e i Numeri." *Il Fatto Quotidiano*, June 12, 2015. http://www.ilfattoquotidiano.it/2015/06/12/migranti -catania-gli-sbarchi-le-persone-e-i-numeri/1769346/.

Broeck, Sabine, and Khalil Saucier. "A Dialogue: On European Borders, Black Movement, and the History of Social Death." *Black Studies Papers* 2, no. 1 (2016): 23–45.

Browne, Simone. *Dark Matters: On the Surveillance of Blackness*. Durham: Duke University Press, 2015.

———. "Digital Epidermalization: Race, Identity and Biometrics." *Critical Sociology* 36, no. 1 (January 1, 2010): 131–50.

Burman, Erica. "Innocents Abroad: Western Fantasies of Childhood and the Iconography of Emergencies." *Disasters* 18, no. 3 (September 1, 1994): 238–53. doi:10.1111/j.1467-7717.1994.tb00310.x.

Bush, Barbara. "'Britain's Conscience on Africa': White Women, Race and Imperial Politics in Inter-War Britain." In *Gender and Imperialism*, edited by Claire Midgley, 200–224. Manchester University Press, 1998.

Calhoun, Greg. "The Idea of Emergency: Humanitarian Action and Global (Dis) Order." In *Contemporary States of Emergency: The Politics of Military and Humanitarian Interventions*, 29–58. New York: Zone Books, 2010.

Callahan, Michael D. *Mandates and Empire: The League of Nations and Africa, 1914–1931*. Sussex Academic Press, 2008.

Cameron, Rob. "Migrants Crisis: Unease as Czech Police Ink Numbers on Skin." *BBC*, September 2, 2015. https://www.bbc.com/news/blogs-eu-34128087.

Campesi, Giuseppe. "Arab Revolts and the Crisis of the European Border Regime. Manufacturing the Emergency in the Lampedusa Crisis." In *Plenary, European Group on the Study of Deviancy and Social Control, 39th Annual Meeting, No Borders, Chambéry, France*, 2011.

———. "The Arab Spring and the Crisis of the European Border Regime: Manufacturing Emergency in the Lampedusa Crisis." EUI Working Papers. European University Institute, 2011.

Campt, Tina. *Other Germans: Black Germans and the Politics of Race, Gender, and Memory in the Third Reich*. Ann Arbor: University of Michigan Press, 2004.

Caplan, Jane. *Written on the Body: The Tattoo in European and American History.* London: Reaktion, 2000.

Caplan, Jane, and John Torpey. *Documenting Individual Identity: The Development of State Practices in the Modern World.* New Jersey: Princeton University Press, 2018.

Césaire, Aimé. *Discourse on Colonialism.* New York: NYU Press, 2001.

Chakravartty, Paula, and Denise Ferreira da Silva. "Accumulation, Dispossession, and Debt: The Racial Logic of Global Capitalism—An Introduction." *American Quarterly* 64, no. 3 (2012): 361–85.

Chattopadhyay, Swati. "'Goods, Chattels and Sundry Items': Constructing 19th-Century Anglo-Indian Domestic Life." *Journal of Material Culture* 7, no. 3 (November 1, 2002): 243–71.

Chew, Vivienne, Melissa Phillips, and Min Yamada Park. "COVID-19 Impacts on Immigration Detention: Global Responses," 2020. doi:10.26183/SWC5-FV98.

Chude-Sokei, Louis. *The Sound of Culture: Diaspora and Black Technopoetics.* Connecticut: Wesleyan University Press, 2015.

Chun, Wendy Hui Kyong. "Introduction: Race and/as Technology; or, How to Do Things with Race." *Camera Obscura* 24, no. 1 (2009): 1–38.

Clarkson, Thomas. *The History of the Abolition of the African Slave-Trade.* Loschberg: Jazzybee, 1808.

Cole, Simon A. *Suspect Identities: A History of Fingerprinting and Criminal Identification.* Cambridge, MA: Harvard University Press, 2009.

Commissione Centri Accoglienza Immigrati. "Commissione parlamentare di inchiesta sul sistema di accoglienza e di identificazione nonché sulle condizioni di trattamiento dei migranti nei centri di accoglienza, nei centri die accoglienza per richiedenti asilo e nei centri di identificaazione ed espulsione." Resoconto stenografico [stenographic report]. Camera dei Deputati, 2016. http://documenti.camera .it/leg17/resoconti/commissioni/stenografici/pdf/69/audiz2/audizione/2016/01/13/ leg.17.stencomm.data20160113.U1.com69.audiz2.audizione.0036.pdf.

Connolly, Kate. "A Laboratory for Refugee Politics: Inside Passau, the 'German Lampedusa.'" *The Guardian*, August 28, 2015. https://www.theguardian.com/ world/2015/aug/28/refugee-politics-passau-german-west-balkan.

Cooper, Frederick, and Cooper Frederick. *Decolonization and African Society: The Labor Question in French and British Africa.* Cambridge University Press, 1996.

Cooper, Frederick, and Ann Laura Stoler. *Tensions of Empire: Colonial Cultures in a Bourgeois World.* Berkeley: University of California Press, 1997.

Crawley, Heaven. "How COVID-19 Became a Cover to Reduce Refugee Rights." *The Conversation.* Accessed July 28, 2021. http://theconversation.com/how-covid -19-became-a-cover-to-reduce-refugee-rights-156247.

Danewid, Ida. "White Innocence in the Black Mediterranean: Hospitality and the Erasure of History." *Third World Quarterly* 38, no. 7 (July 3, 2017): 1674–89.

Datta, Souvid. "A Town at Its Limits." *Atavist*, October 22, 2015. http://www .refugeetrails.com/1.

Davis, Angela Y. *Women, Race & Class.* London: Penguin, 2019.

De Cesari, Chiara. "The Paradoxes of Colonial Reparation: Foreclosing Memory and the 2008 Italy–Libya Friendship Treaty." *Memory Studies* 5, no. 3 (July 1, 2012): 316–26.

De Genova, Nicholas, ed. *The Borders of "Europe": Autonomy of Migration, Tactics of Bordering*. Durham and London: Duke University Press, 2017.

De Genova, Nicholas, Martina Tazzioli, and Soledad Álvarez-Velasco. "Europe/ Crisis: New Keywords of 'the Crisis' in and of 'Europe.'" *Near Futures Online* 1 (2016): 1–16.

Dedering, Tilman. "War and Mobility in the Borderlands of South Western Africa in the Early Twentieth Century." *The International Journal of African Historical Studies* 39, no. 2 (2006): 275–94.

Delcker, Janosch. "The Scandal Hanging over Ursula von Der Leyen." *Politico*, July 15, 2019. https://www.politico.eu/article/the-scandal-hanging-over-ursula-von-der -leyen/.

Deleuze, Gilles, and Félix Guattari. *Thousand Plateaus*. London: A&C Black, 2004.

Deleuze, Gilles, and Claire Parnet. *Dialogues II*. New York: Columbia University Press, 2007.

Derrida, Jacques. *Schurken: zwei Essays über die Vernunft*. Suhrkamp, 2006.

Derrida, Jacques, and Marie-Françoise Plissart. *Droit de Regards*. Paris: Les Éditions de Minuit, 1985.

Derrida, Jacques, and Elizabeth Rottenberg. *Negotiations: Interventions and Interviews, 1971–2001*. Palo Alto: Stanford University Press, 2002.

Deutsche Kolonialgesetzgebung. *Die Deutsche Kolonial-Gesetzgebung. Sammlung Der Auf Die Deutschen Schutzgebiete Bezüglichen Gesetze, Verordnungen, Erlasse Und Internationalen Vereinbarungen*. Berlin: Köbner Gerstmeyer, 1907.

Deutsche Nationalversammlung. "177. Sitzung (20.5.1920)." *Stenographische Berichte NV* 333 (1920): 5694–97.

Deutsche Welle. "Maas: 'Neue Dimension organisierter Kriminalität.'" *DW.COM*. Accessed April 30, 2021. https://www.dw.com/de/maas-neue-dimension -organisierter-kriminalit%C3%A4t/a-18959186.

Dhawan, Nikita, and Maria do Mar Castro Varela. "Human Rights and Its Discontents: Postkoloniale Interventionen." In *Menschenrechte. Demokratie. Geschichte. Transdisziplinäre Herausforderungen an Die Pädagogik*, edited by Julia König and Sabine Seichter, 144–61. Wineheim: Beltz Juventa, 2013.

Di Pasquale, Francesca. "The 'Other' at Home: Deportation and Transportation of Libyans to Italy During the Colonial Era (1911–1943)." *International Review of Social History* 63, no. S26 (August 2018): 211–31. doi:10.1017/ S0020859018000299.

Diehl, Jörg. "Köln: Bilanz Der Silvesternacht–Hunderte Opfer, Fast Keine Täter." *Spiegel Panorama*, March 11, 2019. https://www.spiegel.de/panorama/justiz/ koelner-silvesternacht-ernuechternde-bilanz-der-justiz-a-1257182.html.

Dietze, Gabriele. "Das 'Ereignis Köln.'" *Femina Politica* 25, no. 1 (May 2, 2016): 93–102.

Dijstelbloem, Huub. "The Migration Machine." In *Migration and the New Technological Borders of Europe*, edited by Albert Meijer, Michiel Besters, Huub Dijstelbloem, and Albert Meijer, 1–21. London: Palgrave Macmillan, 2011.

Dikötter, Frank, and Ian Brown. *Cultures of Confinement: A History of the Prison in Africa, Asia, and Latin America*. Ithaca: Cornell University Press, 2018.

Dimitriadi, Angeliki. "Governing Irregular Migration at the Margins of Europe. The Case of Hotspots on the Greek Islands." *Etnografia e Ricerca Qualitativa* 10, no. 1 (2017): 75–96.

Diner, Dan. *Gegenläufige Gedächtnisse: Über Geltung und Wirkung des Holocaust*. Göttingen: Vandenhoeck & Ruprecht, 2007.

Dines, Nick, Nicola Montagna, and Vincenzo Ruggiero. "Thinking Lampedusa: Border Construction, the Spectacle of Bare Life and the Productivity of Migrants." *Ethnic and Racial Studies* 38, no. 3 (February 19, 2015): 430–45. doi:10.1080/01 419870.2014.936892.

Douglas, Mary. *Purity and Danger: An Analysis of Concepts of Pollution and Taboo*. London and New York: Routledge, 2013.

Du Bois, W. E. B. *The World and Africa*. New York: International Publishers, 1947.

Edelman, Lee. *No Future: Queer Theory and the Death Drive*. Durham: Duke University Press, 2004.

Elden, Stuart, and Jeremy Crampton. "Introduction: Space, Knowledge and Power: Foucault and Geography." *Space, Knowledge and Power: Foucault and Geography*, January 1, 2012, 1–16. doi:10.1017/UPO9780748626281.001.

El-Enany, Nadine. *Bordering Britain: Law, Race and Empire*. Manchester University Press, 2021.

El-Tayeb, Fatima. *Schwarze Deutsche: der Diskurs um "Rasse" und nationale Identität 1890–1933*. Frankfurt am Main: Campus, 2001.

European Commission. "Commission Decision on the Establishment of a European Union Emergency Trust Fund for Stability and Addressing Root Causes of Irregular Migration and Displaced Persons in Africa." Brussels, October 20, 2015. https://ec .europa.eu/transparency/regdoc/rep/3/2015/EN/3-2015-7293-EN-F1-1.PDF.

———. "Communication from the Commission to the European Parliament, the European Council, the Council and the European Investment Bank on Establishing a New Partnership Framework with Third Countries under the European Agenda on Migration." COM(2016) 385 final. Strasbourg, June 7, 2016. https://eur -lex.europa.eu/resource.html?uri=cellar:763f0d11-2d86-11e6-b497-01aa75ed71a1 .0001.02/DOC_1&format=PDF.

———. "Examining the Creation of a European Border Surveillance System (EUROSUR)." COM(2008) 68 final. Brussels, February 13, 2008.

———. "Progress Report on the Implementation of the Hotspots in Italy." Strasbourg, 2015. https://eur-lex.europa.eu/resource.html?uri=cellar:c2df43cd-a3e8-11e5-b528 -01aa75ed71a1.0011.03/DOC_1&format=HTML&lang=EN&parentUrn=CELEX: 52015DC0679.

———. "Summary of EMN Ad-Hoc Query No. 588 Eurodac Fingerprinting," 2014.

———. "The Hotspot Approach to Managing Exceptional Migration Flows." Accessed January 4, 2019. https://ec.europa.eu/home-affairs/sites/homeaffairs/files

/what-we-do/policies/european-agenda-migration/background-information/docs/2
_hotspots_en.pdf.

European Council. "European Council Conclusions, EUCO 22/15, 26 June 2015,
Point 4," 2015.

European Parliament, and European Council. "Regulation Establishing the European
Border Surveillance System (EUROSUR)." Brussels: Official Journal of the
European Union, October 22, 2013.

European Union. "Asylum: Deal to Update EU Fingerprinting Database." *The
European Sting*, June 20, 2018. https://europeansting.com/2018/06/20/asylum-deal
-to-update-eu-fingerprinting-database/.

Falk, Francesca. "Invasion, Infection, Invisibility. An Iconology of Illegalized
Immigration." In *Images of Illegalized Immigration*, edited by Christine Bischoff
and Silvia Kafehsy, 83–100. Bielefeld: transcript, 2010.

Fanon, Frantz. *Black Skin, White Masks*. London: Pluto Press, 1986.

———. *The Wretched of the Earth*. New York: Grove Atlantic, 2007.

Farris, Sara R. *In the Name of Women's Rights: The Rise of Femonationalism*.
Durham: Duke University Press, 2017.

Fassin, Didier, and Mariella Pandolfi. *Contemporary States of Emergency: The
Politics of Military and Humanitarian Interventions*. New York: Zone Books, 2010.

Federici, Silvia. *Caliban and the Witch*. New York: Autonomedia, 2014.

Fehrenbach, Heide. *Race after Hitler: Black Occupation Children in Postwar
Germany and America*. Princeton and Oxford: Princeton University Press, 2018.

Fekete, Liz. "The Deportation Machine: Europe, Asylum and Human Rights." *Race
& Class* 47, no. 1 (July 2005): 64–78.

Feldman, Allen. *Archives of the Insensible: Of War, Photopolitics, and Dead Memory*.
University of Chicago Press, 2015.

———. "On the Actuarial Gaze: From 9/11 to Abu Ghraib." *Cultural Studies* 19, no.
2 (March 2005): 203–26.

———. "The Becoming Non-State of the State." *Social Text*, May 21, 2011.
https://socialtextjournal.org/periscope_article/the_state-become-nonstate_-_allen
_feldman/.

———. *Xenophobic Technicities: A Media Archeology*, 2016. https://www.youtube
.com/watch?v=AeqDo59M8MY.

Fiske, John. "Surveilling the City: Whiteness, the Black Man and Democratic
Totalitarianism." *Theory, Culture & Society* 15, no. 2 (May 1, 1998): 67–88.

Flint, Kate. *The Victorians and the Visual Imagination*. Cambridge University Press,
2000.

Flusser, Vilém. *Into the Universe of Technical Images*. Minneapolis and London:
University of Minnesota Press, 2011.

Fosdick, Raymond B. "Passing of the Bertillon System of Identification." *Journal of
Criminal Law and Criminology* 6 (1915): 363–69.

Foucault, M., Arnold I. Davidson, and Graham Burchell. *The Birth of Biopolitics:
Lectures at the Collège de France, 1978–1979*. Berlin: Springer, 2008.

Foucault, Michel. *Discipline and Punish: The Birth of the Prison*. London: Knopf
Doubleday, 2012.

————. *Power/Knowledge: Selected Interviews and Other Writings, 1972–1977.* New York: Pantheon Books, 1980.

————. *Society Must Be Defended: Lectures at the Collège de France, 1975–76.* Penguin, 2004.

Foucault, Michel, and François Ewald. *Society Must Be Defended: Lectures at the Collège de France, 1975–1976.* London: Allen Lane, 2003.

Foucault, Michel, and Paul Rabinow. *The Foucault Reader.* New York: Pantheon Books, 1984.

Freedman, Jane. "Sexual and Gender-Based Violence against Refugee Women: A Hidden Aspect of the Refugee 'Crisis.'" *Reproductive Health Matters* 24, no. 47 (January 1, 2016): 18–26.

Fried, Nico. "Ein Wort Zu Viel." *Süddeutsche,* January 7, 2016. https://www.sueddeutsche.de/politik/politiker-ein-wort-zu-viel-1.2808096.

Friedman, Edle. "Learning the Lessons of the Kindertransport." *The Jewish Chronicle,* December 8, 2015. https://www.thejc.com/comment/comment/learning-the-lessons-of-the-kindertransport-1.63265.

Friese, Heidrun. *Grenzen der Gastfreundschaft: Die Bootsflüchtlinge von Lampedusa und die europäische Frage.* Bielefeld: transcript, 2014.

Fritsche, Andreas. "Strafe für antikoloniale Aktivität (neues deutschland)." Accessed June 1, 2021. https://www.nd-aktuell.de/artikel/76876.strafe-fuer-antikoloniale-aktivitaet.html.

Frontex. "Europe Day–United against Corona Virus with Eyes on the Future." Accessed February 14, 2022. https://frontex.europa.eu/media-centre/news/news-release/europe-day-united-against-corona-virus-with-eyes-on-the-future-r9vMlS.

————. "EUROSUR," 2018. http://frontex.europa.eu/intelligence/eurosur/.

Frosh, Paul. "The Gestural Image: The Selfie, Photography Theory, and Kinesthetic Sociability." *International Journal of Communication* 9 (2015): 1–22.

Gaibazzi, Paolo, Stephan Dünnwald, and Alice Bellagamba. *EurAfrican Borders and Migration Management: Political Cultures, Contested Spaces, and Ordinary Lives.* London: Palgrave Macmillan, 2016.

Gall, Alexander. *Das Atlantropa-Projekt: Die Geschichte einer gescheiterten Vision.* Frankfurt am Main: Campus Verlag, 1998.

Gallois, William. *A History of Violence in the Early Algerian Colony.* Basingstoke: Palgrave Macmillan, 2013.

Galloway, Alexander R. *The Interface Effect.* New Jersey: John Wiley & Sons, 2013.

Galton, Francis. *Finger Prints: The Classic 1892 Treatise.* Mineola: Dover Publications, 2012.

————. "Identification by Finger-Tips." *Nineteenth Century* 30, no. August (1891): 303–11.

Garcia, Raphael Tsavkko. "How the Pandemic Turned Refugees Into 'Guinea Pigs' for Surveillance Tech." *Medium,* January 21, 2021. https://onezero.medium.com/how-the-pandemic-turned-refugees-into-guinea-pigs-for-surveillance-tech-d7cf916551cc.

Garelli, Glenda, and Martina Tazzioli. "The Biopolitical Warfare on Migrants: EU Naval Force and NATO Operations of Migration Government in the Mediterranean." *Critical Military Studies* 4, no. 2 (May 4, 2018): 181–200.

Gates, Kelly. *Our Biometric Future: Facial Recognition Technology and the Culture of Surveillance*. New York: NYU Press, 2011.

Gates, Kelly A. "Biometrics and Post-9/11 Technostalgia." *Social Text* 23, no. 2 (83) (June 1, 2005): 35–53.

The General Act of the Berlin Conference on West Africa. "The General Act of the Berlin Conference on West Africa." *ThoughtCo*, February 26, 1885, sec. ThoughtCo. https://www.thoughtco.com/general-act-of-the-berlin-conference-4070667.

Genova, Nicholas De, and Nathalie Peutz. *The Deportation Regime: Sovereignty, Space, and the Freedom of Movement*. Durham: Duke University Press, 2010.

Gerwarth, Robert, and Stephan Malinowski. "Hannah Arendt's Ghosts: Reflections on the Disputable Path from Windhoek to Auschwitz." *Central European History* 42, no. 02 (2009): 279–300.

Gibson, Mary. *Born to Crime: Cesare Lombroso and the Origins of Biological Criminology*. Praeger, 2002.

Gillespie, Marie, Souad Osseiran, and Margie Cheesman. "Syrian Refugees and the Digital Passage to Europe: Smartphone Infrastructures and Affordances." *Social Media + Society* 4, no. 1 (January 1, 2018): 1–12.

Gilman, Sander L. *On Blackness Without Blacks: Essays on the Image of the Black in Germany*. Boston: G. K. Hall, 1982.

Gilmore, Ruth Wilson. *Golden Gulag: Prisons, Surplus, Crisis, and Opposition in Globalizing California*. Berkeley: University of California Press, 2007.

Gilroy, Paul. "Agonistic Belonging: The Banality of Good, the 'Alt Right' and the Need for Sympathy." *Open Cultural Studies* 3, no. 1 (January 1, 2019): 1–14.

GIZ. "The Coronavirus Pandemic: How Europe Is Learning from Africa." Accessed June 15, 2021. https://www.giz.de/en/mediacenter/92966.html.

Glissant, Édouard. *Poetics of Relation*. Ann Arbor: University of Michigan Press, 1997.

Goffman, Erving. *Stigma: Notes on the Management of Spoiled Identity*. New York: Simon and Schuster, 2009.

Goldberg, David Theo. *The Racial State*. New Jersey: Wiley, 2002.

Goodacre, Hugh. "Conomics, Geography and Colonialism in the Writings of William Petty." In *Open Economics: Economics in Relation to Other Disciplines*, edited by Richard Arena, Sheila Dow, and Matthias Klaes, 18–31. London and New York: Routledge, 2008.

Govan, Fiona. "King Felipe Urges UK End 'Colonial Anachronism' of Gibraltar." *The Local*, September 22, 2016. https://www.thelocal.es/20160922/king-felipe-urges-uk-to-end-colonial-anachronism-of-gibraltar.

Grace, Helen, Amy Chan Kit-Sze, and Wong Kin Yuen. *Technovisuality: Cultural Re-Enchantment and the Experience of Technology*. London and New York: I. B. Tauris, 2015.

Gramsci, Antonio. *The Southern Question*. Guernica Editions, 2005.

Gray, Richard T. *About Face: German Physiognomic Thought from Lavater to Auschwitz*. Detroit: Wayne State University Press, 2004.

Gregory, Derek. *The Colonial Present: Afghanistan. Palestine. Iraq*. New Jersey: Wiley, 2004.

Griffiths, Melanie, and Colin Yeo. "The UK's Hostile Environment: Deputising Immigration Control." *Critical Social Policy*, January 11, 2021, 0261018320980653. doi:10.1177/0261018320980653.

Gronenberg, Frank. "Asylpolitik ist moderner Kolonialismus." *MOZ*, July 20, 2013. https://www.moz.de/nachrichten/brandenburg/artikel-ansicht/dg/0/1/1175522/.

Grosse, Pascal. "What Does German Colonialism Have to Do with National Socialism? A Conceptual Framework." In *Germany's Colonial Pasts*, edited by Eric Ames, Mareia Klotz, and Lora Wildenthal, 115–34. Lincoln, NE, and London: University of Nebraska Press, 2005.

Gueye, Abdoulaye. "The Colony within the Metropole: The Racial Diversity of Contemporary France and the Insertion of the Colonial Past into the National Narrative." *Canadian Journal of African Studies/Revue Canadienne Des Études Africaines* 45, no. 1 (January 1, 2011): 1–16.

Hage, Ghassan. "État de Siège: A Dying Domesticating Colonialism?" *American Ethnologist* 43, no. 1 (2016): 38–49. doi:10.1111/amet.12261.

Haggerty, Kevin D., and Richard V. Ericson. "The Surveillant Assemblage." *British Journal of Sociology* 51, no. 4 (December 2000): 605–22.

Halberstam, J. Jack. *In a Queer Time and Place: Transgender Bodies, Subcultural Lives*. New York: NYU Press, 2005.

Hamood, Sara. *African Transit Migration through Libya to Europe: The Human Cost*. The American University in Cairo, 2006.

Hansen, Peo, and Stefan Jonsson. "Bringing Africa as a 'Dowry to Europe.'" *Interventions* 13, no. 3 (September 1, 2011): 443–63.

———. *Eurafrica: The Untold History of European Integration and Colonialism*. Bloomsbury Publishing, 2014.

Haraway, Donna. "Situated Knowledges: The Science Question in Feminism and the Privilege of Partial Perspective." *Feminist Studies* 14, no. 3 (1988): 575–99.

Hark, Sabine, and Paula-Irene Villa. *Unterscheiden und herrschen: Ein Essay zu den ambivalenten Verflechtungen von Rassismus, Sexismus und Feminismus in der Gegenwart*. Bielefeld: transcript, 2017.

Hartley-Brewer, Julia. "Red Doors and Wristbands: Another Day, Another Comparison to Nazi Germany," January 25, 2016, sec. News. https://www.telegraph.co.uk/news/uknews/immigration/12120009/Red-doors-and-wristbands-Another-day-another-comparison-to-Nazi-Germany.html.

Harvey, David. *The Enigma of Capital: And the Crises of Capitalism*. New York: Oxford University Press, 2010.

———. *The New Imperialism*. New York: Oxford University Press, 2005.

Hayes, Ben. "NeoConOpticon: The EU Security-Industrial Complex." Amsterdam and London: Transnational Institute and Statewatch, 2009.

Hayes, Ben, Chris Jones, and Eric Töpfer. "Eurodrones Inc." Amsterdam and London: Transnational Institute and Statewatch, 2014.

Hayes, Ben, and Matthias Vermeulen. "Borderline: The EU's New Border Surveillance Initiatives: Assessing the Costs and Fundamental Rights Implications of EUROSUR and the 'Smart Borders.'" Berlin: Heinrich Böll Foundation, 2014.

Hayles, Katherine. *Writing Machines*. Massachusetts: MIT Press, 2002.

Head, Naomi. "The Failure of Empathy: European Responses to the Refugee Crisis." *OpenDemocracy*, February 18, 2016. https://www.opendemocracy.net/en/can -europe-make-it/failure-of-empathy-european-responses-to-refugee-crisis/.

Headrick, Daniel R. *The Tools of Empire: Technology and European Imperialism in the Nineteenth Century*. Oxford University Press, 1981.

Hegde, Radha Sarma. *Mediating Migration*. Cambridge and Malden: Polity, 2016.

Heller, Charles. "Perception Management–Deterring Potential Migrants through Information Campaigns." *Global Media and Communication* 10, no. 3 (November 23, 2014): 303–18.

Henry, Sir Edward Richard. *Classification and Uses of Finger Prints*. London: George Routledge and Sons, 1900.

Hernandez, Jesus Campos. *Race, Market Constraints and the Housing Crisis: Critical Links to Segregation and Mortgage Redlining in Sacramento*. Berkeley: University of California, 2012.

Herscher, Andrew. "Surveillant Witnessing: Satellite Imagery and the Visual Politics of Human Rights." *Public Culture* 26, no. 3 (September 1, 2014): 469–500.

Heynen, Robert, and Emily van der Meulen. "Unpacking State Surveillance: Histories, Theories, and Global Contexts." In *Making Surveillance States: Transnational Histories*, 3–30. University of Toronto Press, 2019.

Hilberg, Raul. *Die Vernichtung der europäischen Juden*. Frankfurt am Main: Fischer, 1994.

Hill Collins, Patricia. "Controlling Images and Black Women's Oppression." In *Seeing Ourselves: Classic, Contemporary, and Cross-Cultural Readings in Sociology*, edited by John J. Macionis, Nijole Vaicaitis Benokraitis, and Bruce Douglas Ravelli, 232–39. London: Pearson Education, 2007.

Hobbes, Thomas. *Leviathan*. New York: Barnes & Noble, 2004.

Hoffman, Kelly M., Sophie Trawalter, Jordan R. Axt, and M. Norman Oliver. "Racial Bias in Pain Assessment and Treatment: Recommendations, and False Beliefs about Biological Differences between Blacks and Whites." *Proceedings of the National Academy of Sciences of the United States of America* 113, no. 16 (April 19, 2016): 4296–4301.

hooks, bell. *Black Looks: Race and Representation*. New York and London: Routledge, 2014.

Hulme, Peter. "Cast Away." In *Sea Changes: Historicizing the Ocean*, edited by B. Klein and G. Mackenthun, 187–201. London: Routledge, 2004.

Ingenieur von Zwergern. "Zur Eingeborenenfrage in Deutsch-Südwestafrika." *Koloniale Zeitschrift* 12, no. 49 (1911): 789–90.

Italian Ministry of Interior. "Circular n. 27978," September 23, 2014. https://www .meltingpot.org/IMG/pdf/circolare_impronte.pdf.

Ivits, E. "Silvesternacht in Köln Am Bahnhof: Männer Umzingeln Frauen." *Stern*, January 4, 2016. https://www.stern.de/panorama/stern-crime/silvesternacht-in -koeln-am-bahnhof--maenner-umzingeln-frauen-6631416.html.

Jay, Martin. *Downcast Eyes: The Denigration of Vision in Twentieth-Century French Thought*. Berkeley: University of California Press, 1993.

Jones, Chris. "Market Forces: The Development of the EU Security-Industrial Complex." Amsterdam: Transnational Institute, 2017.

Justice and Home Affairs Ministers. "Discussion Paper European Border and Coast Guard." Informal Meeting of the Justice and Home Affairs Ministers, 25–26 January 2016. Amsterdam, 2016. http://www.statewatch.org/news/2016/jan/eu -council-jha-informal-borders-25-26-1-15.pdf.

Kane, Carolyn L. *Chromatic Algorithms: Synthetic Color, Computer Art, and Aesthetics after Code*. Chicago and London: The University of Chicago Press, 2014.

Kaplan, Martha. "Panopticon in Poona: An Essay on Foucault and Colonialism." *Cultural Anthropology* 10, no. 1 (1995): 85–98.

Kasimis, Charalambos, Apostolos G. Papadopoulos, and Ersi Zacopoulou. "Migrants in Rural Greece." *Sociologia Ruralis* 43, no. 2 (2003): 167–84.

Kawash, Samira. *Dislocating the Color Line: Identity, Hybridity, and Singularity in African-American Narrative*. Stanford University Press, 1997.

Keenan, Thomas, and Sohrab Mohebbi. "It Is Obvious from the Map." In *The System of Systems*, edited by Rebecca Glyn-Blanco, Maria McLintock, and Danae Papazymouri, 120–28. Athens: Davias, 2017.

Khiabany, Gholam. "Refugee Crisis, Imperialism and Pitiless Wars on the Poor." *Media, Culture & Society* 35, no. 5 (2016): 755–62.

Kim-Puri, H. J. "Conceptualizing Gender-Sexuality-State-Nation: An Introduction." *Gender & Society* 19, no. 2 (April 1, 2005): 137–59. doi:10.1177/0891243204273021.

Kirschenbaum, Matthew G. *Mechanisms: New Media and the Forensic Imagination*. Massachusetts: MIT Press, 2008.

Kιvιlcιm, Zeynep. "Migration Crises in Turkey." In *The Oxford Handbook of Migration Crises*, edited by Cecilia Menjívar, Marie Ruiz, and Immanuel Ness, 427–44. New York: Oxford University Press, 2019.

Klein, Naomi. *The Shock Doctrine: The Rise of Disaster Capitalism*. London: Penguin, 2014.

Kokkinidis, Tasos. "Migrant Camp in Lesvos 'a Concentration Camp' Says Human Rights Watch." *Greek Reporter*, October 6, 2017. https://greece.greekreporter.com /2017/10/06/migrant-camp-in-lesvos-a-concentration-camp-says-human-rights -watch/.

Korieh, Chima J. "Hegemonic and Negotiated Encounters: Reflections on Indirect Rule and Protest in Colonial Eastern Nigeria." In *African Agency and European Colonialism: Latitudes of Negotiation and Containment: Essays in Honor of A. S. Kanya-Forstner*, edited by Femi James Kolapo and Kwabena O. Akurang-Parry, 111–20. Lanham and Plymouth: University Press of America, 2007.

Kotzias, Nikos. *Ελλάδα Αποικία Χρέους. Ευρωπαική Αυτοκρατία Και Γερμανική Προτοκραθεδρία*. Athens: Ekdosis Patakis, 2013.

Kreutzer, Guido. *Die schwarze Schmach, der Roman des geschändeten Deutschlands.* Leipzig: Vogel, 1921.

Krüger, Anja. "Ehemaliges KZ als Flüchtlingsunterkunft: Asylsuchende in Buchenwald-Baracke." *Die Tageszeitung: taz*, January 13, 2015, sec. Politik. https://taz.de/!5023890/.

Kundnani, Arun, and Deepa Kumar. "Race, Surveillance, and Empire." *International Socialist Review*, 2010. /issue/96/race-surveillance-and-empire.

Kundrus, Birthe. "Kontinuitäten, Parallelen, Rezeptionen Überlegungen Zur 'Kolonialisierung' Des Nationalsozialismus." *WerkstattGeschichte* 43 (2006): 45–62.

Kuntsman, Adi. *Selfie Citizenship.* Berlin: Springer, 2017.

Kuster, Brigitta. *Grenze filmen: Eine kulturwissenschaftliche Analyse audiovisueller Produktionen an den Grenzen Europas.* Bielefeld: transcript, 2018.

Latonero, Mark, and Paula Kift. "On Digital Passages and Borders: Refugees and the New Infrastructure for Movement and Control." *Social Media + Society* 4, no. 1 (January 1, 2018): 1–11.

Lebzelter, Gisela. "Die 'Schwarze Schmach': Vorurteile–Propaganda–Mythos." *Geschichte Und Gesellschaft* 11, no. 1 (1985): 37–58.

Lentin, Alana. *Racism and Ethnic Discrimination.* New York: The Rosen Publishing Group, 2011.

Lerp, Dörte. *Imperiale Grenzräume: Bevölkerungspolitiken in Deutsch-Südwestafrika und den östlichen Provinzen Preußens 1884–1914.* Frankfurt am Main: Campus Verlag, 2016.

Lester, Eve. *Making Migration Law: The Foreigner, Sovereignty, and the Case of Australia.* Cambridge University Press, 2018.

Leurs, Koen. "Communication Rights from the Margins: Politicising Young Refugees' Smartphone Pocket Archives." *International Communication Gazette* 79, no. 6–7 (November 1, 2017): 674–98.

Leurs, Koen, and Sandra Ponzanesi. "Connected Migrants: Encapsulation and Cosmopolitanization." *Popular Communication* 16, no. 1 (January 2, 2018): 4–20.

Lim, Bliss Cua. *Translating Time: Cinema, the Fantastic, and Temporal Critique.* Durham: Duke University Press, 2009.

Litzkow, Julia. "The Impact of COVID-19 on Refugees and Migrants on the Move in North and West Africa." Copenhagen: Mixed Migration Centre, 2021.

Lorey, Isabell. "Der Traum von Der Regierbaren Stadt." *Transversal*, 2007. https://transversal.at/transversal/1007/lorey/de?hl=policey.

Lupton, Deborah. *Risk.* New York: Routledge, 2013.

Lyman, Rick. "Regulating Flow of Refugees Gains Urgency in Greece and Rest of Europe." *New York Times*, November 25, 2015. https://www.nytimes.com/2015/11/26/world/europe/regulating-flow-of-refugees-gains-urgency-in-greece-and-rest-of-europe.html.

Lyon, David. *Surveillance as Social Sorting: Privacy, Risk and Automated Discrimination.* London and New York: Routledge, 2005.

———. *Surveillance Studies: An Overview.* Cambridge: Polity, 2007.

Mabon, Simon. "Sovereignty, Bare Life and the Arab Uprisings." *Third World Quarterly* 38, no. 8 (August 3, 2017): 1782–99. doi:10.1080/01436597.2017.129 4483.

MacDougall, Ian. "How McKinsey Helped the Trump Administration Carry Out Its Immigration Policies." *New York Times*, December 3, 2019. https://www.nytimes .com/2019/12/03/us/mckinsey-ICE-immigration.html.

Mader, Mary Beth. "Foucault's 'Metabody.'" *Journal of Bioethical Inquiry* 7, no. 2 (June 1, 2010): 187–203.

Madley, Benjamin. "From Africa to Auschwitz: How German South West Africa Incubated Ideas and Methods Adopted and Developed by the Nazis in Eastern Europe." *European History Quarterly* 35, no. 3 (July 2005): 429–64.

Magnet, Shoshana. *When Biometrics Fail: Gender, Race, and the Technology of Identity*. Durham: Duke University Press, 2011.

Maguire, Mark. "The Birth of Biometric Security." *Anthropology Today* 25, no. 2 (2009): 7.

Mamdani, Mahmood. "Settler Colonialism: Then and Now." *Critical Inquiry* 41, no. 3 (March 2015): 596–614.

Mamozai, Martha. *Herrenmenschen*. Leipzig: Rowohlt, 1982.

———. *Schwarze Frau, weisse Herrin: Frauenleben in den deutschen Kolonien*. Leipzig: Rowohlt, 1989.

Marin, Luisa. "The Deployment of Drone Technology in Border Surveillance, between Techno-Securitization and Challenges to Privacy and Data Protection." In *Surveillance, Privacy and Security*, edited by J. Peter Burgess, M. Friedewald, and J. Cas, 107–22. New York: Routledge, 2017.

Maß, Sandra. "Das Trauma des weißen Mannes." *L'Homme* 12, no. 1 (January 2001): 11–33.

———. "Von der 'schwarzen Schmach' zur 'deutschen Heimat.' Die Rheinische Frauenliga im Kampf gegen die Rheinlandbesetzung, 1920–1929." *WerkstattGeschichte* 32 (2002). https://pub.uni-bielefeld.de/publication/1914288.

Massumi, Brian. "National Enterprise Emergency Steps Toward an Ecology of Powers." *Theory, Culture & Society* 26, no. 6 (2009): 153–85.

Mathiesen, Thomas. *On Globalisation of Control: Towards an Integrated Surveillance System in Europe*. London: Statewatch, 1999.

Mbembe, Achille. "Necropolitics." *Public Culture* 15, no. 1 (2003): 11–40.

McClintock, Anne. *Imperial Leather: Race, Gender, and Sexuality in the Colonial Contest*. New York: Routledge, 1995.

McCormick, Ted. *William Petty: And the Ambitions of Political Arithmetic*. Oxford: Oxford University Press, 2009.

McCoy, Alfred W. *Policing America's Empire: The United States, the Philippines, and the Rise of the Surveillance State*. University of Wisconsin Press, 2009.

McGlotten, Shaka. "Black Data." In *No Tea, No Shade: New Writings in Black Queer Studies*, edited by E. Patrick Johnson, 262–68. Durham: Duke University Press, 2016.

McGregor, Gordon. *Die eingeborenen Passmarken von Deutsch Südwest Afrika*. Windhoek: Wissenschaftliche Gesellschaft Namibia Verlag, 2013.

M'charek, Amade. "Dead-Bodies-at-the-Border. Distributed Evidence and Emerging Forensic Infrastructure for Identification." In *Bodies of Evidence: Security, Knowledge, and Power*, edited by Mark Maguire, Ursula Rao, and Nils Zurawski, 89–109. Duke University Press, 2018.

McKenna, Christopher D. "The American Challenge: McKinsey & Company's Role in the Transfer of Decentralization to Europe, 1957–1975." *Academy of Management Proceedings*, no. 1 (August 1997): 226–30.

McKinsey, and IOM. "More than Numbers—How Migration Data Can Deliver Real-Life Benefits for Migrants and Governments," 2018. https://publications .iom.int/books/more-numbers-how-migration-data-can-deliver-real-life-benefits -migrants-and-governments.

Meade, Amanda. "Charlie Hebdo Cartoon Depicting Drowned Child Alan Kurdi Sparks Racism Debate." *The Guardian*, January 14, 2016. http://www.theguardian .com/media/2016/jan/14/charlie-hebdo-cartoon-depicting-drowned-child-alan -kurdi-sparks-racism-debate.

Melzer, Chris. "Flüchtlingskrise in Griechenland—87 Prozent der Kinder wollen gar nicht nach Europa." *Cicero Online*, March 11, 2020. https://www.cicero.de /innenpolitik/fluechtlingskrise-griechenland-lesbos-kinder-madchen-integration -europa.

Mercer, Kobena. *Welcome to the Jungle: New Positions in Black Cultural Studies*. New York: Routledge, 2013.

Meyer, Maria. "Die Schwarze Schmach." *Frauenbeilage Des Hamburger Echo* 4, no. 6 (1922): 1.

Mezzadra, Sandro, and Brett Neilson. *Border as Method, or, the Multiplication of Labor*. Durham and London: Duke University Press, 2013.

Mezzadra, Sandro, and Federico Rahola. "The Postcolonial Condition: A Few Notes on the Quality of Historical Time in the Global Present." In *Reworking Postcolonialism: Globalization, Labour and Rights*, edited by Pavan Kumar Malreddy, Birte Heidemann, Ole Birk Laursen, and Janet Wilson, 36–54. London: Palgrave Macmillan, 2015.

Mirzoeff, Nicholas. *How to See the World: An Introduction to Images, from Self-Portraits to Selfies, Maps to Movies, and More*. London: Hachette, 2016.

———. "Invisible Empire: Abu Ghraib and Embodied Spectacle." *Visual Arts Research* 32, no. 2 (2006): 38–42.

———. *The Right to Look: A Counterhistory of Visuality*. Durham: Duke University Press, 2011.

———. "The Sea and the Land: Biopower and Visuality from Slavery to Katrina." *Culture, Theory and Critique* 50, no. 2–3 (July 2009): 289–305.

"Missing Migrants Project." Accessed March 24, 2020. https://missingmigrants.iom .int/region/mediterranean.

Mitchell, Timothy. *Colonising Egypt*. Berkeley: University of California Press, 1988.

Mitropoulos, Angela. "Invisible Hand(s): Hidden Labor, AI-Driven Capitalism and the COVID-19 Pandemic," edited by Magdalena Taube and Krystian Woznicki. Zagreb: Mi2, 2020.

Modrow, Bastian. "Eine Heldin wider Willen." *Kieler Nachrichten*, July 3, 2019. https://www.kn-online.de/Nachrichten/Schleswig-Holstein/Sea-Watch-Kapitaenin -Carola-Rackete-wird-zur-Heldin-wider-Willen.

Molnar, Petra. "Technology on the Margins: AI and Global Migration Management from a Human Rights Perspective." *Cambridge International Law Journal* 8, no. 2 (December 2019): 305–30. doi:10.4337/cilj.2019.02.07.

Monroy, Matthias. "Frontex and the use of Force." Accessed July 28, 2021. https:// digit.site36.net/2021/04/03/frontex-and-the-use-of-force/.

Monture-Angus, Patricia, and Suzanne M. Stiegelbauer. "Thunder in My Soul: A Mohawk Woman Speaks." *Resources for Feminist Research* 25, no. 1/2 (1996): 52–53.

Moving Europe. "Can't Stop a Movement!" 2017. http://moving-europe.org/cant-stop -a-movement/.

Mulvey, Laura. *Visual Pleasure and Narrative Cinema*. Massachusetts: Afterall Books, 2016.

Neocleous, Mark. "Air Power as Police Power." *Environment and Planning: Society and Space* 31, no. 4 (2013): 578–93.

Nieuwenhuys, Céline, and Antoine Pécoud. "Human Trafficking, Information Campaigns, and Strategies of Migration Control." *American Behavioral Scientist* 50, no. 12 (August 1, 2007): 1674–95.

Noack, Rick. "Leaked Document Says 2,000 Men Allegedly Assaulted 1,200 German Women on New Year's Eve." *Washington Post*, July 11, 2016. https://www .washingtonpost.com/news/worldviews/wp/2016/07/10/leaked-document-says -2000-men-allegedly-assaulted-1200-german-women-on-new-years-eve/.

O'Brien, Gerald V. "Indigestible Food, Conquering Hordes, and Waste Materials: Metaphors of Immigrants and the Early Immigration Restriction Debate in the United States." *Metaphor and Symbol* 18, no. 1 (January 1, 2003): 33–47.

Oeppen, Ceri. "'Leaving Afghanistan! Are You Sure?' European Efforts to Deter Potential Migrants Through Information Campaigns." *Human Geography* 9, no. 2 (2016): 57–68.

O'Malley, Pat, Lorna Weir, and Clifford Shearing. "Governmentality, Criticism, Politics." *Economy and Society* 26, no. 4 (November 1, 1997): 501–17.

Omwenyeke, Sunny. "The 'Fortress Within': Restriction of Movement and Refugee Self-Organisation." *Heimatkunde*, September 18, 2013. https://heimatkunde.boell .de/2013/11/18/%E2%80%98fortress-within%E2%80%99-restriction-movement -and-refugee-self-organisation.

Operation Commander Op Sophia. "EUNAVFOR MED–Operation SOPHIA: Six Monthly Report: June, 22nd to December, 31st 2015." 5653/16. Brussels: European External Action Service (EEAS), February 17, 2016. https://wikileaks .org/eu-military-refugees/EEAS.

Opitz, May, May Ayim, Katharina Oguntoye, and Dagmar Schultz. *Showing Our Colors: Afro-German Women Speak Out*. University of Massachusetts Press, 1992.

Ott, Stephanie. "How a Selfie with Merkel Changed Syrian Refugee's Life." Accessed June 23, 2021. https://www.aljazeera.com/features/2017/2/21/how-a-selfie-with -merkel-changed-syrian-refugees-life.

Oxford Languages. "Deterrence." Accessed July 15, 2021. https://languages.oup.com /google-dictionary-en/.

Oxford Learner's Dictionaries. "Selfie." Accessed February 13, 2020. https://www .oxfordlearnersdictionaries.com/definition/english/selfie.

Palmer, Richard John. *The Control of Plague in Venice and Northern Italy: 1348– 1600*. Canterbury: University of Kent, 1978.

Parenti, Christian. *The Soft Cage: Surveillance in America, From Slavery to the War on Terror*. New York: Hachette, 2007.

Park, K.-Sue. "Money, Mortgages, and the Conquest of America." *Law & Social Inquiry* 41, no. 4 (2016): 1006–35. doi:10.1111/lsi.12222.

Parker, Noel, and Nick Vaughan-Williams. "Lines in the Sand? Towards an Agenda for Critical Border Studies." *Geopolitics* 14, no. 3 (August 21, 2009): 582–87.

Patterson, Charles. *Eternal Treblinka: Our Treatment of Animals and the Holocaust*. New York: Lantern Books, 2002.

Patterson, Orlando. *Slavery and Social Death*. Cambridge, MA: Harvard University Press, 1985.

Perera, Suvendrini. "Oceanic Corpo-Graphies, Refugee Bodies and the Making and Unmaking of Waters." *Feminist Review* 103, no. 1 (2013): 58–79.

Piazza, Pierre. "Bertillonage: The International Circulation of Practices and Technologies of a System of Forensic Identification." *Criminocorpus. Revue d'Histoire de La Justice, Des Crimes et Des Peines*, April 18, 2011. http://journals .openedition.org/criminocorpus/2970.

Pinney, Christopher. *Photography and Anthropology*. London: Reaktion Books, 2012.

Plaza Girls. "Zine Issue 2." *Zine Issue 2*. Accessed January 4, 2019. https://www .plazagirls.com/the-zine.

Poley, Jared. *Decolonization in Germany: Weimar Narratives of Colonial Loss and Foreign Occupation*. Oxford: Peter Lang, 2007.

Pollard, Sidney, and Colin Holmes. *Documents of European Economic History*. London: Edward Arnold, 1968.

Pollozek, Silvan, and Jan Hendrik Passoth. "Infrastructuring European Migration and Border Control: The Logistics of Registration and Identification at Moria Hotspot." *Environment and Planning D: Society and Space* 37, no. 4 (August 1, 2019): 606–24. doi:10.1177/0263775819835819.

Pommerin, Reiner. "Zur Praxis Nationalsozialistischer Rassenpolitik. Sterilisierung Der 'Rheinlandbastarde.'" In *Schwarze Weißheiten. Vom Umgang Mit Fremden Menschen*, edited by Fansa Mamoun, 157–62. Schriftenreihe Des Landesmuseums Für Natur Und Mensch, Heft 19. Oldenburg, 2001.

Ponzanesi, Sandra, and Bolette B. Blaagaard. "In the Name of Europe." *Social Identities* 17, no. 1 (January 1, 2011): 1–10.

Ponzanesi, Sandra, and Koen Leurs. "On Digital Crossings in Europe." *Crossings: Journal of Migration & Culture* 5, no. 1 (March 1, 2014): 3–22.

Poschardt, Ulf. "Kalaschnikows, Sprenggürtel Und Jetzt Die Sexuelle Gewalt." *Die Welt*, January 15, 2016. https://www.welt.de/politik/deutschland/article151065691/ Kalaschnikows-Sprengguertel-und-jetzt-die-sexuelle-Gewalt.html.

Poster, Mark. *What's the Matter with the Internet?* Minneapolis: University of Minnesota Press, 2001.

Potyondi, Stephen. "The Discovery of the Street: Urbanism, Gentrification, and Cultural Change in Early Nineteenth-Century Paris." University of Alberta, 2011. doi:10.7939/R3P99K.

Pratt, Mary Louise. *Imperial Eyes: Travel Writing and Transculturation*. New York: Routledge, 2003.

Preciado, Paul B. "Learning from the Virus." Accessed May 25, 2021. https://www.artforum.com/print/202005/paul-b-preciado-82823.

Probyn, Elsbeth. "Writing Shame." In *The Affect Theory Reader*, edited by Melissa Gregg and Gregory J. Seigworth, 320–31. Durham: Duke University Press, 2010.

Puar, Jasbir K. "Abu Ghraib: Arguing against Exceptionalism." *Feminist Studies* 30, no. 2 (2004): 522–34. doi:10.2307/20458978.

———. "Homonationalism as Assemblage: Viral Travels, Affective Sexualities." *Jindal Global Law Review* 4, no. 2 (2013): 23–43.

Pugliese, Joseph. *Biometrics: Bodies, Technologies, Biopolitics*. New York and London: Routledge, 2012.

———. "Biometrics, Infrastructural Whiteness, and the Racialized Zero Degree of Nonrepresentation." *Boundary 2* 34, no. 2 (June 1, 2007): 105–33.

———. "Crisis Heterotopias and Border Zones of the Dead." *Continuum* 23, no. 5 (October 2009): 663–79.

———. *State Violence and the Execution of Law: Biopolitical Caesurae of Torture, Black Sites, Drones*. New York: Routledge, 2013.

Rapefugees.net. "Vergewaltigungskarte." *Rapefugees*, n.d. www.rapefugees.net.

Razack, Sherene. "Domestic Violence as Gender Persecution: Policing the Borders of Nation, Race, and Gender." *Canadian Journal of Women and the Law* 8 (1995): 45–63.

———. "How Is White Supremacy Embodied? Sexualized Racial Violence at Abu Ghraib." *Canadian Journal of Women and the Law* 17, no. 2 (2005): 341–63.

Redfield, Peter. "Foucault in the Tropics: Displacing the Panopticon." In *Anthropologies of Modernity: Foucault, Governmentality, and Life Politics*, edited by Jonathan Xavier Inda, 50–79. Sheffield: Blackwell, 2005.

Rediker, Marcus. *The Slave Ship: A Human History*. New York: Penguin, 2007.

Reiner, Robert, Stuart Hall, Chas Critcher, Tony Jefferson, John Clark, and Brian Roberts. "Policing the Crisis: Mugging, the State, and Law and Order." *The British Journal of Sociology* 29, no. 4 (December 1978): 511.

Rettberg, Jill Walker. "Biometric Citizens: Adapting Our Selfies to Machine Vision." In *Selfie Citizenship*, edited by Adi Kuntsman, 89–96. Cham: Springer International Publishing, 2017.

———. *Seeing Ourselves Through Technology: How We Use Selfies, Blogs and Wearable Devices to See and Shape Ourselves*. London: Palgrave Macmillan, 2014.

Risam, Roopika. "Now You See Them: Self-Representation and the Refugee Selfie." *Popular Communication* 16, no. 1 (January 2, 2018): 58–71.

Rizzo, Lorena. "Shades of Empire: Police Photography in German South-West Africa." *Visual Anthropology* 26, no. 4 (July 2013): 328–54.

Robinson, Cedric J. *Black Marxism: The Making of the Black Radical Tradition.* Chapel Hill: University of North Carolina Press, 2000.

Rodríguez, Encarnación Gutiérrez. "The Coloniality of Migration and the 'Refugee Crisis': On the Asylum-Migration Nexus, the Transatlantic White European Settler Colonialism-Migration and Racial Capitalism." *Canada's Journal on Refugees/ Refuge: Revue Canadienne Sur Les Réfugiés* 34, no. 1 (2018): 16–34.

Rosenberg, Daniel, and Travis D. Williams, eds. *Raw Data Is an Oxymoron.* Massachusetts: MIT Press, 2013.

Rosman, Rebecca. "Racism Row as French Doctors Suggest Virus Vaccine Test in Africa." Accessed July 28, 2021. https://www.aljazeera.com/news/2020/4/4/racism -row-as-french-doctors-suggest-virus-vaccine-test-in-africa.

Rügemer, Werner. *The Capitalists of the 21st Century: An Easy-to-Understand Outline on the Rise of the New Financial Players.* tredition, 2019.

Sameer, Ahmed. "Why I Fight against the Residence Obligation Law." *The VOICE Refugee Forum Germany*, 2004. http://www.thevoiceforum.org/ahmed-eng.

Sat1. "Die Schande von Köln." *Akte*, January 12, 2016. https://www.sat1.de/tv/akte/ video/2016-die-schande-von-koeln-clip.

Saucier, P. Khalil, and Tryon P. Woods. "Ex Aqua: The Mediterranean Basin, Africans on the Move, and the Politics of Policing." *Theoria* 61, no. 141 (January 1, 2014): 55–75.

Scarry, Elaine. *The Body in Pain: The Making and Unmaking of the World.* New York: Oxford University Press, 1987.

Scheer, Ursula. "Übergriffe in Köln: Frauen, versteckt euch!" *Frankfurter Allgemeine Zeitung*, June 1, 2016. https://www.faz.net/1.3999586.

Scherer, Steve. "'No Fingerprints!' Chant Migrants in Italy as EU Cracks Down." *Reuters*, December 17, 2015. https://www.reuters.com/article/us-europe-migrants -lampedusa-fingerprint-idUSKBN0U02H720151217.

Schiebinger, Londa L. *Nature's Body: Gender in the Making of Modern Science.* New Jersey: Rutgers University Press, 2004.

Schmitt, Carl. *Land und Meer: Eine weltgeschichtliche Betrachtung.* Stuttgart: Klett-Cotta, 2008.

Schnee, Heinrich. *Deutsches Koloniallexikon: Vol. III.* Leipzig: Quelle and Meyer, 1920.

Schneider, William H. "Smallpox in Africa during Colonial Rule." *Medical History* 53, no. 2 (April 2009): 193–227. doi:10.1017/S002572730000363X.

Schuster, Julia. "A Lesson from 'Cologne' on Intersectionality: Strengthening Feminist Arguments against Right-Wing Co-Option." *Feminist Theory* 22, no. 1 (January 1, 2021): 23–42. doi:10.1177/1464700120921077.

Schwenkenbecher, Jan. "Ein Algorithmus, der Flüchtlinge über ein Land verteilt." *Süddeutsche*, January 19, 2018. https://www.sueddeutsche.de/wissen/asyl-ein -algorithmus-der-fluechtlinge-ueber-ein-land-verteilt-1.3832486.

Sekula, Allan. "The Body and the Archive." *October* 39, no. Winter Issue (1986): 3–64.

Sengoopta, Chandak. *Imprint of the Raj: How Fingerprinting Was Born in Colonial India*. London: Pan, 2004.

Shahabuddin, Mohammad. "The Colonial 'Other' in the Nineteenth Century German Colonization of Africa, and International Law." *African Yearbook of International Law Online/Annuaire Africain de Droit International Online* 18, no. 1 (2010): 15–39.

Sharp, Ingrid, and Matthew Stibbe. *Aftermaths of War: Women's Movements and Female Activists, 1918–1923*. Leiden: Brill, 2011.

Shatz, Omer, and Juan Branco. "Communication to the Office of the Prosecutor of the International Criminal Court, Pursuant to the Article 15 of the Rome Statute," 2019. https://www.statewatch.org/news/2019/jun/eu-icc-case-EU-Migration -Policies.pdf.

Shields, Michael. "Swiss, like Danes, Seize Assets from Refugees to Recoup Costs." *Reuters*, January 14, 2016. https://www.reuters.com/article/uk-europe-migrants -swiss-idUKKCN0US2X620160114.

Shoniregun, Charles A., and Stephen Crosier. *Securing Biometrics Applications*. Berlin: Springer, 2008.

Silva, Denise Ferreira da. "Fractal Thinking." *Accessions* 2 (2017). https://accessions .org/article2/fractal-thinking/.

———. "No-Bodies: Law, Raciality and Violence." *Griffith Law Review* 18, no. 2 (2009): 212–36.

Singha, Radhika. "Settle, Mobilize, Verify: Identification Practices in Colonial India." *Studies in History* 16, no. 2 (August 1, 2000): 151–98.

Solove, Daniel J. *Nothing to Hide: The False Tradeoff Between Privacy and Security*. New Haven: Yale University Press, 2011.

Spalek, Basia. *Communities, Identities and Crime*. Bristol: Policy Press, 2008.

Spectator Germanicus. "Eingeborenensorgen in Deutschsüdwest." *Süddeutsche Monatshefte* 10, no. 2 (1913): 249–53.

Spiegel Online. "Streit Um Sea-Watch-Kapitänin: Salvini Pöbelt, Rackete Verlässt Italien." *Spiegel Online*, July 19, 2019, sec. Politik. https://www.spiegel.de/ politik/ausland/carola-rackete-und-matteo-salvini-sea-watch-kapitaenin-hat-italien -verlassen-a-1278080.html.

Spijkerboer, Thomas, and Elies Steyger. "European External Migration Funds and Public Procurement Law." *European Papers* 4, no. 2 (2019): 493–521.

Stafford, Barbara Maria. *Body Criticism: Imaging the Unseen in Enlightenment Art and Medicine*. Massachusetts: MIT Press, 1993.

Stallybrass, Peter, and Allon White. *The Politics and Poetics of Transgression*. Ithaca: Cornell University Press, 1986.

Stanley-Becker, Isaac. "How McKinsey Quietly Shaped Europe's Response to the Refugee Crisis." *Washington Post*, July 24, 2017. https://www.washingtonpost.com /world/europe/how-mckinsey-quietly-shaped-europes-response-to-the-refugee -crisis/2017/07/23/2cccb616-6c80-11e7-b9e2-2056e768a7e5_story.html.

Steinmetz, George. *The Devil's Handwriting: Precoloniality and the German Colonial State in Qingdao, Samoa, and Southwest Africa*. University of Chicago Press, 2007.

Steyerl, Hito. *The Wretched of the Screen*. Berlin: Sternberg Press, 2012.

Stiegler, Bernard. *Technics and Time: The Fault of Epimetheus*. Vol. 1. Palo Alto: Stanford University Press, 1998.

Stoffels, Michael. "Residenzpflicht. Zur Tradition einer rassistischen Auflage für Ausländer." In *Leben unter Vorbehalt: institutioneller Rassismus in Deutschland*, edited by Margarete Jäger, 69–67. Duisburg: DISS, 2002.

Stoler, Ann Laura. *Carnal Knowledge and Imperial Power: Race and the Intimate in Colonial Rule*. Berkeley: University of California Press, 2002.

———. *Duress: Imperial Durabilities in Our Times*. Durham: Duke University Press, 2016.

———. "Making Empire Respectable: The Politics of Race and Sexual Morality in 20th-Century Colonial Cultures." *American Ethnologist* 16, no. 4 (November 1989): 634–60.

Storm, Darlene. "Faception Can Allegedly Tell If You're a Terrorist Just by Analyzing Your Face." *Computerworld*, 2016. https://www.computerworld.com/article/3075339/faception-can-allegedly-tell-if-youre-a-terrorist-just-by-analyzing-your-face.html.

Stupp, Catherine. "EU Maritime Agency Gets Ready to Use Drones to Monitor Refugee Boats." *Euractiv*, March 7, 2016. https://www.euractiv.com/section/justice-home-affairs/news/eu-maritime-agency-gets-ready-to-use-drones-to-monitor-refugee-boats/.

Svirsky, Marcelo. *Agamben and Colonialism*. Edinburgh University Press, 2012.

Swift, Graham. *Out of This World*. Basingstoke and Oxford: Picador, 2012.

Symons, Emma-Kate. "Cologne Attacks: 'This Is Sexual Terrorism Directed towards Women.'" *Women in the World*, January 19, 2016. https://womenintheworld.com/2016/01/19/cologne-attacks-this-is-sexual-terrorism-directed-towards-women/.

Taku, Charles. *Conférence de La Défense Du Droit Pénal*, 2012. https://www.youtube.com/watch?v=QAZr9EzfSqE#t=132.

Tan, Nikolas F., and Thomas Gammeltoft-Hansen. "The End of the Deterrence Paradigm? Future Directions for Global Refugee Policy." *Journal on Migration and Human Security* 5, no. 1 (2017): 28–56.

Tate, Trudi. *Modernism, History and the First World War*. Penrith: Heb Humanities-Ebooks, 2013.

Taussig, Michael. *Mimesis and Alterity: A Particular History of the Senses*. New York and London: Routledge, 1993.

———. *Shamanism, Colonialism, and the Wild Man*. Chicago and London: The University of Chicago Press, 1987.

Taylor, Adam. "Refugees in One of Britain's Poorest Towns Say the Red Doors on Their Housing Make Them Targets." *Washington Post*, January 20, 2016. https://www.washingtonpost.com/news/worldviews/wp/2016/01/20/refugees-in-one-of-britains-poorest-towns-say-the-red-doors-on-their-housing-makes-them-targets/.

Tazzioli, Martina. "EUROSUR, Humanitarian Visibility and (Nearly) Real-Time Mapping in the Mediterranean." *ACME: An International Journal for Critical Geographies* 15, no. 3 (2016): 561–79.

———. "The Government of Migrant Mobs: Temporary Divisible Multiplicities in Border Zones." *European Journal of Social Theory* 20, no. 4 (2017): 30–45.

Tazzioli, Martina, and Glenda Garelli. "The EU Hotspot Approach at Lampedusa." *OpenDemocracy*, February 23, 2016. https://www.opendemocracy.net/can-europe -make-it/glenda-garelli-martina-tazzioli/eu-hotspot-approach-at-lampedusa.

Theweleit, Klaus. *Male Fantasies*. Minneapolis: University of Minnesota Press, 1987.

———. *Male Fantasies Vol. 2*. Minneapolis: University of Minnesota Press, 1989.

Thobani, Sunera. "Empire, Bare Life and the Constitution of Whiteness: Sovereignty in the Age of Terror." *Borderlands* 11, no. 1 (2012): 1–30.

Thorwarth, Katja. "Der Hass der weißen Männer: Carola Rackete triggert das Maskulinisten-Ego." *https://www.fr.de*, July 22, 2019, sec. Meinung. https:// www.fr.de/meinung/carola-rackete-scheint-maskulinisten-ego-ordentlich-triggern -12829860.html.

Ticktin, Miriam. "A World without Innocence." *American Ethnologist* 44, no. 4 (November 2017): 577–90.

———. "Invasive Others: Toward a Contaminated World." *Social Research: An International Quarterly* 84, no. 1 (2017): xxi–xxxiv.

———. "Sexual Violence as the Language of Border Control: Where French Feminist and Anti-Immigrant Rhetoric Meet." *Signs: Journal of Women in Culture and Society* 33, no. 4 (2008): 863–89.

Tifentale, Alise. "The Selfie: Making Sense of the 'Masturbation of Self-Image' and the 'Virtual Mini-Me.'" *Selfiecity*, 2014. https://d25rsf93iwlmgu.cloudfront.net/ downloads/Tifentale_Alise_Selfiecity.pdf.

Tiqqun. *The Cybernetic Hypothesis*. Minneapolis: MIT Press, 2020.

Todo, Lorenzo. "Revealed: 2,000 Refugee Deaths Linked to Illegal EU Pushbacks." *The Guardian*, May 5, 2021. http://www.theguardian.com/global-development /2021/may/05/revealed-2000-refugee-deaths-linked-to-eu-pushbacks.

Toland, John. *Adolf Hitler: The Definitive Biography*. New York: Knopf Doubleday, 2014.

Tranter, Kieran. "The Laws of Technology and the Technology of Law." *Griffith Law Review* 20, no. 4 (2011): 753–62.

Traore, Mohamet. *Schwarze Truppen im Ersten Weltkrieg: Zwischen Rassismus, Kolonialismus und Nationalismus*. Hamburg: Diplomica Verlag, 2014.

Travis, Alan. "EU-UK Naval Mission on People-Smuggling Led to More Deaths, Report Says." *The Guardian*, November 7, 2017. https://www.theguardian.com/ world/2017/jul/11/eu-naval-tactics-operation-sophia-stop-people-smuggling-cause -more-deaths-report-says.

Turner, Patricia. *I Heard It Through the Grapevine: Rumor in African-American Culture*. Berkeley: University of California Press, 1994.

Van der Ploeg, Irma. "Genetics, Biometrics and the Informatization of the Body." *Annali-Istituto Superiore Di Sanita* 43, no. 1 (2007): 44–50.

Vaughan-Williams, Nick. *Europe's Border Crisis: Biopolitical Security and Beyond*. Oxford University Press, 2015.

Vialatte, Alexandre, and Henri Pourrat. *Correspondance Alexandre Vialatte–Henri Pourrat: 1916–1959*. Clermont-Ferrand: Presses Université Blaise Pascal, 2003.

Waits, Mira Rai. "The Indexical Trace: A Visual Interpretation of the History of Fingerprinting in Colonial India." *Visual Culture in Britain* 17, no. 1 (January 2, 2016): 18–46.

Wang, Ylun, and Michael Kosinski. "Deep Neural Networks Are More Accurate Than Humans at Detecting Sexual Orientation from Facial Images." *Journal of Personality and Social Psychology* 114, no. 2 (2018): 246–301.

Weber, Beverly. "The German Refugee 'Crisis' After Cologne: The Race of Refugee Rights." *English Language Notes* 54, no. 2 (September 1, 2016): 77–92.

Weheliye, Alexander G. *Habeas Viscus: Racializing Assemblages, Biopolitics, and Black Feminist Theories of the Human.* Durham: Duke University Press, 2014.

WHO. "WHO Recommendations for International Traffic in Relation to COVID-19 Outbreak," 2020. https://www.who.int/news-room/articles-detail/updated-who -recommendations-for-international-traffic-in-relation-to-covid-19-outbreak.

Wiener, Norbert. *The Human Use of Human Beings: Cybernetics and Society.* London: Hachette, 1988.

Wigger, Iris. "'Black Shame'—the Campaign against 'Racial Degeneration' and Female Degradation in Interwar Europe." *Race & Class* 51, no. 3 (January 2010): 33–46.

———. *The "Black Horror on the Rhine": Intersections of Race, Nation, Gender and Class in 1920s Germany.* London: Palgrave Macmillan, 2017.

———. "The Interconnections of Discrimination: Gender, Class, Nation, and Race and the 'Black Shame on the Rhine.'" *European Societies* 11, no. 4 (September 2009): 553–82.

Wilcox, Lauren. "Embodying Algorithmic War: Gender, Race, and the Posthuman in Drone Warfare." *Security Dialogue* 48, no. 1 (2017): 11–28.

Wildenthal, Lora. "Race, Gender, and Citizenship in the German Colonial Empire." In *Tensions of Empire: Colonial Cultures in a Bourgeois World*, edited by Ann Laura Stoler and Frederick Cooper, 263–83. Berkeley: University of California Press, 1997.

Wilders, Geert. *No Way. You Will Not Make the Netherlands Home*, 2015. https://www .youtube.com/watch?v=wgCSw1JKl7A.

Winkle, Stefan. *Geisseln der Menschheit: Kulturgeschichte der Seuchen.* Artemis & Winkler, 2005.

Wood, David Murakami. "The 'Surveillance Society': Questions of History, Place and Culture." *European Journal of Criminology* 6, no. 2 (March 1, 2009): 179–94. doi:10.1177/1477370808100545.

Wright, John. *The Trans-Saharan Slave Trade.* New York: Routledge, 2007.

Wu, Xiaolin, and Xi Zhang. "Automated Inference on Criminality Using Face Images." *Preprint ArXiv:1611.04135*, 2016, 4038–52. https://emilkirkegaard.dk/en /wp-content/uploads/Automated-Inference-on-Criminality-using-Face-Images.pdf.

Young, Brigitte, and Willi Semmler. "The European Sovereign Debt Crisis: Is Germany to Blame?" *German Politics and Society* 29, no. 1 (March 1, 2011): 1–24.

Yuval-Davis, Nira. *Gender and Nation.* London: SAGE Press, 1997.

Zaccaria, Paola. "(Trans)MediterrAtlantic Embodied Archives." *JOMEC Journal* 0, no. 8 (November 1, 2015): 1–18.

Zestos, George K. *The Global Financial Crisis: From US Subprime Mortgages to European Sovereign Debt*. New York: Routledge, 2015.

Ziada, Ammar. "Where Did the Syrian 'Ya Batel' Tattoo Disappear in Europe?" *Enab Baladi*, July 10, 2016. https://english.enabbaladi.net/archives/2016/07/syrian-ya -batel-tattoo-disappear-europe/.

Zimmerer, Jürgen. "Annihilation in Africa: The 'Race War' in German Southwest Africa (1904–1908) and Its Significance for a Global History of Genocide." *Bulletin of the GHI Washington* 37 (2005): 51–57.

———. *Deutsche Herrschaft über Afrikaner: Staatlicher Machtanspruch und Wirklichkeit im kolonialen Namibia*. Münster: LIT Verlag, 2004.

———. *Von Windhuk nach Auschwitz? Beiträge zum Verhältnis von Kolonialismus und Holocaust*. Münster: LIT Verlag, 2011.

Žižek, Slavoj. "The Cologne Attacks Were an Obscene Version of Carnival." *New Statesman America*, 2016. https://www.newstatesman.com/world/europe/2016/01 /slavoj-zizek-cologne-attacks.

# Index

# About the Author

Anouk Madörin is a feminist researcher based in Berlin. Before joining the University of Potsdam as a lecturer in cultural studies, she was a doctoral fellow of the DFG research training group Minor Cosmopolitanisms and a visiting scholar at the Department of Media, Communications, Creative Arts, Language, and Literature at Macquarie University, Sydney. Anouk holds a PhD in cultural studies and has studied gender studies and cultural history and theory in Basel, Berlin, and at NYU's Department of Social and Cultural Analysis in New York City. Interested in the gendered, sexual, and racial genealogies of power, Anouk works at the intersection of feminist and media theory, postcolonialism, critical migration, and border studies, and has published on the racial securitization of Europe's borders, the sexual politics of border control, and the colonial history of new media.

www.ingramcontent.com/pod-product-compliance
Lightning Source LLC
Chambersburg PA
CBHW022318280326
41932CB00010B/1144